He that hath truth on his side is a fool as well as a coward if he is afraid to own it because of other men's opinions.
Daniel Defoe (1660-1731)

Fraud and falsehood only dread examination. Truth invites it.
Samuel Johnson (1709 – 1784)

"Mormonism believes its "Priesthood" has divine authority from God to conduct all aspects of Mormonism in this life and the life to come. This concept is paramount in understanding that **the Mormon "Priesthood" authority reaches beyond the grave**; an aspect that leverages a very real, controlling power over the living. **As the controlling authority for the "Church," which is where salvation lies for the Mormon, allegiance to the "Church" and its controlling authority (the "Priesthood") cannot be underestimated.**" Rocky Hulse

"It is sometimes urged that the permanent realization of such a desire is impossible, since the Latter-day Saints hold as a principle of their faith that God now reveals Himself to man, as in ancient times; that the priesthood of the Church constitute a body of men who have, each for himself, in the sphere in which he moves, special right to such revelation; that the President of the Church is recognized as the only person through whom divine communication will come as law and doctrine to the religious body; that such revelation may come at any time, upon any subject, spiritual or temporal, as God wills; and finally that, in the mind of every faithful Latter-day Saint, such revelation, in whatsoever it counsels, advises or commands, is paramount. Furthermore it is sometimes pointed out that the members of the Church are looking for the actual coming of a Kingdom of God on earth, that shall gather all the kingdoms of the world into one visible, divine empire, over which the risen Messiah shall reign. **All this, it is held, renders it impossible for a 'Mormon' to give true allegiance to his country, or to any earthly government.**" Elder Brigham H. Roberts, Ordained as one of the First Seven Presidents of the Seventy in October 1888, Mormon Church Historian from 1901 until his death in 1933.

When Salt Lake City Calls

Is There A Conflict Between Mormonism And The Public Trust?

By

Rocky Hulse

JAcl; SALLY,

I HoPE you ENJOY THE Book!

Rocky Hul

12/ic/07

Editing by Michael Musegades
Cover by Maria Schneider

xulon PRESS

Printed in the United States of America

ISBN 978-1-60477-220-3

Editing by Michael Musegades
Cover by Maria Schneider

www.xulonpress.com

Keys To Abbreviated Titles

CN – *Church News* (Weekly Church Magazine, comes in
    newspaper form)
CR – *Conference Reports*
DS – *Doctrines of Salvation*
D & C – *Doctrines and Covenants*
ER – *Encyclopedia of Religion*
HC – *History of the Church*, (Seven Volumes)
IE – *Improvement Era* (Monthly Church Magazine)
JD – *Journal of Discourses*
JST – *Joseph Smith Translation*
MD – *Mormon Doctrine*
TPJS – *Teachings of the Prophet Joseph Smith*

ACKNOWLEDGMENTS

Twenty eight years ago I had just returned from the Persian Gulf onboard the *USS Hoel* (DDG-13), having been involved in operations where we rescued U.S. Embassy and Western European oil field workers from Iran; those we didn't rescue became the American Embassy Hostages. On a bull-riding weekend in Southern California, I met a blonde beach bunny named Helen. She didn't like Sailors, and she didn't like cowboys; but, she liked me. For 27 years, 26 of those as a Sailor's wife, she's rode the waves of life with me. Her Sailor has finally come home from the sea; yet, for the better part of the last year it seems almost like I've been out there still, spending countless hours wrapped up in this book. I thank her for her patience and for loving this cowboy/Sailor.

There's another Sailor involved in this project, Mike Musegades. I am not a writer. I'm comfortable sitting in the Combat Information Center (CIC) of a United States Ship going in harms way. I'm at home conducting Anti-Submarine, Anti-Surface, and Anti-Air Warfare operations. My enlisted specialty before I was commissioned as a Chief Warrant Officer was Electronic Warfare (EW). I'm at home there as well, sitting in the EW Module analyzing electronic signals and extracting minute pieces of information that mean a great deal in the overall picture of military intelligence. My 33 years of Naval Service dealt in facts and analysis. My study of Mormonism has produced a lot of facts that I have analyzed and needed to be put to paper; enter Mike Musegades. Thanks Mike for the countless hours you gave of your time to edit this book. Your editorial comments and suggestions were invaluable. Thanks also to Jenneane, Michele, and Lila, for the time I took Mike away from you.

A special thanks to Maria Schneider for graciously accepting the task of designing the book cover. Your ideas and talent are very visible and much appreciated.

I wish to acknowledge Jay Forrester, Pastor Doug Rettig and Don Gee for their help in keeping the Nauvoo Christian Visitors Center open for business and allowing me to work on this project. In the midst of this book we took on a major renovation project on the visiting areas of the Center—so many Christian folks pitched in to paint, patch, and repair— thank you!! God bless you all.

Sandra Tanner, Bill McKeever, Jim Valentine, and Fred Wheeler all provided encouragement and helpful suggestions—Thanks!

Preface

The old cliché, "Don't judge a book by its cover," is certainly applicable to this work. In today's "politically correct" world, resist the temptation to dismiss this book offhand as the author's bigoted sentiments because he doesn't like a particular Mormon candidate for office. Nothing could be further from the truth. This book will present documented evidence that most Americans are simply unaware of. Presenting documented evidence to educate people about the beliefs and teachings of a religion does not make one a bigot, nor does it make one a persecutor of those holding to the views the evidence elucidates. It simply makes me a reporter of the information and allows you as the reader to judge it as you will.

The idea of a conflict existing between a Mormon's responsibilities in an elected, or appointed, public office and their religious beliefs is not a whimsical contrivance by the author. The conflict does exist. Absolute obedience to the Mormon Priesthood, and the belief that Mormon leaders are "prophets, seers, and revelators," who are God's living oracles on earth and take precedence over everything else, is the foundation from which Mormonism springs. These foundational beliefs of Mormonism are alive and well today and are part and parcel of the faith, and are in direct conflict with Mormon politicians and government officials being independent and not under the absolute control of a religious hierarchy. The evidence for this conflict will be presented here.

This book is not intended to be an all-encompassing, exhaustive treatise on Mormon origins, history or doctrines. There are many notable works on those areas readily available. This book is intended to be a quick read, with enough documentation to develop a reasoned, logical answer for the question: "Can we as Americans trust Mormons in public office to act independent of their religious hierarchy with respect to the responsibilities of that given office and the good of the American people?"

The evidence to support the doctrine of absolute allegiance to the Mormon Priesthood and those revered as "prophets, seers and revelators" will be reinforced by reviewing two very significant historical events which were a direct result of these Mormon Church doctrinal and cultural positions: from history past, the Mountain Meadows Massacre and from recent history, the Mark Hofmann bombings (The Mormon Murders).

It is a decided position by this author to provide numerous, perhaps redundant, quotes on the primary doctrinal positions of Mormonism from which the premise of this book is drawn. Why? This book is sure to be attacked because of the very nature of its subject. An overabundance of quotes is intended to show that the subject of this book is not based on some obscure quote by some obscure Mormon; rather, it is based on the continuous, systematic doctrinal position of the Mormon Church since its beginning to the present day.

FULL DISCLOSURE – I was born and raised as a sixth generation Mormon on my father's side, fourth on my mother's. When in my mid-twenties, and serving in the U. S. Navy, I was challenged that Mormonism was not what I was brought up to believe. That challenge rankled my fur and I set out to prove that Mormonism was exactly what I had been indoctrinated to believe: "The only true and living church on the face of the whole earth"; a restoration of the "Church" that Jesus had set up while He was living, and had subsequently fallen into apostasy and was lost from the earth until God's chosen servant, Joseph Smith, restored it to the world. I studied the history and origins of Mormonism for four years. The evidence against the Mormonism I had been indoctrinated into was overwhelming. On January 1, 1986, I was saved as a Christian and subsequently asked to have my name removed from the rolls of the Mormon Church; it took almost three years to accomplish this.

My wife, Helen, and I are currently the Directors of the Nauvoo Christian Visitors Center in Nauvoo, Illinois; a Christian apologetics ministry specializing in defending Christianity from the attacks levied against it by Mormon doctrine.

Because I was once a Mormon, left it, and now accurately report the teachings and doctrines it espouses, I will surely be attacked by Mormons, and many non-Mormons alike, for writing this book. I ask you to look at the evidence and ignore the *ad hominem* attacks that will be levied. The evidence will speak for itself; simply because I was born and raised in the Mormon Church and I'm intimately familiar with its teachings and then chose to leave, shouldn't nullify the evidence presented herein. I am not a bigot if I am presenting researched, fully documented and accurately reported information about the doctrines of a religion that are simply not compatible with the democratic foundations we Americans adhere to and expect from our elected and appointed government officials. This book is neither an endorsement, nor non-endorsement, of any candidate or appointee of a public office; rather, it is an exposé of conflicting allegiances which are mandated upon those who profess a belief in Mormonism and the teachings of Joseph Smith. This book is not about a person or persons; it is about principles required by Mormon doctrine.

No one is without bias, and I don't claim to bring this documented evidence forward from an unbiased position. I do have a bias: I have studied Mormonism as few have, and I have access to documentation that few people will ever have. The evidence presented here is but a sampling of the plethora of quotes from Mormon writings that support the principles that I will attempt to formulate in the pages of this book. Mormonism is complicated, and the beliefs of Mormonism are tucked away in thousands of volumes of writing. A careful examination of the evidence proves that Mormon doctrine, along with the Mormon Church required covenants of Baptism, taking the Sacrament, its "Priesthood," and most significantly the covenants in its secret Temple Ceremonies are at odds with the traditional American values that our politicians and government appointees are independent of control by a church, an institution, or any person or persons, except for the American people as a whole.

All I ask from you is an objective evaluation of the evidence. Let the evidence speak for itself.

Rocky Hulse

CONTENTS

Chapter One

OVERVIEW OF MORMONISM, ITS ORIGINS AND HISTORY

One must have a general understanding of Mormonism, its doctrines and beliefs, in order to grasp the complicated aspects of its influence. Mormonism is not Catholicism, Protestantism, nor any of the denominational, or nondenominational forms of Christianity, it is a religious system unto itself. Mormonism is a complex entity which interweaves business enterprises with religious beliefs and political ambition. This chapter is a simplistic overview to provide the reader with some basics to allow a better understanding of the whole and is certainly not intended to be an in-depth study.

NEW YORK

Mormonism began on December 23, 1805 when Joseph Smith, Jr., was born in Sharon, Vermont. When Joseph was approximately ten years old his family relocated to Palmyra in Western New York. When just fourteen years of age, Joseph claimed to have received a vision from heaven in which God the Eternal Father (an exalted man with a body of flesh and bones)[1] and his Son, Jesus Christ, appeared to him. Joseph wrote that he went into the woods to pray and ask "18. ...which of all the sects was right—and which I should join. 19. I was answered that I must join none of them, for they were all wrong; and the Personage who addressed me said that all their creeds were an abomination in his sight; that those professors were all corrupt;...."[2] In this first sentence of verse 19, the founder of Mormonism, Joseph Smith, claims that all churches are wrong, all creeds are an abomination (Christian theology comes from the creeds), and all professors of Christianity are corrupt—ergo, all Christian churches are false, all Christian theology is an abomination in Jesus' sight, and all Christians are corrupt. This declaration set Mormonism on a collision course with Christianity everywhere it went, and continues on this course to this very day.

In 1830 the *Book of Mormon*, the source of the nickname "Mormon," was first published; 5,000 copies were initially printed. Joseph Smith claimed an angel named Moroni first appeared to him in September of 1823 and told him of an ancient record of the inhabitants of this continent written upon gold plates.[3] Moroni subsequently gave these plates of gold to Joseph in September of 1827 from which he translated the Book of Mormon. According to Smith, upon completion of the translation the angel Moroni returned and took the gold plates to heaven; therefore, neither physical validity of the plates, nor verification of the translation can be accomplished.

By revelation from God, Joseph Smith is commanded to organize the "Church of Christ"[4] on April 6, 1830, in Fayette, New York. On May 3, 1834, Joseph and the governing Elders of the new church overrule the "revelation" and change the name of the church to "The Church of the Latter-day Saints."[5] Then, on April 26, 1838, Joseph receives another "revelation" providing an altogether different name for the church: "The Church of Jesus Christ of Latter-day Saints,"[6] which remains to this day.

KIRTLAND, OHIO

To escape "the power of the enemy," in January of 1831 Joseph received "revelations" to move the new church from New York "to the Ohio."[7] The three existing New York branches (small congregations) then relocated to Kirtland, Ohio. As the Mormon Church began to grow, it was commanded by "revelation" to expand its boundaries "in this land, which is the land of Missouri, which is the land which I have appointed and consecrated for the gathering of the saints. Wherefore, this is the land of promise, and the place for the city of Zion. And thus saith the Lord your God, if you will receive wisdom here is wisdom. Behold, the place which is now called Independence is the center place; and a spot for the temple is lying westward, upon a lot which is not far from the court-house."[8] Many prophecies and teachings were given by Joseph Smith concerning Missouri. Among those was that the "Garden of Eden" was located there and was called "Adam-ondi-Ahman."[9] Joseph further taught that the "Second Coming" of Jesus would be to "Adam-ondi-Ahman."[10] Tenth Mormon Prophet Joseph Fielding Smith taught "When Christ comes in fulfillment of this promise, *there will be on the earth two great cities made holy with holy sanctuaries, or temples.* One will be the city of Jerusalem in the land of Judah, which shall be rebuilt; the other the city of Zion, or the New Jerusalem, in the land of Joseph" (Independence, Jackson County, Missouri).[11]

As you can see by the above quotes, great emphasis was placed on Missouri, and remains to this day. However, as the Mormon Church was building up Zion in Missouri, Kirtland, Ohio was growing as well. In May of 1833 the construction of a temple was begun, with its dedication commencing on

March 27, 1836. The building of this edifice had come at a great sacrifice, both physical and financial. The gathering of Mormon converts to Kirtland had fueled land speculation prices. The debts of the Mormon Church were mounting, so in November of 1836 Joseph Smith decided to solve some of these financial problems by establishing a bank called the Kirtland Safety Society Bank. However, the State of Ohio refused to grant a charter.

"Smith was furious, claiming that God had told him that the bank was to be opened. Nothing would stop him from obeying the Lord. According to Smith, the license had been denied simply because they were Mormons. So Joseph proceeded to open his institution not as the Kirtland Safety Society "Bank," but rather, as the Kirtland Safety Society *Anti*-Bank*ing* Company, complete with currency that had the prefix "anti" and the suffix "ing" lightly stamped around the bold-typed word "BANK." Smith actually believed that his debts, along with those of his followers, could be wiped out by merely printing these notes and using them to pay creditors.

The bills, however, were practically worthless because Smith had virtually no silver/gold coinage to back up the paper he issued. His entire capital stock consisted of nothing but land valued at inflated prices....

Smith spread the word that he had $60,000 in hard coinage to back the paper notes, and could lay his hands on $600,000 more if necessary. In reality he had barely $6,000. He also said that he had only printed up about $10,000 in bills, when at least $150,000 had been distributed....

Smith opened for business after installing himself and Sidney Rigdon [1st Counselor to Joseph] as the institution's main officers, while supporting positions within the Society's corporate structure were filled by most of his twelve apostles....

Less than one month after opening, Smith's currency was exchanging at 12 ½ cents on the dollar. The authorities quickly heard about the scandal and on February 1, 1837, a writ was sworn out against Joseph Smith, Jr., and Sidney Rigdon accusing the two men of "illegal banking and issuing unauthorized bank paper." Their trial was scheduled for the court's fall session....

They were found guilty of violating state banking laws and fined $1,000 each, plus small costs....

...Soon afterward, the final nail in the Kirtland congregation's coffin was procured in the form of an arrest warrant for Smith on the charge of banking fraud, a much more serious offense than the one for which he and Rigdon had already been convicted (i.e., illegal banking). Smith knew he was guilty, but to be taken back to court could end his dream of establishing God's kingdom on earth.

So, in the dead of night, January 12, 1838, Smith and Rigdon fled Kirtland on horseback, in hopes of finding peace and safety in Far West (Caldwell County [Missouri]) the newly established LDS refuge near Zion....

In his history, Smith would write that he was "obliged to flee" his persecutors, just as the Apostles and Prophets of old were forced to do..."[12]

MISSOURI

During the period from 1831-1838 the Mormon Church was primarily located in two areas: Kirtland, Ohio and Independence/Far West, Missouri. Until 1838, most of their leaders and key people remained in Kirtland. With the failure of the Kirtland Safety Society Bank and the turmoil surrounding the defrauding of so many people in its wake, the Church moved completely to Missouri. Even though Missouri had been designated as the location of "Zion" by revelation in 1831, all had not gone well for the "saints" there either.

> "But from the moment they arrived in Independence, the Mormons were looked upon as troublemakers. Their new home was a frontier town populated primarily by rough, illiterate, and anti-social hunters, tradesmen, trappers, gamblers, and assorted ruffians. Such individuals did not take kindly to being disdainfully termed "Gentiles" and being told that they would one day have to evacuate the area so God's kingdom of righteousness could be established....
> We are daily told [by the Mormons]...that we, (the Gentiles,) of this country are to be cut off, and our lands appropriated by them for inheritances. Whether this is to be accomplished by the hand of the destroying angel, the judgments of God, or the arm of power, they are not fully agreed among themselves."[13]

The straw that broke the camel's back for the Mormons in Jackson County, Missouri was the publishing of Joseph Smith's "Book of Commandments." This publication of the Mormon Prophet's supposed revelations from God incited the Missourians to drive the Mormons out of Jackson County:

> "The main reason why the printing press was destroyed, was because they published the Book of Commandments. It fell into the hands of the world, and the people of Jackson county, Missouri, saw from the revelations that they were considered by the church as intruders upon the land of Zion, as enemies to the church, and that they should be cut off out of the land of Zion and

22

sent away. The people seeing these things in the Book of Commandments became more enraged, tore down the printing press, and drove the church out of Jackson county."[14]

The Missourians were outraged by Joseph Smith's revelations from God declaring that Jackson County was to be Zion and all Missourians were to be removed from it, so they drove the Mormons out with a vengeance. The Mormons were accepted by the citizens of Clay County, just north of Jackson County, as religious refugees. By January 1, 1834, nearly every Mormon had left Jackson County and relocated to Clay County. By the time Joseph Smith and Sidney Rigdon had fled from the Ohio banking scandal and arrived in Missouri in 1838, the "saints" had secured an agreement to live in Caldwell County, just north of Clay County, Missouri. This agreement had brought a time of peace between the old Missouri residents and the "saints." The arrival of Joseph Smith soon ended that peaceful existence.

Soon after his arrival, Joseph began to expand Mormon settlements outside of the agreed Caldwell County refuge; again with revelations predicting the ultimate reign of Mormonism in the land. There was much dissent both inside the Mormon camp as well as with the Missourians. Many Mormons left the "Church," were labeled as apostates and were reviled by Church leadership. Joseph Smith, as the Prophet, and Sidney Rigdon as 1st Counselor, expended much energy in putting down those who dissented their leadership, trying their best to hold the flock together. This flurry of words might not have escalated into violence had not the approval been given for the formation of a militant organization, a secret police society, known as the "Danites":

"Threats of legal action by the apostates prompted even harsher replies from both Rigdon and Smith, who declared that they "had been harassed to death, as it were, for seven or eight years, and they were determined to bear it no longer, for they would rather die than suffer such things." Joseph went so far as to say that "he did not intend in [the] future to have any process served on him, and the officer who attempted it should die; that any person who spoke or acted against the presidency or the church should leave the country or die." As he put it, "any person who said a word against the heads of the Church, should be driven over these prairies as a chased deer by a pack of hounds."

To back up his threats, Joseph permitted the formation of a secret group of enforcers to "sustain church leaders without question." More bluntly, they were organized "for the purpose of plundering and murdering the enemies of the Saints." Smith apparently sanctioned the brotherhood as a primary weapon "in the hands of God, of bringing forth the millenial kingdom." But according to Kenneth Winn, adjunct history professor at Washington University, Smith's secret cadre of ruffians and assassins was little more than "an aggressive, malicious, secret police force...a nineteenth-century version of storm-troopers." They called themselves 'Danites.'"[15]

What really drew the "line in the sand" and pitted Mormonism against the Missourians, was the belief being espoused in Mormonism that it was above the law:

"Conflict on a large scale between the Mormons and the Missourians around Caldwell County might have been avoided had Smith and his followers not become so militaristic. Anxiety among non-Mormon settlers also increased when they realized that at some point the Saints had decided to no longer subject themselves to civil authority. The Danites led the way by pledging oaths of allegiance and protection to one another no matter what offenses they might commit in the eyes of Gentiles. Lyman Wight, for example, known for his fiery temperament, instructed new Danite recruits as follows:

> [I]f any brother have stolen a horse, or committed any other offence, and is arraigned before a justice of the peace for trial, you must, at the risk of your lives, rescue him, and not permit him to be tried by the Gentile law."[16]

This pitting of a "Theocratic State" against the civil authority already in place, even in frontier Missouri, was bound to clash; and clash it did. Mormon history today generally ignores the ingredients of Mormonism that contributed to these events and places the blame squarely on the Missourians.

Mormons often remind all who will listen that Governor Lilburn Boggs, of Missouri, issued an "extermination order" on October 27, 1838, which is true. However, they fail to mention that President Sidney Rigdon delivered a speech in Far West, Missouri, on July 4, 1838, 115 days earlier, which issued the first "extermination" statements directed at the Missourians:

> "But from this day and this hour we will suffer it no more. We take God and all the holy angels to witness, this day, that we warn all men, in the name of Jesus Christ to come on us no more for ever, for from this hour we will bear it no more; our rights shall no more be trampled on with impunity; the man, or the set of men who attempt it, do it at the **EXPENSE OF THEIR LIVES**. And that mob that comes on us to disturb us, it shall be between us and them **A WAR OF EXTERMINATION**; for we will follow them until the **LAST DROP OF THEIR BLOOD IS SPILLED**; or else **THEY WILL**

HAVE TO EXTERMINATE US, for WE WILL CARRY THE SEAT OF WAR TO THEIR OWN HOUSES AND THEIR OWN FAMILIES, AND ONE PARTY OR THE OTHER SHALL BE UTTERLY DESTROYED."[17] (Emphasis added.)

It should be noted that the word "extermination," in Governor Boggs Order, was not defined "to kill" as we might apply it today with respect to insects or vermin; rather, its meaning was to "remove, or displace."

The inevitable happened, when the theocratic state being established by Joseph Smith tried to overrun the Missouri civil society already in place, the battle lines were drawn. Many skirmishes between Missourians and Mormons caused the governor to call out the militia. Mormons and Missouri mobs clashed repeatedly, both committing senseless and lawless acts against each other. The ensuing result was a face off between the militia of Missouri and the Mormons at Far West in what could have been a battle with the worst possible consequences. However, Mormon leaders agreed to surrender and were taken to jail. The remaining Mormons began to leave the State and crossed the Mississippi River at Quincy, Illinois; ultimately settling just north of Quincy in Commerce, Illinois.

Joseph Smith and his brother Hyrum, as well as other senior Mormon leaders, were tried for various crimes, including murder and treason. The prosecution's witnesses included primary Mormon leaders and dissenters who had left the Mormon ranks. The primary witness against Joseph Smith was the leader of the Danites, Sampson Avard. Sampson's testimony clearly indicated that Joseph Smith had directed the illegal activities of the secret police society. After six months of incarceration, Joseph and his brother Hyrum bribed the Sheriff with a jug of whiskey and $800.

On April 15, 1839, the sheriff and his men were passed out drunk and allowed the Mormon leaders to escape.

NAUVOO

Even while Joseph and other Mormon leaders were in jail in Missouri, his followers began establishing their new Zion in Commerce, Illinois. Initially, Illinois provided a welcome sanctuary for the refugee Mormons; however, the mixing of the theocratic state, with the civil state was to bring clashes once again between Mormons and their neighbors. In 1840, the Mormons changed the name of Commerce to Nauvoo, and it became known as the City of Joseph. In just three years the population rose to approximately 10,000 people, second in size only to Chicago.

Many factors contributed to the ultimate demise of the Mormon Zion in Nauvoo. However, the greatest impact to the demise was Nauvoo's city charter. The charter granted town officials judicial privileges, the ability to create an army (known as the Nauvoo Legion – over which Joseph Smith appointed himself as General), and the right to enact very rigid laws governing almost every facet of life in Nauvoo. Initially, Nauvoo flourished, but that tranquility was short-lived. Dissension among the Mormon people spilled over into the surrounding population. Many dissenters left and became part of the local population. Their stories of abuse of power and implementing strange religious practices contrary to the laws of the state of Illinois brought conflict once more to the Mormon people.

The Nauvoo period of history in Mormonism is of primary significance. It was here that many of the unique Mormon doctrines were first implemented. It was here that polygamy was first introduced to the Church as a whole, however this was done clandestinely. It was here that the major doctrines of baptism for the dead, celestial marriage (marriage for time and all eternity), the endowment ceremony (allowing one to become a God in the next life), and the plurality of Gods was first taught. Nauvoo was also, where Joseph Smith first set his sights on a political kingdom to usher in the second coming of Christ.

Joseph Smith petitioned Congress for monetary restitution for the losses the Mormons had suffered in Missouri. The President and Congress listened to his pleas, but refused to take action because of their unwillingness to meddle in the issue of states rights. Their hesitation in acting upon the petitions by Joseph Smith allowed the state of Missouri to provide testimony from the trial of Joseph Smith for treason. This testimony ended any opportunity the Mormons may have had for Congress to act in their favor.

Joseph Smith believed the only way to vindicate the Saints was for him to run for, and be elected, President of the United States. He announced his candidacy, selected Sidney Rigdon as his Vice Presidential running mate and then ordered the elders of the church to campaign for him. He also petitioned Congress in 1843 for the ability to raise a 100,000 man army, but this request was denied. His vision of becoming President of the United States was the catalyst for establishing a secret organization called the Council of Fifty. This secret organization was put in place to establish a world government vested in the Mormon Church:

"Although the petition was denied, Smith continued pursuing his dream of establishing an earthly kingdom by setting up a shadow-government on March 11, 1844. He called his body of behind-the-scenes rulers his Council of Fifty, which according to one member was created as "the Municipal department of the Kingdom of God set up on the Earth, and from which all Law emanates, for the rule, government & control of all Nations, Kingdoms & towns, and People under the whole heavens." According to Wilford Woodruff, the Council's stated purpose was to 'organize the political kingdom of God in preparation for the second coming of Christ.'"[18]

Once again, Mormonism's attempted mixing of a Theocratic and Civil government and their defiance of the laws of the land placed them at odds with society. In 1833 Illinois enacted laws prohibiting polygamy. Ignoring the laws of the land, Joseph Smith instituted and practiced polygamy, which placed the Mormon Church on a collision course with the State of Illinois. Abandoning civil law, coupled with the abuse of power as demonstrated in the liberties taken with the City Charter of Nauvoo, led to the conflicts between the local citizens and the Mormons.

Dissenters from the highest ranks of Mormon leadership pooled their resources and purchased a printing press. They produced a single issue of a newspaper called the *Nauvoo Expositor*, which accurately reported that Joseph Smith and other Church leaders were secretly practicing polygamy and that Joseph Smith was teaching the doctrine of plurality of Gods. This was information that Joseph Smith did not want the rank-and-file Mormon membership to know. Therefore, as the Mayor of Nauvoo he declared the Nauvoo Expositor to be a nuisance and ordered its destruction. Approximately 200 Mormons responded to his call and ransacked the Nauvoo Expositor building pulling the pi and type and all printing supplies into the street, where they were burned. This total disregard for the First Amendment and the laws of the State of Illinois led to Joseph Smith's arrest and incarceration in the Carthage Jail.

Joseph and his brother, Hyrum were arrested on charges of treason. John Taylor, and Willard Richards were arrested for inciting a riot. While incarcerated, a local mob formed and rushed the jail killing Joseph and his brother Hyrum and seriously wounding John Taylor. A local Mormon, Cyrus

Wheelock, had smuggled a pepper-box pistol and a single shot pistol into the jail, which Joseph Smith and his brother Hyrum retained respectively. When the mob rushed the jail Joseph went to the door and discharged all six barrels of the pepperbox pistol, only three successfully fired; nonetheless, he killed two men and wounded a third. Mormonism lauds Joseph Smith as a martyr. Was he murdered, yes? Was he martyred, no? Martyrs do not leave this world in a gunfight in which they are a participant.

Joseph Smith's death caused a power vacuum in the church. Many of those in leadership tried to establish themselves as Joseph Smith's rightful heir to the Mormon Church position of "Prophet." At this point in Mormon history numerous splinter groups formed and separated themselves from the main body. Brigham Young eventually won this power struggle and became the de facto new leader of Mormonism.

The tension and conflicts between Mormonism – its doctrines and practices – and its abuses of the law with its neighbors, eventually led to an agreement between Mormon and civil leaders, for the Mormons to depart the state after the spring thaw in 1846. Mormon leadership did not wait for the spring thaw and instead departed Nauvoo the first week of February, in the dead of winter subjecting their people to great hardships as they traveled across Southern Iowa. Mormon history claims that they were driven from their homes due to persecution. A closer look at history shows conflicting information:

> "Warrants pending for the arrest of Brigham Young and other leaders on charges of counterfeiting were among the reasons for the early departure of the Saints from the "city of Joseph" in February rather than in the spring as originally proposed."[19]

30

"...Government records indeed indicate that Young, along with apostles Willard Richards, John Taylor, Parley Pratt, Orson Hyde, and others were involved in making counterfeit coinage dubbed 'Nauvoo Bogus.'

Nauvoo's counterfeiting operation actually may have started under Joseph's leadership, since Edward Bonney and Marinus G. Eaton—two out of the only three non-Mormons on his Council of Fifty—were known counterfeiters. Bogus money also had been passed by Mormons Theodore Turley, Cyrus Chase, Rufus Adams, George Reader, Peter Haws (Council of Fifty), Warren Snow (future bishop in Utah), and Dominicus Carter (future member of Stake Presidency in Utah). Moreover, a number of individuals claimed that Joseph knew about, and approved, the use of bogus presses and money dies in the city.

When U.S. Marshals finally reached Nauvoo in December 1845 to arrest Young, he went into hiding in hopes of possibly circumventing the law as Joseph had done so many times. But when faced with the possibility of federal troops showing up, Young decided the exodus west could no longer wait. Young announced his response to the new threat on February 3, 1846, before a crowd of Saints that had gathered in the newly finished temple. He did not try to explain away the counterfeiting charges, nor declare that he would allow the courts to prove his innocence. Instead, Young simply stated that he would be taking his family westward as soon as possible."[20]

UTAH

The Mormons left Nauvoo and headed west; first to Winter Quarters, just west of modern day Omaha, Nebraska, then on to the Great Salt Lake Basin, where they established today's Salt Lake City, Utah. When they arrived in the Salt

Lake Basin, it was part of Mexico. Now, outside the boundaries of the United States in a very remote location, they had freedom to practice polygamy unfettered by governments opposed to such a practice. In 1850 however, Utah became a territory of the United States. Once again Mormons came under the governing rules of the United States; and once again, the conflicts between Mormon doctrine and civil authority began.

Upon their arrival in the Salt Lake Valley, Brigham Young began to establish a theocratic Mormon state. When Utah became a United States territory and non-Mormon government officials arrived and began to enforce the laws of the United States, the scene was set for another confrontation between Mormonism and the United States government. 1857/58 found Utah in a state of war with the United States. The President of the United States, James Buchanan, dispatched federal troops under the initial command of Brg. Gen. William Harney to suppress the Mormon uprising in Utah. Brigham Young, who had refused to relinquish his position as Governor of the Territory of Utah in 1854 when his term ended, prepared the Mormons for war:

> "Young, for all intents and purposes, had severed Utah's ties with the US government. The very next day he even held a strategy meeting with his top officer of the Nauvoo Legion, Lt. Gen. Daniel Wells. Together they agreed that Mormon soldiers would "waylay our enemies, attack them from ambush, stampede their animals, take the supply trains, cut off detachments, and parties sent to canyons for wood, or on other service." Thus began the Utah War of 1857/58."[21]

The initial U.S. campaign against Utah was poorly managed. The U.S. soldiers were scattered across the country and delayed the army's assembly and departure. When the

10th Infantry finally left from Fort Leavenworth, it was very late in the season to complete the 1200 mile journey. Brg. Gen. Harney began the journey, but was detached to Kansas with his Second Dragoons to quell civil unrest. Colonel Johnson was assigned as the new commanding officer upon Brg. Gen. Harney's departure, but took several weeks to catch up to the troops. The assembled army was placed under the temporary command of Colonel Edmund Alexander who was inexperienced and allowed his supply train to be spread out across the countryside, which made it vulnerable to attack by the Mormons.

When Colonel Johnson finally arrived he found that his army's supplies had been pillaged by Mormon raids, and he was forced to lay up for the winter outside of Utah at a base called Camp Scott. The winter was especially harsh, and with diminished supplies the U.S. troops suffered terribly. During this time Brigham Young taunted Colonel Johnson incessantly, prompting him to write Washington:

"The Mormons have placed themselves in rebellion against the Union, and entertain the insane design of establishing a form of government thoroughly despotic, and utterly repugnant to our institutions.... I have ordered that wherever they are met in arms, that they be treated as enemies."[22]

President Buchanan sent an unofficial emissary, Thomas L. Kane, to persuade Brigham Young to avoid the impending conflict. Brigham Young initially refused the olive branch. However, when the Mormons were offered a full pardon for their various acts of rebellion and treason Young changed his mind and accepted an agreement to install the newly appointed Governor of the Utah Territory and U.S. Army peacekeeping troops. The new governor, Alfred Cumming, and other federal appointees, found the Utah Territory to be a hostile and uninviting environment.

John Cradlebaugh, newly appointed Territorial Supreme Court Judge, was utterly frustrated in his attempts to bring to justice the perpetrators of the Mountain Meadows Massacre (detailed in Chapter Nine). His disappointment is evident in the following statement:

> "There seems to be a combined effort on the part of the community to screen the murderers from the punishment due for the murder they have committed.... [W]hen officers seek to arrest persons accused of crimes they are not able to do so; the parties are screened and secreted by the community.... witnesses are screened; others are intimidated by persons in that community.... Such acts and conduct go to show that the community there do not desire to have criminals punished."[23]

The Civil War focused attention away from the rogue Territory of Utah. The Mormons provided no troops to either side of the conflict, but rather, sat back and predicted that the United States would fall as a just recompense to their treatment of "God's people," the Mormons. When the nation did not fall as a result of the Civil War, a post war uneasy truce set in. Federal authorities wrestled with the constant abrasive division between the civil and the theocratic governance of Mormon Utah. Governor Alfred Cumming summed up this dichotomy well:

> "There is nothing to do. Alfred Cumming is Governor of the Territory, but Brigham Young is governor of the people."[24]

The next several years saw Mormonism struggle to deal with its repugnant doctrine of polygamy. Many petitions for statehood would fall to the wayside because of the unwillingness of Mormons, at the direction of their leadership, to abide Federal Law and cease the unlawful practice of polygamy. With the deaths of Brigham Young and John Taylor, their second and third prophets respectively, the way was cleared for this distasteful practice to be done away with. The Mormon Church was brought to its knees when the Edmunds-Tucker Act was passed in March of 1887 making polygamy a felony and disincorporating the Mormon Church. On May 19, 1890, a five to four decision by the Supreme Court upheld the government's ability to seize the property of the Mormon Church:

> "In *Church of Jesus Christ of Latter-day Saints v. the United States*, the high court passed down a 5-4 decision on May 19, 1890, in support of the government action. The majority opinion stated: "Congress had before it—a contumacious organization, wielding by its resources an immense power in the Territory of Utah, and employing those resources and that power in constantly attempting to oppose, thwart and subvert the legislation of Congress and the will of the government of the United States."[25]

Fourth Mormon Prophet Wilford Woodruff, was between a rock and a hard place. He could continue to allow the practice of polygamy and see the Government dismantle the Mormon Church, or discontinue the practice and abide by the laws of the land. He therefore issued what is called "Official Declaration – 1," wherein he declares to the Mormon people that it is no longer required of them to practice polygamy. The crux of the October 6, 1890, declaration is as follows:

> "Inasmuch as laws have been enacted by Congress forbidding plural marriages, which laws have been pronounced constitutional by the court of last resort, I

hereby declare my intention to submit to those laws, and to use my influence with the members of the Church over which I preside to have them do likewise.

There is nothing in my teachings to the Church or in those of my associates, during the time specified, which can be reasonably construed to inculcate or encourage polygamy; and when any Elder of the Church has used language which appeared to convey any such teaching, he has been promptly reproved. And I now publicly declare that my advice to the Latter-day Saints is to refrain from contracting any marriage forbidden by the law of the land."[26]

The roots of polygamy ran deep however, and the road away from polygamy was a rough one. Mormon Prophet Woodruff's Declaration to cease practicing polygamy begins with "To Whom It May Concern"; Joseph Smith's revelation to practice polygamy says "thus saith the Lord":

1. VERILY, thus saith the Lord unto you my servant Joseph, that inasmuch as you have inquired of my hand to know and understand wherein I, the Lord, justified my servants Abraham, Isaac, and Jacob, as also Moses, David and Solomon, my servants, as touching the principal and doctrine of their having many wives and concubines—
2. Behold, and lo, I am the Lord thy God, and will answer thee as touching this matter.
3. Therefore, prepare thy heart to receive and obey the instructions which I am about to give unto you; for all those who have this law revealed unto them must obey the same.
4. For behold, I reveal unto you a new and an everlasting covenant; and if ye abide not that covenant, then are

ye damned; for no one can reject this covenant and be permitted to enter into my glory.[27]

History shows that polygamy did not end with this *"Declaration"* and polygamous marriages simply went "underground" as polygamous colonies were established in Canada and Mexico where the governments disregarded the practice of polygamy. **Polygamy was the rallying cry; however, the issue wasn't truly polygamy, the issue was the political domination in direct opposition to the U.S. Government:**

> "Polygamy was the catalyst for change in the LDS Church, and the issue that rallied the country, but for some the deeper issue was political. Senator Frederick T. Dubois of Idaho wrote in his autobiography, **"Those of us who understand the situation were not nearly so much opposed to polygamy as we were to the political domination of the church. We realized, however, that we could not make those who did not come actually in contact with it, understand what this political domination meant. We made use of polygamy."**
>
> The United States could not accept a quasi-independent nation-state in its midst, an independent theocratic kingdom, or a secular government on paper behind which stood a shadow church government that determined its laws and lawmakers, or a court system in which religious authority decided secular disputes. Gentiles in Utah were outsiders, and if they were vigorously critical, they were suspect. "LDS publications applauded physical attacks on anti-Mormons until 1889, the year the First Presidency also publicly abandoned its ideals of a political theocracy," writes D. Michael Quinn.
>
> The key word, perhaps, is "publicly" abandoned. The church wanted statehood in large part because

Utah would essentially run its own affairs as a state, whereas the federal government and its appointees had considerable latitude in running a territory. **Gentiles in the Intermountain West and across the country fought statehood, fearing that with a clear Mormon majority obediently following the church's direction, the church would control the secular affairs of Utah as well as those of nearby areas with a significant LDS population. <u>Mormons, after all, had followed the commands of Joseph Smith and then Brigham Young in politics as well as belief, and it was not unreasonable to assume they would continue to obey their leaders' dictates</u>.**"[28] (emphasis added.)

With the "Manifesto" in place, publicly the Mormon Church was complying with Federal Law and thus the wheels of "statehood" began to move again. On January 4, 1896, Utah became the 45th state. In the years 1894 to 1896 the Church began to receive what was left of its properties back after the dispersal of the Edmunds-Tucker Act of 1887 and the Supreme Court ruling of May 19, 1890. The Church was in serious financial difficulty and the prospect of bankruptcy loomed on its horizon.

Conservative fiscal policies and major divestitures of Church holdings in commercial ventures brought the Church back to solvency by 1907 when it began the present day practice of reinvesting in private businesses. Today the Mormon Church's worth is estimated at over $60 Billion and its wealth and business holdings are kept in absolute secrecy. The last public financial disclosure of the Mormon Church was in 1959.

Statehood and the railroad brought business and non-Mormon diversity to Utah. Mormons served in the Spanish-American War of 1898, and in all follow-on conflicts on par with their fellow Americans. Finally out of the lime-light, brought about by their defiance of U.S. Law, Mormon Utah began to grow and prosper in step with the rest of the States. One major difference remained however, its absolute dominance by the Mormon Church. Many residents of Utah, not Mormon by faith, define their residency as "Living under the Zion Curtain."

WHAT'S THE POINT?

It is important to have a perspective of Mormon origins and history from a source other than the Mormon Church. The Mormon Church sanitizes its history and rather than providing accurate information to its members and the public, only that which is "faith promoting" is allowed to be printed:

> "Mormon teachers are required to present the currently acceptable, faith-promoting, official view of history, Apostle Boyd Packer said in a famous speech to the annual Church Educational System Religious Educators' Symposium in 1981. Packer, giving marching orders to CES seminary and institute teachers, gave four "cautions": (1) "There is no such thing as an accurate, objective history of the Church without consideration of the spiritual powers that attended this work"; (2) "There is a temptation... to want to tell everything, whether it is worthy or faith-promoting or not. Some things that are true are not very useful"; (3) "In an effort to be objective, impartial, and scholarly, a writer or a teacher may unwittingly be giving equal time to the adversary.... In the church we are not neutral. We are one-sided. There is a war going on, and we are engaged in it"; (4) The fact that something is already in print or available from another source is no excuse for using potentially damaging mate-

rials in writing, speaking, or teaching: 'Do not spread disease germs!'"[29]

"The church has always tried to retain a proprietary hold over the telling of its own history. The earliest clear example of this is the checkered history of mother Lucy Mack Smith's B*iographical Sketches of Joseph Smith, the Prophet, and His Progenitors for Many Generations,* first published by Apostle Orson Pratt in Liverpool in 1853. Brigham Young was unhappy with the book and ordered the printing destroyed."[30]

"The most serious problems occur when the church suppresses evidence that is contrary to official interpretation. "Faithful history" tends to be apologetic and celebratory, to downplay or avoid sensitive aspects of Mormon history. It is not, for example, politically correct to suggest that Mormons, while victims, were not always innocent victims, or that though holiness may be an affront to the observer, ordinary Saintly holiness was not usually the cause of Mormon persecutions."[31]

Whenever you deal with Mormon history, you have to be like Paul Harvey; you have to get: "The rest of the story!" A thorough review of the transcribed article in Appendix One from the *NILES' NATIONAL REGISTER* of August 31, 1844, will provide some insightful observations of the real reasons there was conflict between the Mormons and the states they had resided in until their removal from Illinois. The keen perceptions by the writer of this article were virtually clairvoyant with respect to their application in connection with the Mountain Meadows Massacre, the Utah War of 1857/58 and the conflicts surrounding the problems of Utah Statehood. In each case, the writer's observations were correct: "they have always manifested a disposition to resist or evade the general laws of the state when applied to restrain their action. Such is the testimony against them in other states, and such is our own experience of them in Illinois. The causes of this insubordination and turbulence on their part are neither obscure nor uncertain; they are found to be in their peculiar tenets of faith and principles of government."[32]

[1] Joseph Fielding Smith, *Teachings of the Prophet Joseph Smith* (Salt Lake City: Deseret Book Co., 1938), 345.

[2] *Pearl of Great Price*, Joseph Smith 2:18-19, 1977.

[3] Ibid., 2:30-34.

[4] *Doctrine and Covenants* 20:1-2, 1977. (Hereafter referred to as *D & C*)

[5] Joseph Smith, *History of the Church of Jesus Christ of Latter-day Saints* (Salt Lake City: Deseret News, 1970), 2: 62-63.

[6] *D & C* 115:4

[7] Ibid., 37:1,3; 38:32.

[8] Ibid., 57:1-3.

[9] Bruce R. McConkie, *Mormon Doctrine* (Salt Lake City: Bookcraft, 1966), 20.

[10] Ibid., 694.

[11] Joseph Fielding Smith, *Doctrines of Salvation: Sermons and Writings of Joseph Fielding Smith*, 3 vols., ed. Bruce R. McConkie, (Salt Lake City: Bookcraft, 1954-56) 3:72.

[12] Richard Abanes, *One Nation Under Gods: A History of the Mormon Church* (New York: Four Walls Eight Windows, 2002) 136-139, 141.

[13] Ibid., 104.

[14] David Whitmer, *An Address To All Believers In Christ* (Richmond, Missouri, 1887), 54.

[15] Abanes, *One Nation Under Gods: A History of the Mormon Church*, 151.

[16] Ibid., 154-155.

[17] B. H. Roberts, *Comprehensive History of the Church* (Salt Lake City, Deseret News Press, 1930) 1:441.

[18] Abanes, *One Nation Under Gods: A History of the Mormon Church*, 186-7.

[19] *BYU Studies*, vol. 8 (1967-1968), Number 2 – Winter 1968, 214.

[20] *One Nation Under Gods: A History of the Mormon Church*, 216-7.

[21] Ibid., 256-7.

[22] Ibid., 260.

[23] Ibid., 265.

[24] Ibid., footnote 54, 572.

[25] Richard N. Ostling and Joan K. Ostling, *Mormon America: The Power and the Promise*, (HarperCollins Publishers Inc., San Francisco, 1999) 77-8.

[26] *D & C Official Declaration—1*

[27] Ibid., 132:1-4.

[28] Ostling, *Mormon America: The Power and the Promise*, 78-9.

[29] Ibid., 249.

[30] Ibid., 250.

[31] Ibid., 251.

[32] *NILES' NATIONAL REGISTER.*, Fifth Series.—No. 27.—Vol. XVI], Baltimore, August 31, 1844., [Vol. LXVI.—Whole No. 1,718, page 433. (copy in possession of the author).

Chapter Two

MORMON DOCTRINES

This chapter will be a brief overview of Mormon doctrines and organization. It is important for you to have a foundation to work from so you may fully grasp the primary concern of this book, which is deeply rooted in Mormon doctrine.

You have to understand the organization of the Mormon Church in order to understand the power behind it. First, let's look at the "First Presidency." So, who, and what, is the "First Presidency?" It is the absolute top of the leadership and power pyramid. The Mormon Church's First Presidency is made up of:

THE PROPHET
(OR PRESIDENT)

/ \

1ST COUNSELOR   2ND COUNSELOR

Directly under the First Presidency is the Quorum of the Twelve Apostles; often referred to as the Council of the Twelve. The President of the Quorum of the Twelve also wields great power in the Church.

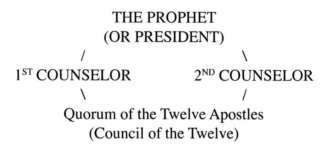

THE PROPHET
(OR PRESIDENT)

/ \

1ST COUNSELOR   2ND COUNSELOR

\ /

Quorum of the Twelve Apostles
(Council of the Twelve)

These fifteen men, the three men of the First Presidency and the Twelve Apostles, are revered by Mormons as the very "Oracles of God" on earth and are referred to as "The Brethren":

> "Men who receive revelations or oracles for the people are themselves called *oracles*. (2 Sam. 16:23.) Members of the First Presidency, [and] Council of the Twelve ... – because they are appointed and sustained as prophets, seers, and revelators to the Church – are known as the *living oracles*."[1]

These fifteen men, according to Mormonism, have a special spiritual endowment in connection with teaching people:

> "Although the Church has many men who serve as "General Authorities," only the First Presidency and the members of the Quorum of the Twelve Apostles are sustained as prophets, seers, and revelators."[2]
>
> "It should be in mind that some of the General Authorities have had assigned to them a special calling; they possess a special gift; they are sustained as prophets, seers, and revelators, which gives them a special spiritual endowment in connection with their teaching the people. They have the **right**, the **power**, and **authority**

to declare the mind and will of God to his people…"[3] (emphasis added.)

Twice a year in the General Conference of the Mormon Church, held the first week of April and the first week of October in Salt Lake City, these fifteen men, "The Brethren," are sustained by the members of the Church in attendance; they are asked to "sustain" these men by a physical vote, denoted by the lifting of the "right arm to the square" (taken from the swearing of oaths in their secret temple ceremony, which is a plagiarism of Scottish Rite Masonry). This vote is also conducted at the regional level throughout the Church twice a year in their "Stake Conferences." Chapter Five deals exclusively with the primacy of this doctrine.

It is important to understand this principle of "speaking for God," because the majority of Mormon doctrine comes from the teachings of these men from their General Conference "talks" or from their books or other writings. Mormon Church instructional manuals are replete with excerpts from these Conference "talks" and writings.

Mormonism also brings forth what it calls additional scripture to the Bible. Mormonism claims the Book of Mormon, The Doctrine and Covenants, and The Pearl of Great Price, as additional books of divine scripture.

As stated in Chapter One, Mormonism teaches that the Book of Mormon was recorded on plates of gold that were revealed by an angel to Joseph Smith so he could translate them. They are reported to have been written in "reformed Egyptian"; however, the angel "Moroni" took the plates away after the translation so no verification may be accomplished. The Book of Mormon is purported to be a history of two groups of people; one from the Tower of Babel, and the other, a group of Jews from Jerusalem around 600 B.C. Both groups are reported to have sailed by boats to the Americas and are the ancestors of the indigenous peoples of the Americas. DNA conclusively proves that the indigenous peoples of the Americas are not of Jewish descent; they are of Asiatic and Mongolian descent. No physical evidence has ever been found to validate the claims made by The Book of Mormon. The only "proof" to validate The Book of Mormon, is a request made in the book itself. In Moroni, the last book in The Book of Mormon, Chapter 10 verse 4 it reads: "And when ye shall receive these things, I would exhort you that ye would ask God, the Eternal Father, in the name of Christ, if these things are not true; and if ye shall ask with a sincere heart, with real intent, having faith in Christ, he will manifest the truth of it unto you, by the power of the Holy Ghost." So, in Mormonism, The Book of Mormon is merely validated by feelings with no evidence supporting the book. Mormonism disregards the volumes of evidence which scientifically, archaeologically, historically or linguistically, disprove the book.

The Doctrine and Covenants is primarily a collection of the prophecies Joseph Smith claimed God gave directly to him (135 out of 138 Sections, plus two "Official Declarations," are believed to be revelations from God). This book has been extensively revised since its original publication and many of the "prophecies" never happened; thus, in accordance with the Bible (Deuteronomy 18:21-22), Joseph Smith is a false prophet.

The Pearl of Great Price is composed of three books: 'Selections From The Book Of Moses,' 'The Book of Abraham' and the book 'Joseph Smith—History.'

Selections From The Book Of Moses, is reported to be extracts from the Book of Genesis from Joseph Smith's Translation of the Bible. Joseph Smith never had any of the ancient manuscripts of the Bible from which to do a translation. He simply sat down with the Bible and rewrote it however his imagination desired. There is no manuscript evidence whatsoever to justify this rewriting of the text.

The Book of Abraham was reported to be a translation of ancient Egyptian papyrus that came into Joseph Smith's possession in 1835. He translated the papyrus into The Book of Abraham. The papyri were believed to have been lost; however the Metropolitan Museum of Art in New York City found the papyri in its archives in November of 1967. The papyri were transferred to the Mormon Church and subsequent translation has shown they are a common funerary text known as "The Book of the Breathings," or "The Book of the Dead." The Book of Abraham translation of these papyri by Joseph Smith has been clearly shown to be fraudulent. (This book is the source in Mormonism for its doctrine of "Pre-existence." Mormonism teaches that all humans were born as "spirit children" to God the Father, through a sexual relationship with one of his polygamous wives in the "Spirit World." This doctrine of "Pre-existence" is the source of the racist teaching that people of color are born that way because of their lack of valiancy in that pre-earth life. This doctrine is fully covered in Appendix Five.)

The Joseph Smith—History, is an extract from The History of Joseph Smith the Prophet (*History of the Church*, Vol. 1, Chapters 1-5). The book details the history leading up to and including Joseph Smith's reported "First Vision," which is the beginning of Mormonism. This "First Vision" is day one, hour one, minute one, second one, of Mormonism. In the "First Vision" Joseph Smith states that he didn't know what church to join, so he went out in the woods to pray and ask God which church was right. He says God the Father and Jesus Christ (two distinct individuals) appeared to him in a vision. He says that God the Father pointed to Jesus and said "This is My Beloved Son. Hear Him!"[4] He goes on to say that when he asked which of all the "sects was right," Jesus told him the following: "19. I was answered that I must join none of them, for they were all wrong; and the Personage who addressed me said that all their creeds were an abomination in his sight; that those professors were all corrupt;" that: "they draw near to me with their lips, but their hearts are far from me, they teach for doctrines the commandments of men, having a form of godliness, but they deny the power thereof."[5] In one sentence Joseph Smith says Jesus Christ told him: All churches are wrong; all Christian Creeds are an abomination (Christian Creeds are Christian Doctrine); and all professors of Christianity are corrupt. Wow! The very first moment of Mormonism, the "First Vision" is an all out attack on Christianity! The mantra of Mormonism today is "We don't say anything bad about any other religion." Nothing could be further from the truth. Verse 19 of Joseph Smith's "First Vision" is a part of the Mormon Canon today. No one can join the Mormon Church and be baptized without professing a belief in the "First Vision" of Joseph Smith. The "First Vision" is the very foundation of Mormonism—without it, there is no Mormon Church.

COMPARING MORMONISM TO THE EIGHT ESSENTIAL FUNDAMENTALS OF CHRISTIANITY

Mormon doctrine is very complex and involved. In a single chapter, I cannot begin to provide but the very basics of Mormon Doctrine. To give you an express comparison, I will use a quick list which I borrowed from Bob Anderson of Watchman Fellowship, called the Eight Essential Fundamentals of Christianity. Watchman Fellowship uses this list to provide a basic look to see how various religious groups line up with the essential fundamentals of Christianity as defined in the Bible:

1. The Deity of Christ
2. The Trinity
3. Bodily Resurrection
4. Salvation by Grace
5. Sufficiency of Scripture
6. Universality of Sin
7. The Atonement
8. The Virgin Birth

Table 1: The Eight Essential Fundamentals of Christianity

Noting differences between the various denominations on non-essentials, when these "essential fundamentals" are compared to Catholic, Protestant and most non-denominational Christian Churches, with few exceptions, they all can agree on these basic tenets of Christianity. Using this doctrinal comparison list, it is possible to identify various religious sects as non-Christian without any bigotry or bias. Knowing that I will be called a bigot for making an accurate, factual comparison of Mormon Doctrine to this list, I'll take the heat because I believe it is imperative for the reader to understand some of these doctrinal positions in order to fully grasp the principles that will be discussed in later chapters. So, how does Mormonism compare to the "Eight Fundamentals of Christianity?"

1. The Deity of Christ	NO
2. The Trinity	NO
3. Bodily Resurrection	NO (with qualification)
4. Salvation by Grace	NO
5. Sufficiency of Scripture	NO
6. Universality of Sin	NO
7. The Atonement	NO
8. The Virgin Birth	NO

Table 2: Comparing Mormon Doctrine to the Eight
Essential Fundamentals of Christianity.

Christianity comes from the Bible. Using the Bible as the standard, let's look more closely at these Eight Essential Fundamentals:

1. THE DEITY OF CHRIST:

CHRISTIANITY: "In the beginning was the Word, and the Word was with God, and the Word was God."[6] "And the Word was made flesh, and dwelt among us, (and we beheld his glory, the glory as of the only begotten of the Father,) full of grace and truth."[7] Christian doctrine says that Jesus is God incarnate (God come in the flesh).

MORMONISM: "**Jesus is man's spiritual brother**. We dwelt with Him in the spirit world as members of that large society of eternal intelligences, which included our

Heavenly Parents and all the personages who have become mortal beings upon this earth or who ever shall come here to dwell. In that spirit-creation, when we became children of God, **Jesus was the "first born," and so He is our eldest brother**."[8] (emphasis added.) "Although **he was a God**, even the Son of God, with power and authority to create this earth and other earths, yet there were some things lacking which he did not receive until after his resurrection."[9] (emphasis added.) Mormon doctrine clearly contradicts Christianity and teaches that Jesus is "a God," and man's older brother—not in fact, God incarnate.

2. THE TRINITY:

CHRISTIANITY: The Christian doctrine of the Trinity cannot be explained in a few paragraphs or even a few pages; nonetheless, it is a foundational teaching of Christianity, because it is taught in the Bible from Genesis to Revelation. The word "Trinity" is not found in the Bible; however, the principle, for which we have coined the word "Trinity," is unquestionably found there. "Part of the problem of understanding the trinity is the inadequacy of human words to express divine reality. For instance, we speak of "Persons" in the Godhead. We use this term because it describes a being who has intellect, emotion, and will. We can understand this. But we must be careful in applying such terms to God. "Three persons" is the usual expression, but it is an imperfect term, denoting separate moral or rational individuals. There are not three individuals but *three personal self distinctions* within *one* divine essence."[10]

"Thus saith the Lord the King of Israel, and his redeemer the Lord of hosts; I *am* the first, and I *am* the last; and beside me *there is* no God."[11] This, plus many other Biblical scriptures clearly tell us there is only "one" God. "Go ye therefore, and teach all nations, baptizing them in the name [singular] of the Father, and of the Son, and of the Holy Ghost:"[12] (bracketed word added.) In this passage Matthew was specific in choosing the singular word "name," instead of "names." Matthew clearly understood the Trinitarian nature of God – God is one being, but exists in three persons.

MORMONISM: "**The Father has a body of flesh and bones as tangible as man's**; the Son also; but the **Holy Ghost** has not a body of flesh and bones, but **is a personage of Spirit**. Were it not so, the Holy Ghost could not dwell in us".[13] (emphasis added.) Mormonism teaches that there are three distinct individual Gods that make up the Godhead – denying the Christian belief of "one God." Mormonism also teaches that God the Father has a body of flesh and bones and is an exalted man who once lived on another planet in another galaxy, far, far away: "**God himself was once as we are now, and is an exalted man, and sits enthroned in yonder heavens! That is the great secret....and that he was once a man like us; yea, that God himself, the Father of us all, dwelt on an earth, the same as Jesus Christ himself did; and I will show it from the Bible**."[14] (emphasis added.)That principle cannot be found in the Bible and is a contradiction to Christianity. However, it is part and parcel of Mormonism.

3. BODILY RESURRECTION:

CHRISTIANITY: "And this is the will of him that sent me, that every one which seeth the Son, and believeth on him, may have everlasting life: and I will raise him up at the last day."[15] "Jesus said unto her, I am the resurrection, and the life: he that believeth in me, though he were dead, yet shall he live:"[16] The concept of "resurrection" is foundational in Christianity. However, Christianity teaches that part of the resurrection is judgment. People will be judged and resurrected to live with Jesus Christ for eternity if they trusted on Jesus, and what he did on the Cross of Calvary, and placed their sins on him, or be sent to Hell if they did not, thereby dying in their sin. "And many of them that sleep in the dust of the earth shall awake, some to everlasting life, and some to shame *and* everlasting contempt."[17]

MORMONISM: "In the resurrection, some are raised to be angels, others are raised to become Gods."[18] "Contrary to the views found in the uninspired teachings and creeds of modern Christendom, there are in eternity *kingdoms of glory* to which all resurrected persons (except the **sons of perdition**) [see note] will eventually go. These are named: *celestial, terrestrial,* and *telestial*—the glory of each being beyond mortal comprehension. (D. & C. 76; 1 Cor. 15:39-42; Rev. 21.)"[19] (bracketed information and emphasis added.) Mormonism contradicts Christianity, teaching that there are different levels of heaven, called *"kingdoms of glory."* These are the "Celestial Kingdom, the Terrestial Kingdom, and the Telestial Kingdom," highest to lowest respectively; Mormonism also teaches that hell only exists prior to the resurrection and then is abolished thereafter—all in direct contradiction to the Bible: "Highest among the kingdoms of glory hereafter is the *celestial kingdom.*"[20] "Those attaining a terrestrial kingdom will be inheritors of *terrestrial glory* which differs from celestial glory 'as that of the moon differs from the sun in the firmament.'"[21] "That glory granted the inhabitants of the lowest kingdom of glory is called *telestial glory.*"[22] "Hell will have an end."[23] Yes, Mormons believe in the resurrection from the dead; however, the Christian doctrine of being everlastingly resurrected to heaven or hell is directly contradicted by Mormon doctrine.

NOTE – WHO ARE "SONS OF PERDITION?"

In the above quote it says that all men will be resurrected and go to *"kingdoms of glory," "*except the **sons of perdition**." So, who are the "sons of perdition?" The quick answer: <u>ANYONE WHO DARES TO LEAVE THE MORMON CHURCH</u>! Anyone who leaves the Mormon Church is labeled an apostate. Brigham Young made the following statement concerning apostates:

"The Lord is merciful, but, when He comes to His Kingdom on the earth, He will banish traitors from His presence, and they will be sons of perdition. Every apostate who ever received this gospel in faith, and had the Spirit of it, will have to repent in sackcloth and ashes, and sacrifice all he possesses, or be a son of perdition, go down to hell, and there dwell with the damned; and those who persecute and destroy the people of God, and shed the blood of innocence, will be judged accordingly."[24] (emphasis added.)

Anyone who leaves the Mormon Church is called an apostate. They will not go to any of the "Three Degrees of Glory." They will be cast into "Outer Darkness" with Satan and the demons. Mormon Apostle Bruce R. McConkie addresses the destiny of those who become "sons of perdition":

"Their destiny, following their resurrection, is to be cast out with the devil and his angels, to inherit the same kingdom in a state where 'their worm dieth not, and the fire is not quenched.'"[25]

President Joseph Fielding Smith teaches that only those who have "known the light," can become a "son of perdition." In this next quote he specifically associates membership in the Mormon Church with having "known" or "received" the light:

"I think I am safe in saying that no man can become a Son of Perdition until he has known the light.

Those who have never received the light are not to become Sons of Perdition. They will be punished if they rebel against God. They will have to pay the price of their sinning, but **it is only those who have the light through the priesthood and through the power of God and <u>through their membership in the Church</u> who will be banished forever from his influence into outer darkness to dwell with the devil and his angels.** That is a punishment that will not come to those who have never known the truth. Bad as they may suffer, and awful as their punishment may be, they are not among that group which is to suffer the eternal death and banishment from all influence concerning the power of God."[26] (emphasis added.)

I was born into the Mormon Church. As an adult I was challenged that what I had been brought up to believe about the Mormon Church wasn't true. I began to do some investigation. I wanted evidence with which to refute the challenge. My research uncovered a world of Mormonism I had never seen. I found the origins, history and doctrines of Mormonism had been altered, changed, rewritten, and falsified—all without note or mention.

In the Mormon faith, members are taught from the time they are "knee high to a toadstool" that being an apostate to Mormonism is the worst fate this world has to offer. Within the bounds of Mormon Doctrine, Hitler, with the blood of over six million innocent people on his hands, has the opportunity to ascend in the next life and become a God. Not so with an apostate to Mormonism, their fate is to be cast into outer darkness and spend eternity with Satan and the demons.

Confronted with the overwhelming evidence that the Mormonism I had grown up in was a fraud, I had a very difficult decision to make. I knew that if I decided to leave, I would be branded an apostate and viewed by Mormons as less of a human being than Adolf Hitler. For me, truth overruled scorn, and I asked to have my name removed from the rolls of the Mormon Church.

Over the years I have talked with many Mormons who have come to the same point in their lives as I did with respect to the evidence about Mormonism's origins, history and doctrines. Yet, they will not take the step I have taken to leave. The price is too high. They will not risk losing their families, job or status in the Church and community in which they live. So, they just go through the motions, trapped in a system they dare not challenge.

4. <u>SALVATION BY GRACE:</u>

CHRISTIANITY: "For by grace are ye saved through faith; and that not of yourselves: *it is* the gift of God: Not of works, lest any man should boast."[27] "And if by grace, then *is it* no more of works: otherwise grace is no more grace. But if *it be* of works, then is it no more grace: otherwise work is no more work."[28] Christianity believes salvation comes in Christ alone, through faith alone, by grace alone.

MORMONISM: Spencer W. Kimball, the 12th Mormon prophet, stated that grace was "a fallacious doctrine," in his book *The Miracle of Forgiveness*: "**One of the most fallacious doctrines originated by Satan and propounded by man is that man is saved alone by the grace of God**; that belief in Jesus Christ alone is all that is needed for salvation."[29] "However, one of the **untrue doctrines** found in modern Christendom is the concept that man can **gain salvation** (meaning in the kingdom of God) **by grace alone** and without obedience. This **soul-destroying doctrine** [salvation by grace] has the obvious effect of lessening the determination of an individual to **conform to all of the laws and**

ordinances of the gospel, such conformity being essential if the sought for reward is in reality to be gained."[30] (bracketed information and emphasis added.) Mormonism believes "for we know that it is by grace that we are saved, after all we can do."[31] This Book of Mormon verse, 2 Nephi 25:23, coupled with the above quotes from a Mormon Prophet and Apostle, clearly show that Mormonism teaches that salvation by grace alone is false teaching. Mormonism teaches that one must live all the commandments of God to be 'saved.' This belief is purely contradictory to Christianity as the Bible clearly taught us that only one man fulfilled the "Law," the God-man, Jesus Christ.

5. SUFFICIENCY OF SCRIPTURE:

CHRISTIANITY: "Heaven and earth shall pass away, but my words shall not pass away."[32] "The grass withereth, the flower fadeth: but the word of our God shall stand for ever."[33]

MORMONISM: Joseph Smith, founding prophet of Mormonism originally penned "Fourteen Articles of Faith." In the revised "Articles of Faith," number eight reads: "8. We believe the Bible to be the word of God as far as it is translated correctly; we also believe the Book of Mormon to be the word of God."[34] (Note that the Bible is given qualifications for validity; however, the Book of Mormon is not.)

Joseph Smith did not believe the Bible could be trusted: "Ignorant translators, careless transcribers, or designing and corrupt priests have committed many errors."[35]

One of the original Mormon Twelve Apostles, Orson Pratt, said, "Who, in his right mind, could, for one moment, suppose the Bible in its present form to be a perfect guide? Who knows that even one verse of the Bible has escaped pollution?"[36]

It should be noted that since the first publications of the additional books of Mormon scripture (The Book of Mormon, The Doctrine and Covenants (originally published as The Book of Commandments), and The Pearl of Great Price), thousands of additions and deletions have been made to those texts; even though Mormonism claims they were given by direct revelation and were perfectly delivered to their prophets.

6. UNIVERSALITY OF SIN:

CHRISTIANITY: It is a foundational teaching in Christianity that through Adam's sin in the Garden of Eden, a sinful nature was passed on to the human race; this is evident in David's statement in Psalms 51: "Behold, I was shapen in iniquity; and in sin did my mother conceive me."[37] David wasn't condemning his mother as conceiving him in some kind of sinful relationship, he was speaking of the Biblical concept that man has a sinful nature. "Among whom also we all had our conversation in times past in the lusts of our flesh, fulfilling the desires of the flesh and of the mind; and were by nature the children of wrath, even as others."[38] Christianity sees the heart of man as wicked: "The heart *is* deceitful above all *things*, and desperately wicked: who can know it?"[39] Christianity teaches that all men are sinners: "For all have sinned, and come short of the glory of God;"[40] Anyone who says they are not sinners, or haven't sinned, are fooling themselves: "If we say that we have no sin, we deceive ourselves, and the truth is not in us."[41]

MORMONISM: The doctrine of man having a sinful nature doesn't exist in Mormonism; it teaches that part of God's overall plan was that Adam would disobey Him and eat of the fruit in the Garden: "Adam fell that men might be; and men are that they might have joy."[42] Brigham Young expounded on this principle: "Some may regret that our first parents sinned. This is nonsense. If we had been there, and they had not sinned, we should have sinned. I will not blame Adam or Eve, why? **Because it was necessary that sin should enter the world**; no man could ever understand the principle of exaltation without its opposite; no one could ever receive an exaltation without being acquainted with its opposite. How did Adam and Eve sin? Did they come out in direct opposition to God and to His government? No. But they transgressed a command of the Lord, and through that transgression sin came into the world. The Lord knew they would do this, and **He had designed that they should**."[43] (emphasis added.) In Mormonism, Adam and Eve fell upward. In the January 2006 issue of the Mormon Church's official magazine, *Ensign*, the 10th Mormon Prophet, Joseph Fielding Smith, is quoted as agreeing with Brigham Young: "When Adam was placed in the Garden of Eden, he was in the presence of God our Eternal Father. He talked with the Father and the Father with him. But something happened, **and it had to happen**: Adam partook of certain fruit. My Bible, the King James Version, [speaks in a commentator's note] of Adam's Fall [as] "man's shameful fall." **Well, it wasn't a shameful fall at all**."[44] (emphasis added.) Mormon scripture contradicts the Bible in saying that man is innocent before God: "Every spirit of man was innocent in the beginning; and God having redeemed man from the fall, men became again, in their infant state, innocent before God."[45]

7. THE ATONEMENT:

CHRISTIANITY: Christianity wouldn't be Christianity without the atoning sacrifice of Jesus Christ upon the Cross of Calvary. Foundational to a Christian belief is that Jesus Christ gave His life, and shed His blood, as a substitute sacrifice for the sins of mankind. "But God commendeth his love toward us, in that, while we were yet sinners, Christ died for us. Much more then, being now justified by his blood, we shall be saved from wrath through him."[46] It is the belief of Christianity that if one accepts this act of Christ the Savior for us on Calvary, then our sins are washed away in Him and His righteousness becomes our righteousness: "For he hath made him *to be* sin for us, who knew no sin; that we might be made the righteousness of God in him."[47] Christianity holds that **ALL** sin was paid for on the Cross of Calvary – **NOT JUST SOME SIN – ALL SIN!!** "But if we walk in the light, as he is in the light, we have fellowship one with another, and the blood of Jesus Christ his Son cleanseth us from all sin."[48]

MORMONISM: It is a foundational teaching of Mormonism that Jesus' Blood **does not** cover all sin. Brigham Young taught: "It is true that the blood of the Son of God was shed for sins through the fall and those committed by men, yet **men can commit sins which it can never remit**."[49] (emphasis added.) Joseph Smith taught this principle as well: *"Joseph Smith taught that there were certain sins so grievous that man may commit, that they will place the transgressors beyond the power of the atonement of Christ. If these offenses are committed, then the blood of Christ will not cleanse them from their sins even though they repent. Therefore, their only hope is to have their own blood shed to atone, as far as possible, in their behalf.* This is scriptural doctrine, and is taught in all the standard works of the Church."[50] (*italics* in the original.) 10th Mormon Prophet, Joseph Fielding Smith, agrees with both Joseph and Brigham: *"But man may commit certain grievous sins—according to his light and knowledge—that will place him beyond the reach of the atoning blood of Christ. If then he would be saved he must make sacrifice of his own life to atone—so far as in his power lies—for that sin, for the blood of Christ alone under certain circumstances will not avail."*[51] (*italics* in the original.) This teaching of Mormonism absolutely contradicts the Biblical teachings of Christianity.

8. THE VIRGIN BIRTH:

CHRISTIANITY: The Virgin Birth of the Savior is another foundational teaching of Christianity which begins in the Messianic Prophecies of the Old Testament: "Therefore the Lord himself shall give you a sign; Behold, a virgin shall conceive, and bear a son, and shall call his name Immanuel."[52] Matthew and Luke tell us about this miracle: "Now the birth of Jesus Christ was on this wise: When as his mother Mary was espoused to Joseph, before they came together, she was found with child of the Holy Ghost."[53] "And the angel said unto her: Fear not, Mary: for though hast found favor with God. And, behold, thou shalt conceive in thy womb, and bring forth a son, and shalt call his name JESUS. Then said Mary unto the angel, How shall this be, seeing I know not a man? And the angel answered and said unto her, The Holy Ghost shall come upon thee, and the power of the Highest shall overshadow thee: therefore also that holy thing which shall be born of thee shall be called the Son of God."[54]

MORMONISM: Again, Mormon doctrine contradicts Biblical Christian doctrine. Numerous quotes from Mormonism are available to substantiate this contradiction. This Mormon doctrine tends to infuriate not only Christians, but uninformed Mormons as well. I will provide several basic quotes here and then place some more lengthy quotes with commentary in Appendix Two. Mormon doctrine teaches that God is an exalted man, and, in the "Pre-existence," sired all of the people who will ever live on this planet. Some very awkward circumstances come out of the Mormon explanation of Jesus' birth. To understand some of the following quotes, the reader needs to know that Mormon doctrine identifies the name of God the Father as Elohim. Brigham

Young denied the Biblical teaching that Mary "was found with child of the Holy Ghost" when he said:

"I have given you a few leading items upon this subject, but a great deal more remains to be told. Now remember from this time forth, and for ever, that **JESUS CHRIST WAS NOT BEGOTTEN BY THE HOLY GHOST**."[55] (emphasis added.)

10th Mormon Prophet Joseph Fielding Smith agrees with Brigham Young:

"They tell us the Book of Mormon states that **Jesus was begotten of the Holy Ghost. I CHALLENGE THAT STATEMENT. The Book of Mormon teaches NO SUCH THING! NEITHER DOES THE BIBLE**."[56] (emphasis added.)

In this next statement by Brigham Young, he clearly says that Jesus was conceived the same way that mortal men are conceived; the phrase "was begotten of his Father, as we were of our Fathers," is quite clear and specific:

"**The birth of the Saviour was as natural as are the births of our children;** it was the result of **natural action**. **He** partook of flesh and blood—**was begotten of his Father, as we were of our fathers**."[57] (emphasis added.) Mormon Apostle, Bruce R. McConkie in his epic work, Mormon Doctrine, reinforces the above statements: "These name-titles all signify that our Lord is the only Son of the Father in flesh. Each of the words is to be understood literally. **Only means only; Begotten means begotten; and Son means son. Christ was begotten by an Immortal Father in the same way that mortal men are begotten by mortal fathers**."[58] (emphasis added.)

The 13th Mormon Prophet, Ezra Taft Benson, who served as Prophet until his death in 1995, used an even more specific term in Jesus' conception, "sired":

"Jesus Christ is the Son of God in the most literal sense. **The body in which He performed His mission in the flesh was SIRED** by that same Holy Being we worship as God, our Eternal Father. He was not the son of Joseph, **nor was He begotten by the Holy Ghost. He is the Son of the Eternal Father**!"[59] (emphasis added.)

In the April 2002 edition of *Ensign,* under "Gospel Classics" we are given "A Doctrinal Exposition by the First Presidency and the Quorum of the Twelve Apostles" in an article titled "The Father & the Son." In the article it states:

"Jesus Christ applies to Himself both titles, "Son" and "Father." Indeed, He specifically said to the brother of Jared: "Behold, I am Jesus Christ. I am the Father and the Son" (Ether 3:14). **Jesus Christ is the Son of Elohim BOTH AS SPIRITUAL AND BODILY OFFSPRING**; that is to say, **Elohim is LITERALLY THE FATHER OF THE SPIRIT OF JESUS CHRIST AND ALSO THE BODY** in which Jesus Christ performed His mission in the flesh, and which body died on the cross and was afterward taken up by the process of resurrection, and is now the immortalized tabernacle of the external spirit of our Lord and Savior. No extended explanation of the title "Son of God" as applied to Jesus Christ appears necessary."[60] (emphasis added.)

To try and explain away the obvious incest implications brought about by the Mormon doctrines that God is an exalted man, sired all of humanity in a "Pre-existent" spirit world, including Mary the mother of Jesus, and that Jesus was conceived the same way mortal men are conceived, Mormon Apostle Orson Pratt gave us the following explanation:

"The fleshly body of Jesus required a Mother as well as a Father. Therefore, the Father and Mother of Jesus, according to the **flesh,** must have been associated together in the **capacity of Husband and Wife**; hence **the Virgin Mary must have been, for the time being, the** *lawful* **wife of God the Father**: we use the term *lawful* Wife, because it would be blasphemous in the highest degree to say that He overshadowed her or begat the Saviour unlawfully. It would have been unlawful for any *man* to have interfered with Mary, who was already espoused to Joseph; for such a heinous crime would have subjected both the guilty parties to death, according to the law of Moses. **But God** having created all men and women, **had the most perfect right to do with His own creation, according to His holy will and pleasure**: He had a lawful right to overshadow the Virgin Mary in the capacity of a husband, and beget a Son, although she was espoused to another; **for the law which He gave to govern men and women was not intended to govern Himself, or to prescribe rules for his own conduct**."[61] (*italics* in the original, emphasis added.)

That explanation, that God can do what he calls sin in His Holy Word the Bible, because He is God, is a totally blasphemous statement.

This last, hideous statement is a quote by Mormon Apostle Melvin J. Ballard explaining the role of the Holy Ghost in Jesus' conception. Having already seen the above, four different Mormon Prophets (including the current Prophet, Gordon B. Hinckley) deny that Mary was with child by the Holy Ghost, Apostle Ballard, who has "the **right**, the **power**, and **authority to declare the mind and will of God** to his people..."[62] (emphasis added.), provides a distasteful explanation of the conception of Jesus:

"ONE of the great questions that I have referred to that the world is concerned about, and is in confusion over, is as to whether or not **his was a virgin birth**, a birth wherein divine power interceded. **Joseph Smith** made it perfectly clear that Jesus Christ told the absolute truth, as did those who testify concerning him, the Apostles of the Lord Jesus Christ, wherein he is declared to be the very Son of God. And if God the Eternal Father is not the real Father of Jesus Christ, then are we in confusion; then is he not in reality the Son of God. But we declare that he *is* the Only Begotten of the Father in flesh.

Mary told the story most beautifully when she said that an angel of the Lord came to her and told her that she had found favor in the sight of God, and had come to be worthy of the fulfillment of the promises heretofore made, to become the **virgin mother** of the Redeemer of the world. She afterwards, referring to the event, said: "God hath done wonderful things unto me." "And the Holy Ghost came upon her," is the story, "and she came into the presence of the highest." **No man or woman can live in mortality and survive the presence of the Highest except by the sustaining power of the Holy Ghost. So it** [the Holy Ghost] **came upon her to prepare her for** [what?] **admittance into the divine presence**, and the power of the Highest, who is the Father [**an exalted man of flesh and bones**], was present, and overshadowed her [**physical sexual act**], and the holy Child that was born of her was called the Son of God.

Men who deny this, or who **think that it degrades our Father**, have no true conception of the sacredness of the most marvelous power which God has endowed mortal men—**the power of creation [ability to have** children]. Even though that power may be abused and may become a mere harp of pleasure to the wicked, nevertheless it is the most sacred and holy and divine function with which God has endowed man. Made holy, it is retained by the Father of us all, and **in his exercise of that great and marvelous creative power** and function, **he did not debase himself, degrade himself, nor debauch his daughter** [if there was no physical act between Father and daughter, there wouldn't be any debasing, degrading, or debauchery]. **Thus Christ became the literal Son of a divine Father, and no one else was worthy to be his father**."[63] (bracketed information and emphasis added.)

TWO OTHER IMPORTANT DOCTRINAL POINTS

Two other Mormon doctrinal points need to be discussed here in order to understand later chapters of this book, specifically Chapter Nine "Mountain Meadows Massacre." These two doctrines are: Innocent Blood and Blood Atonement.

INNOCENT BLOOD: Children under the age of eight-years-old are considered in Mormonism to be innocent and free from any sin. As discussed in the Eight Fundamentals of Christianity, Number (6) Universality of Sin, Mormonism does not believe that man has a sinful nature. The Mormon definition of "innocence": (1) In the gospel sense, innocence is the state of purity and freedom from sin which men must possess to gain salvation in the kingdom of God. (Alma 11:37.) Little children live in a state of perfect innocence and consequently are saved without works on their part.[64] (emphasis added.) (2) Attainment of the age and state of accountability is a gradual process. Thus the Lord says "power is not given unto Satan to tempt little children, until they begin to become accountable before me." (D. & C. 29:47.) Children who develop normally become accountable "**when eight years old**" (D. & C. 68:27)...[65] (emphasis added.)

BLOOD ATONEMENT: Mormonism teaches that there are some sins so grievous that the "Blood of Christ," cannot cover, or atone, for them. *"Joseph Smith taught that there were certain sins so grievous that man may commit, that they will place the transgressors beyond the power of the atonement of Christ. If these offenses are committed, then the blood of Christ will not cleanse them from their sins even though they repent. Therefore their only hope is to have their own blood shed to atone, as far as possible, in their behalf. This is scriptural doctrine, and is taught in all standard works of the Church."*[66] (*italics* in the original.)

WHAT'S THE POINT?

A basic understanding of Mormon doctrines is required in order to discuss almost any aspect of the influence the religion has on its members. Mormonism is very different from the Christian denominations found in the U.S. and around the world. Christian sects do not require oaths and covenants of obedience to gain, or maintain, membership (these will be discussed in follow-on chapters). One cannot begin to understand the inner workings of Mormonism without a basic knowledge of its core beliefs; nor, grasp the significance that these beliefs do not come from the Bible, but from an absolute dependence on their "living oracles."

When Mormonism is compared to the Eight Essential Fundamentals of Christianity, its doctrines do not align with any of those fundamentals. When statements are made that Mormonism is not Christian, those making the statements are vilified, when in reality they are simply making those statements based on a "Doctrinal" comparison between Mormonism and the Bible. So, are those of us who investigate, and with documented evidence make claims about

Mormonism based on that documented research, bigots? No! We are simply being accurate in a "Doctrinal" comparison; that doesn't make us bigots, it makes us investigative reporters.

Is Mormonism Christian? Evidence is what it is—let the evidence stand on its own merit.

¹ *Teachings of the Living Prophets*, Student Manual Religion 333, Published by The Church of Jesus Christ of Latter-day Saints (Salt Lake City, Utah, 1982) 6.
² Ibid., 8.
³ Ibid., 9.
⁴ *The Pearl of Great Price*, Published by The Church of Jesus Christ of Latter-day Saints, Salt Lake City, Utah, U.S.A., 1989) Joseph Smith 1:17. (Hereafter *POGP*)
⁵ Ibid., Joseph Smith 1:19.
⁶ *Bible*, King James Version, (B. B. Kirkbride Bible Co., Inc, Indianapolis, Indiana, 1982) John 1:1. (hereafter *KJV*),
⁷ *KJV*, John 1:14.
⁸ Milton R. Hunter, *The Gospel Through the Ages*, Stevens and Walls, Inc., (Salt Lake City, 1945) 21.
⁹ Joseph Fielding Smith, *Doctrines of Salvation: Sermons and Writings of Joseph Fielding Smith*. 3 vols., compiled by Bruce R. McConkie. (Bookcraft, Salt Lake City, 1954-56) 1:33.
¹⁰ Paul E. Little, *Know What You Believe*, Cook Communications Ministries (Colorado Springs, Colorado, 2003) 30.
¹¹ *KJV*, Isaiah 44:6.
¹² *KJV*, Matthew 28:19.
¹³ *The Doctrine and Covenants Of The Church Of Jesus Christ Of Latter-day Saints, Containing Revelations Given To Joseph Smith, The Prophet With Some Additions By His Successors In The Presidency Of The*

Church, Published by The Church of Jesus Christ of Latter-day Saints (Salt Lake City, Utah 1989) 130:22. (hereafter *Doctrine & Covenants*)

[14] Joseph Smith, *Teachings of the Prophet Joseph Smith,* compiled by Joseph Fielding Smith, (Deseret Book Company, Salt Lake City, Utah, 1974) 345-6.

[15] *KJV,* John 6:40.

[16] Ibid., John 11:25.

[17] Ibid., Daniel 12:2.

[18] Smith, *Teachings of the Prophet Joseph Smith,* 312.

[19] Bruce R. McConkie, *Mormon Doctrine,* Bookcraft (Salt Lake City, Utah, 1966) 420.

[20] Ibid., 116.

[21] Ibid., 784.

[22] Ibid., 778.

[23] Ibid., 349.

[24] Brigham Young in Evans, ed., *Journal of Discourses,* 12:63. (26 volumes)

[25] *Mormon Doctrine,* 746.

[26] Joseph Fielding Smith, Conference Report, October 1958, p. 21, as found on the CD "LDS Library 2006" by Deseret Book.

[27] *KJV,* Ephesians 2:8-9.

[28] Ibid., Romans 11:6.

[29] Spencer W. Kimball, *The Miracle of Forgiveness,* (Bookcraft, Salt Lake City, Utah, 1969) 206.

[30] McConkie, *Mormon Doctrine,* 670-671.

[31] *The Book of Mormon,* Published by The Church of Jesus Christ of Latter-day Saints (Salt Lake City, Utah, 1989) 2 Nephi 25:23.

[32] *KJV,* Matthew 24:35.

[33] Ibid., Isaiah 40:8.

[34] *POGP,* 60.

[35] Smith, *Teachings of the Prophet Joseph Smith,* 327.

[36] Orson Pratt, *Divine Authenticity of the Book of Mormon. From a series of pamphlets*. Liverpool, England: n.p., 1851.

[37] *KJV*, Psalms 51:5

[38] Ibid., Ephesians 2:3.

[39] Ibid., Jeremiah 17:9.

[40] Ibid., Romans 3:23.

[41] Ibid., I John 1:8.

[42] *The Book of Mormon*, 2 Nephi 2:25.

[43] Brigham Young in Watt, ed., *Journal of Discourses*, 10:312.

[44] *Ensign*, Published Monthly by The Church of Jesus Christ of Latter-day Saints, (Salt Lake City, Utah) January 2006, 52.

[45] *D & C* 93:38.

[46] *KJV*, Romans 5:8-9.

[47] Ibid., II Corinthians 5:21.

[48] Ibid., I John 1:7.

[49] Brigham Young in Watt, ed., *Journal of Discourses*, 4:54.

[50] Smith, *Doctrines of Salvation*, 1:135.

[51] Ibid., 1:134.

[52] *KJV*, Isaiah 7:14.

[53] Ibid., Matthew 1:18.

[54] Ibid., Luke 1:30-31; 34-35.

[55] Brigham Young in Watt, ed., *Journal of Discourses*, 1:51.

[56] Smith, *Doctrines of Salvation*, 1:19

[57] Brigham Young in Watt, ed., *Journal of Discourses*, 8:115.

[58] McConkie, *Mormon Doctrine*, 546-547.

[59] Ezra Taft Benson, *I Know that my Redeemer Lives: Latter-day Prophets Testify of the Savior*, Deseret Book, page 205, as quoted in Church News, December 18, 2004, pg 16.

[60] *Ensign*, April 2002, 14.

[61] Orson Pratt, *The Seer (1853-1854)*, (photo reprint) (Photographs obtained from the LDS Historical Department, Published by EBORN BOOKS, 1990, copy 161 of 1000) 158.

[62] *Teachings of the Living Prophets*, 9.

[63] Melvin J. Ballard, *Sermons and Missionary Services of Melvin Joseph Ballard*, Deseret Book Company (Salt Lake City, Utah, 1949) 166-167.

[64] McConkie, *Mormon Doctrine*, 381.

[65] Ibid., 853.

[66] Smith, *Doctrines of Salvation*, 1:135.

Chapter Three

THE MORMON PRIESTHOOD

To understand the conflict between Mormonism and governmental positions of authority, one must understand the Mormon concept of "Priesthood." Mormonism is very different from either Catholicism or Protestantism with respect to its "Priesthood." As in most Mormon doctrinal items, the common words of Christianity take on a very different meaning. Christianity and Mormonism share a common vocabulary; however, they each have their own dictionaries. The Mormon Priesthood is the single, all controlling entity without which, Mormonism disintegrates and ceases to function.

The Mormon Priesthood is an all male system. A young Mormon male, if found worthy (very few are not), will be ordained into the following offices: "Deacon" at age twelve, "Teacher" at fourteen, and "Priest" at sixteen. All of these offices, Deacon, Teacher, and Priest, are found in the lower or Aaronic Priesthood. On any Sunday across the world, these boys gather at Priesthood Meeting, along with their adult male counterparts, in their individual "quorum" meetings. Each office (Deacon, Teacher, Priest, Elder, etc.) meets and associates in its "quorum." The "quorum" is a primary

Priesthood organizational structure within the Mormon Church. All members of each Priesthood office (Deacon, Teacher, Priest, Elder, Seventy, High Priest) at the Ward or Stake level are organized into 'quorums.' At the highest levels of the Church, the First Presidency is the Presiding Quorum of the Church. The Twelve Apostles of the Church are commonly referred to as The Quorum of the Twelve.

At the age of nineteen, usually in association with his departure on a two year "mission" as a full time missionary for the LDS Church, a young Mormon male will be ordained as an Elder in the Melchizedek Priesthood (higher Priesthood). As you can already see, the Christian church would not recognize twelve year old "Deacons," fourteen year old "Teachers," sixteen year old "Priests," or nineteen year old boys as "Elders." Those positions in Christianity are held by older, more mature in the faith believers, not mere boys. Those positions in Christianity are also relatively few in number, not encompassing every male member twelve years old and above.

Joseph Fielding Smith, 10th Prophet of the Mormon Church made the following statement about the Mormon Priesthood in his book *"Religious Truths Defined"*:

"Priesthood is the power of God. It is everlasting because God is everlasting. By this power the heavens exist and worlds without number have been created, are being created, and will be created. Through priesthood, all things move in their times and seasons. Without it, nothing would exist. **Priesthood is authority delegated to man by which he is permitted to officiate in the ordinances of the gospel as an official representative of God**."[1] (emphasis added.)

As can be clearly seen by this quote, Mormonism views its "Priesthood" as the power given to men by God to "offi-

cially" represent Him. This definition is taken literally by the
Mormon Church.

During the General Conference Priesthood Session,
March 31, 2007, President Thomas S. Monson, First
Counselor in the First Presidency, quoted the above prophet's
father, Joseph F. Smith, 6th Prophet of the Mormon Church:

> "...We who hold the priesthood are, in the words
> of the Apostle Peter, "a chosen generation, a royal
> priesthood."
>
> President Joseph F. Smith defined the priesthood as
> "the power of God delegated to man by which man can
> act in the earth for the salvation of the human family,
> ...**by which [men] may speak the will of God as if the
> angels were here to speak it themselves; by which men
> are empowered to bind on earth and it shall be bound
> in heaven, and to loose on earth and it shall be loosed
> in heaven**." President Smith added, "**[The priesthood]
> is sacred, and it must be held sacred by the people**."
>
> My brethren, the priesthood is a gift which brings
> with it not only **special blessings but also solemn
> responsibilities. It is our responsibility to conduct our
> lives so that we are ever worthy of the priesthood we
> bear**."[2] (emphasis added.)

These last two quotes very clearly delineate the Mormon
belief that their priesthood holders are acting directly for
God. These priesthood holders exercise their God given
power to act for Him specifically and directly on earth.

Let's look at the *Encyclopedia of Mormonism* for a more
in-depth Mormon Church definition of its Priesthood:

> THE SOURCE OF PRIESTHOOD POWER. Jesus
> Christ is the great High Priest of God; Christ is therefore
> the source of all true priesthood authority and power on

this earth (Heb. 5- 10). **Man does not take such priest-hood power unto himself; it must be conferred by God through his servants** (Heb. 5:4; D&C 1:38).

Before the world was created, Jesus Christ, the great Jehovah and firstborn of God the Father in the spirit world, covenanted to use the power he had obtained from the Father to implement God's program for the eternal happiness of all God's children (cf. TPJS, p. 190). The actual name of the priesthood is "the Holy Priesthood after the Order of the Son of God"; but to avoid the too-frequent repetition of the name of deity, it is called by other names, particularly the Melchizedek Priesthood; i.e., it is the same authority held by that righteous king and high priest (Gen. 14:18; Heb. 5:6; Alma 13:6, 17-19; D&C 107:1-4; 124:123).

As the divine Savior, Mediator, and Redeemer, Jesus sets the example for all priesthood performance. "Therefore, what manner of men ought ye to be?" Jesus asked his Nephite disciples whom he had ordained: "Verily I say unto you, even as I am" (3 Ne. 27:27).

DEFINITIONS. Joseph Smith defined priesthood as "an everlasting principle, [which has] existed with God from eternity, and will to eternity, without beginning of days or end of years,...holding the keys of power and bless-ings. **In fact, [the Melchizedek] Priesthood is a perfect law of theocracy**" (TPJS, pp. 157, 322). It is the power and authority by which The Church of Jesus Christ of Latter-day Saints is organized and directed.

The word "priesthood" has several meanings for Latter-day Saints:

1. **Priesthood is power, the power of God, a vital source of eternal strength and energy delegated to men to act in all things for the well-being of**

mankind, both in the world and out of it (DS 3:80; Romney, p. 43).

2. **Priesthood is authority, the exclusive right to act in the name of God as his authorized agents** and to perform ordinances for the purpose of opening certain spiritual blessings to all individuals.
3. Priesthood is the right and responsibility to preside within the organizational structure of the Church, but only in a manner consistent with the agency of others.
4. Sometimes the word priesthood is used to refer to the men of the Church in general (as in "the priesthood will meet in the chapel").

Priesthood power may be exercised only under the direction of the one holding the right, or keys, to authorize its use. Priesthood power functions in accord with the characteristics and attributes of God himself, namely persuasion, long-suffering, gentleness, meekness, love unfeigned, righteousness, virtue, knowledge, justice, judgment, mercy, and truth (D&C 121:41; Lectures on Faith 4). It ceases to exist in a man who uses it to obtain the honors of the world, or to gratify pride, or to cover sin or evil, or to exercise unrighteous dominion (D&C 121:33-37).

Priesthood embraces all forms of God's power. It is the power by which the cosmos was ordered, universes and worlds were organized, and the elements in all their varied structures and relationships were put into place. **Through the priesthood, God governs all things**. By this power, the gospel is preached and understood, and the ordinances of exaltation for both the living and the dead are performed (see Plan of Salvation). **Priesthood is the channel for obtaining revelation, the channel through which God reveals himself and his glory, his**

intents and his purposes, to mankind: The priesthood holds "the key of the mysteries of the kingdom, even the key of the knowledge of God" (D&C 84:19-20; cf. TPJS, pp. 166-67). It conveys the mind and will of God; and, when employed by his servants on his errand, it functions as if by the Lord's own mouth and hand (D&C 1:38).

Thus, the LDS doctrine of priesthood differs from all other views. Priesthood is not vocational or professional (see Clergy). It is not hereditary, passed by inheritance from father to son (even the levitical priesthood was conferred by ordination). It is not offered for money (see Priestcraft). It is not held by a group of specialists who are separated from the community (all worthy Latter-day Saint men are eligible to be ordained to the priesthood). And yet it is not a "priesthood of all believers," as in the Protestant conception (ER 11:529).

HISTORY, ORDERS, AND OFFICES OF THE PRIESTHOOD. Whenever the government of God has existed on the earth, it has functioned through this priesthood power, held by righteous men chosen of God, as were Aaron (Heb. 5:4) and Joshua (Num. 27:18-19). In times of apostasy and wickedness, God has not permitted his servants to confer the priesthood on the unworthy, and it has been lost from the earth. When necessary, the priesthood has been restored with each new dispensation of the gospel.

Following the ascension of Jesus Christ and the death of his apostles, apostasy occurred in the Christian church and priesthood authority was taken from the earth. However, after preparation by God through the lives of earnest and sincere reformers and seekers, mankind again received priesthood authority from angelic ministers who held the keys to this power. Beginning on May

15, 1829, heavenly messengers conferred priesthood authority upon Joseph Smith and Oliver Cowdery in a series of visitations (see Aaronic Priesthood: Restoration of; Melchizedek Priesthood: Restoration of; Doctrine and Covenants: Section 110). These restorations included the Aaronic Priesthood (D&C 13), the Melchizedek Priesthood (D&C 27), the keys of the gathering of Israel (D&C 110:11), the keys of the fulfillment of the Abrahamic Covenant (D&C 110:12), the keys of the binding and sealing power (D&C 110:13-16), and the keys of all dispensations of the gospel "from Michael or Adam down to the present time" (D&C 128:21). **These keys of presiding authority have been in turn conferred upon each succeeding prophet and President of the Church. All priesthood power and authority function today under the direction of the president of the church**, who holds all priesthood keys and powers (see First Presidency; Quorum of the Twelve Apostles; Succession in the Presidency).[3] (emphasis added.)

The above quote from the *Encyclopedia of Mormonism* gives some insight into the understanding, the belief, of Mormons with respect to their "Priesthood." Quite literally, in Mormonism, the "Priesthood" is everything, and controls everything! In the above quote under "THE SOURCE OF PRIESTHOOD POWER," we find the following: "Man does not take such priesthood power unto himself; it must be conferred by God through his servants." Also as seen in the above quoted section "HISTORY, ORDERS, AND OFFICES OF THE PRIESTHOOD," the Mormon Church believes that heavenly messengers (John the Baptist for the Aaronic Priesthood and Peter, James, and John for the Melchizedek Priesthood) came to earth in 1829 and physically conveyed the two orders of the Mormon Priesthood to Joseph Smith and Oliver Cowdrey. **Therefore, Mormons believe they "alone" have the direct "Priesthood" authority from God by lineal descent**. This descent in Mormonism is a belief in the physical transmission of this power, as given to Joseph Smith by John the Baptist and Peter, James and John, and then lineally to each successor to the Mormon position of "Prophet" by the Mormon Twelve Apostles who were originally given that authority by Joseph Smith before his death. The physical ordinations then conducted by "worthy" male members to other "worthy" male members continues this "Priesthood" authority under the reigning power, authority, and keys of the current Mormon Prophet in his "dispensation."

Once you understand that Mormons believe that they alone have the "Priesthood" on the earth today, it is easier to understand the position the Mormon "Priesthood" holds in its "Kingdom of God on earth." In the above quote from the *Encyclopedia of Mormonism* we read: "DEFINITIONS. Joseph Smith defined priesthood as "an everlasting principle, [which has] existed with God from eternity, and will to eternity, without beginning of days or end of years,...holding the keys of power and blessings. **In fact, [the Melchizedek] Priesthood is a perfect law of theocracy**" (TPJS, pp. 157, 322). It is the power and authority by which The Church of Jesus Christ of Latter-day Saints is organized and directed."

As you can see, Joseph Smith calls the Melchizedek Priesthood "a perfect law of theocracy" (Webster's defines theocracy as: a government by a person or persons claiming to rule with divine authority). **Mormonism believes its "Priesthood" has divine authority from God to conduct all aspects of Mormonism in this life and the life to come. This concept is paramount in understanding that the Mormon "Priesthood" authority reaches beyond the grave; an aspect that leverages a very real, controlling power over the living. As the controlling authority for the**

"**Church,**" **which is where salvation lies for the Mormon, allegiance to the "Church" and its controlling authority (the "Priesthood") cannot be underestimated.** Mormon Apostle Mark E. Petersen stated in the article titled "Salvation comes through the Church," printed in the Mormon Church's monthly magazine "*Ensign*":

> "When the Savior established his church during his mortal ministry, and as it was further developed by the twelve apostles of that day, one important fact became conspicuously clear, which is: **that salvation comes through the Church.** It does not come through any separate organization or splinter group nor to any private party as an individual. **It comes only through the Church itself** as the Lord established it. It was **the Church** that was organized for the perfecting of the Saints. It was **the Church** that was given for the work of the ministry. It was **the Church** that was provided to edify the body of Christ, as Paul explained to the Ephesians. Therefore it was made clearly manifest that **salvation is in the Church, and of the Church, and is obtained only through the Church.**"[4] (emphasis added.)

Apostle Petersen's statement here that "**salvation is in the Church, and of the Church, and is obtained only through the Church**" and not through Jesus Christ was printed when he was the fourth most senior Mormon in the "Church" and third in line to become their "Prophet."

In Christianity, one's faith is vested in Jesus Christ and him alone. In Christianity, one's denomination can, and should be, very important to them; however, in Christianity, the denomination, or church one attends, doesn't save them – Jesus Christ saves them. In Mormonism, however, "**The Mormon Church**" saves them and their leaders are revered as God's direct "oracles" on earth. **Allegiance to**

the "Mormon Church," its oracles and the "Priesthood" power they hold, is doctrinal!

The "Mormon Priesthood" is the foundation upon which the Mormon Church is built. The 10th Mormon Prophet, Joseph Fielding Smith, said that <u>all Church authority and offices are but an appendage to the Mormon Priesthood</u>:

ALL OFFICES ARE APPENDAGES TO PRIESTHOOD. When an elder is ordained, he receives the Melchizedek Priesthood and then the office of elder, seventy, or high priest, as the case may be, and the *office* which he receives designates the *nature* of his duties. Not only is the office of bishop and elder an *appendage* to the priesthood but so is every other office, for they all grow out of the priesthood. *The apostle, high priest, seventy, and every other office is an appendage to the priesthood.*

The Lord has, himself, declared that *all authorities or offices in the Church are appendages to the priesthood.* That is to say, *they are circumscribed by priesthood and grow out of it.*[5] (*italics* in the original.)

Something that cannot be ignored is the "<u>covenant</u>" of the Mormon Priesthood. In Section 84 of the additional Mormon scripture, the Doctrine and Covenants, we read this direct revelation from God to Joseph Smith concerning the "Priesthood":

35. And also all they who receive this priesthood receive me, saith the Lord;
36. For he that receiveth my servants receiveth me;
37. And he that receiveth me receiveth my Father;
38. And he that receiveth my Father receiveth my Father's kingdom; therefore all that my Father hath shall be given unto him.

39. And this is according to the **oath and covenant** which belongeth to the priesthood.
40. Therefore, **all those who receive the priesthood, receive this oath and covenant** of my Father, which he cannot break, neither can it be moved.
41. **But whoso breaketh this covenant after he hath received it, and altogether turneth therefrom, shall not have forgiveness of sins in this world nor in the world to come.**[6] (emphasis added.)

As can be seen by these verses that Mormons hold as holy scripture, given by direct revelation from God, any Mormon male who accepts ordination in any Mormon Priesthood office, is bound by an oath and covenant. Notice that anyone who receives the Mormon Priesthood receives also the **servants of the Lord: the Mormon Priesthood leadership**. Receiving the Mormon Priesthood leadership is part of the **oath and covenant – so, if a Mormon Priesthood holder fails to "receive my servants," he breaks his covenant and will have no forgiveness of his sins in this world or the world to come**. Do you see the control that is exercised over the male population in Mormonism? If they fail to follow their "Priesthood" leadership, they are breaking their "**oath and covenant**" and could jeopardize their eternity by not being forgiven of their sins.

What is expected as part and parcel of verse 36 of Section 84 of the *Doctrine and Covenants,* "For he that receiveth my servants receiveth me," is nothing less than complete obedience to those servants:

OBEDIENCE REQUIRED OF ELDERS AS WELL AS APOSTLES. What the Lord has revealed in relation to the priesthood teaches us that the elder, even if he is not given some special responsibility, is under just as great a responsibility to be true to "every word that proceedeth forth from the mouth of God," [Remember Mormon Prophets and Apostles are believed to be God's oracles on earth – they have "the right and authority to speak the mind and the will of God." So when these men speak it is "every word that proceedeth forth from the mouth of God."] as is the man who is called to preside over a stake, or even over the Church. *The apostle is under no greater commandment to be true to his covenant and membership in the Church than is the ordinary elder, or seventy, or any other individual holding the priesthood.* It is true the apostle has a greater responsibility to be true to gospel principles and commandments. Especially is this so, if the elder has received the ordinances of the house of the Lord….[the house of the Lord in Mormonism is defined as a Mormon temple where Mormons swear four different oaths of allegiance to the Mormon Church (see Chapter Six)]

The punishment for the violation of this covenant of the priesthood will come as readily and as surely upon the ordained elder as it will upon the apostle in the Church, who may turn away into forbidden paths and to the neglect of duty.[7] (*italics* in the original, bracketed information and emphasis added.)

Here the 10th Mormon Prophet, Joseph Fielding Smith, unequivocally states that violation of Mormon Priesthood covenants are absolute and punishment will come to any and all who may violate them. To neglect ones "Priesthood Duty" is to violate the covenant of the Mormon Priesthood.

Mormonism believes it is truly different from the rest of the world because of its Priesthood; its ability to act (officiate) in the name of God. Jonathan Golden Kimball, one of the Seven Presidents of Seventy (this position is directly under the office of Apostle) makes this point perfectly:

"You owe first allegiance to your quorums and quorum meetings, for there is where you get your authority and power. **Why is it that we are different from other men in the world? It is not because we have greater knowledge and information, but because we hold the Priesthood**."[8] (emphasis added).

As seen in the previously cited quote, reference [4], to this chapter, Mormon Apostle Mark E. Petersen is quoted in the July 1973 *Ensign* magazine as saying: **"that salvation comes through the Church,"**; **"It comes only through the Church itself"**; and **"salvation is in the Church, and of the Church, and is obtained only through the Church."** There is no doubt about what this Mormon Apostle is trying to convey: The Church, The Church, The Church. As we have also seen in this chapter, "The Church" is completely controlled and governed by the "Priesthood;" and the "Priesthood" is what makes Mormonism different from the rest of the world. Understanding that principle, I would like to provide numerous references which clearly show a Mormon's allegiance to their "Church," "Priesthood," and "Prophet." I'm not trying to put you to sleep here. I'm trying to stave off the marginalizing of these principles of Mormonism by those who would say I'm building a case on some single, obscure quote.

Mormon Apostle Jeffrey R. Holland, speaking to a gathering of Native Americans on the Navajo Reservation in Arizona makes a key point in the belief of "allegiance" to the Mormon Church:

"A key point of Elder Holland's message was universal in nature yet particularly applicable to Native Americans: **"We must be Latter-day Saints first, and any other identity second**."

Elder Holland spoke of his Irish ancestry and of Elder Didier being from Belgium, and said, "**I must be a Latter-day Saint first**, and an Irishman second. **Elder Didier must be a Latter-day Saint first**, and a Belgian second. And **you must be a Latter-day Saint first, and an Indian second**.

Everybody comes from a culture; we keep the good part and make it compatible with our first loyalty—and **our first loyalty forever is the gospel of Jesus Christ [Mormonism]**."[9] (bracketed information and emphasis added.)

It is quite clear in the above quote that Mormon Apostle Holland is telling these Mormon Native Americans that they are Mormons first and foremost above all else. Their "**first loyalty**" is to the "Latter-day Saint (LDS)"—Mormon Church! "**We must be Latter-day Saints first, and any other identity second**." Where does that place Mormon elected or appointed Government Officials?

Mormon Apostle Richard G. Scott:

"I testify that you will remove barriers to happiness and find greater peace as you **make your first allegiance your membership in the Church of Jesus Christ**,...."[10] (emphasis added.)

Here Mormon Apostle Scott testifies to the Mormon people at General Conference that allegiance to their membership in the Mormon Church will bring happiness and peace.

Mormon Apostle L. Tom Perry:

"With the partaking of the sacrament [communion], we accept Jesus as our Lord and Savior and **obligate**

86

ourselves to keep his commandments by covenant. **This makes the partaking of the sacrament a renewal of the covenants we made at the time of baptism into the Church**. Thus, by the sacrament, we declare repeatedly, ordinarily weekly, **our allegiance to the plan of salvation and its obligations and blessings**....As members of the Church, we should delight in the privilege of partaking of the sacrament, and thereby affirming our faith in our Lord and Savior and our **allegiance to the Church of Jesus Christ**."[11] (bracketed information and emphasis added.)

Mormon Apostle Perry reminds the Mormon people at General Conference that each week as they take the Mormon sacrament (communion) they re-obligate themselves by covenant to allegiance to the Mormon Church.

Mormon Council of Seventy member Loren C. Dunn:

"I was talking to a priesthood leader just last weekend. We had finished our Saturday night leadership meeting, which was on missionary work, and he said to me, 'You know, you are really a missionary General Authority.' And I said, 'No, I don't consider myself a missionary General Authority. If I can be remembered for anything (and I hope that somehow, somewhere I can), I would settle for that which my father taught me and for which I feel he was known, and that is **one who is willing to give allegiance to and follow a prophet of God**. And if that can be my lot, then I feel I will have accomplished the thing the Lord has sent me to do.'"[12] (emphasis added.)

The Council of Seventy is directly below a Mormon Apostle in the organizational structure of the Mormon Church. Council of Seventy members are considered

"General Authorities" of the Mormon Church. Here, General Authority Dunn wants his lot in life to be remembered as his willingness to give his allegiance to the Mormon Prophet.

Mormon Council of Seventy member Ronald E. Poelman:

"**We should obey the commandments and counsel of Church leaders**; but also through study, through prayer, and by the influence of the Holy Spirit, **we should seek and obtain an individual, personal witness that the principle or counsel is correct and divinely inspired. Then we can give enlightened, enthusiastic obedience, utilizing the Church as a means through which to give allegiance, time, talent, and other resources without reluctance or resentment.**"[13] (emphasis added.)

General Authority Poelman's point is clear: Obey the commandments and counsel of Church leaders; know that it is divinely inspired; then give enlightened, enthusiastic obedience, and allegiance to the Church without reluctance or resentment.

Mormon Apostle Mark E. Petersen:

"**For our own sake, for the sake of our families, for the sake of this restored church of Jesus Christ to which we give our allegiance**, but also to earn the blessing of heaven, let us serve the Lord and keep his commandments."[14] (emphasis added.)

Mormon Apostle Petersen makes it plain: the stakes are high, and for your sake and your families sake, you will give allegiance to the Mormon Church.

15[15] Mormon Prophet Gordon B. Hinckley:

"As the work grows, we may expect a strengthening of the efforts of the adversary against it. **Our best defense is the quiet offense of allegiance to the teachings which have come to us from those whom we have sustained as prophets of God.**"[15] (emphasis added.)

As of this writing, September of 2007, Gordon B. Hinckley is the current serving Mormon Prophet. His point: the best defense against the adversary is allegiance to the teachings of Mormon Prophets.

3[3] Mormon Prophet John Taylor:

"In politics as in everything *else we want to know the will of God, and then do it*....Do we not believe in the voice of the people? Yes; but we believe in the voice of God first, in the middle, and in the end.... We do not think we have wisdom to manage our political affairs without the interposition of the Most High.... **I very much doubt the right of men to do as they please when they profess to be Latter-day Saints; because we have covenanted together to keep the commandments of God and obey the holy priesthood**. (John Taylor. 1867, JD-11:355-6)."[16] (*italics* in the original, emphasis added.)

"...The time has come for decisive action: and whether you are called to act in a religious, civil, or military capacity, it is all in the kingdom of God and the will of God is to be done upon the earth as angels do it in heaven.
We are not fit to occupy our places in the kingdom, either as High Priests, or as Seventies, or as Apostles, or as anything else, **except we are willing and obedient**:

and the same thing applies to our families. **Then let us seek to submit ourselves to the law of God and do it.**"[17] (emphasis added.)

These are very telling statements by Mormon Prophet John Taylor with respect to politics, Mormon leadership, and control by covenant of the Mormon people. He says that, "In politics as in everything *else we want to know the will of God, and then do it*," and, "We are not fit to occupy our places in the kingdom...except we are willing and obedient....let us seek to submit ourselves to the law of God and do it." As we have already seen, in Chapter Two, the Mormon Leadership, "The Brethren," are God's living "oracles" on earth and speak directly for him—they are the "law of God" on earth. The last sentence of note [16] above is paramount in understanding the control of the Mormon Priesthood: "I very much doubt the right of men to do as they please when they profess to be Latter-day Saints; because we have covenanted together to keep the commandments of God and obey the holy priesthood." This Mormon Prophet makes it crystal clear: **As a Mormon, you do not have the right to do as you please**. **As a Mormon, you have covenanted to keep the commandments of God and obey the holy priesthood**.

Albert P. Rockwood, one of the First Seven Presidents of the Quorum of the Seventy, made a statement of absolute control by the Mormon Church Priesthood to all occupations, both civil and military:

"all men holding the Priesthood employed in civil or military occupations were amenable to that priesthood for their acts."[18]

13th Mormon Prophet Ezra Taft Benson:

"If we keep the commandments, we will refrain from joining secret orders and lodges. **Our first allegiance will be to the Church and the priesthood quorums**. We will attend our meetings. We will take our families with us to the sacrament meeting and sit with them and worship with them. If we keep the commandments, we will pay our tithes and offerings, our fast offerings, and our welfare contributions. We will respond to the calls in the Church, and **we will not resign from office when called under the authority of the Holy Priesthood. We will follow the counsel of the leadership of the Church** and call our families together periodically in home evenings in order that the home might be safeguarded and the solidarity of the family increased. We will read the scriptures in our homes as the Lord has admonished us. **We will not violate the sacred covenants we have taken upon ourselves in the waters of baptism and in the temples of the Lord, nor will we desecrate or cast to one side the garments of the Holy Priesthood**. We will attend to our temple work. We will become saviors on Mount Zion in very deed."[19] (emphasis added.)

13th Mormon Prophet Benson candidly states that a Mormon's "first allegiance will be to the Church and the priesthood quorums." He goes on to make some very blunt points: (1) When called to a position in the Church (office), all "callings" are done through the "Holy Priesthood," you will not resign; (2) You will follow the "counsel of the leadership of the Church"; (3) You will not violate the covenants of Baptism into the Mormon Church; (4) You will not violate the covenants made in the Mormon Temple.

1st Counselor in the First Presidency Marion G. Romney:

"<u>I conceive the blessings of the gospel to be of such</u> <u>inestimable worth that the price for them must be</u> <u>very exacting</u>, and if I correctly understand what the Lord has said on the subject, it is. The price, however, is within the reach of us all, because it is not to be paid in money nor in any of this world's goods but in righteous living. <u>What is required is wholehearted devotion to</u> <u>the gospel and unreserved allegiance to the Church</u> <u>of Jesus Christ of Latter-day Saints</u>. Speaking to this point, the Prophet taught ". . . that those who keep the commandments of the Lord and walk in his statutes to the end, are the only individuals" who shall receive the blessings."[20] (emphasis added.)

1st Counselor Romney, in General Conference, relays that the "price" of blessings in the Mormon Church is very high. That price is: "wholehearted devotion" to Mormonism, and "unreserved allegiance to the Church."

Notice the overriding theme in the quotes listed above: The Church, The Church, The Church. The "Church" is everything; and, the only way to serve the Church is absolute allegiance to it—which means, absolute allegiance to its leadership, the "Priesthood." That Priesthood culminates in those that the Church sustains as "prophets, seers, and revelators"—the "Brethren."

10th Mormon Prophet, Joseph Fielding Smith, delivers a very stern warning to any Mormon Church member who should dare to speak out against Mormon Priesthood Leadership:

"<u>It is a serious thing for any member of this Church</u> <u>to raise his voice against the priesthood, or to hold</u> <u>the priesthood in disrespect; for the Lord will not</u> <u>hold such guiltless; so he has promised, and he will</u> <u>fulfill....</u>"[21] (emphasis added.)

2nd Mormon Prophet, Brigham Young, makes plain the Mormon perception that the "Priesthood" has once again been "restored" to the earth and will never again be taken away. If Mormons will but practice their religion, and follow the Priesthood, "they will live, and not be cut off":

> "I can tell you something more, brethren and sisters, and friends, and the United States, and all the world; **the Lord Almighty will not suffer His Priesthood to be again driven from the earth**, even should He permit the wicked to kill and destroy this people. The Government of the United States and all the kings of the world may go to war with us, but God will preserve a portion of the meek and humble of **this people to bear off the Kingdom to the inhabitants of the earth, and will defend His Priesthood**; for it is the last time, the last gathering time; and **He will not suffer the Priesthood to be again driven from the earth**. They may massacre men, women, and children; but the Lord will not suffer them to destroy the Priesthood; and **I say to the Saints, that, if they will truly practise their religion, they will live, and not be cut off**."[22] (emphasis added.)

"KEYS" TO THE MORMON PRIESTHOOD

Another principle that needs to be understood is the "Keys" to the Mormon Priesthood. Understanding what is meant by "Keys" and the importance that these "Keys" hold with respect to the Mormon Church Hierarchy is crucial in understanding the complete concept of the Mormon Priesthood. The most basic definition of Mormon Priesthood Keys is: the authority to act. Let's look at the definition as given in the *Encyclopedia of Mormonism*:

Keys of the Priesthood

The keys of the priesthood refer to the right to exercise power in the name of Jesus Christ or to preside over a priesthood function, quorum, or organizational division of the Church. Keys are necessary to maintain order and to see that the functions of the Church are performed in the proper time, place, and manner. They are given by the laying on of hands in an ordination or setting apart by a person who presides and who holds the appropriate keys at a higher level. Many keys were restored to men on earth by heavenly messengers to the Prophet Joseph Smith and Oliver Cowdery.

The keys of the kingdom of God on earth are held by the apostles. The president of the church, who is the senior apostle, holds all the keys presently on earth and presides over all the organizational and ordinance work of the Church (D&C 107:8-9, 91-92). He delegates authority by giving the keys of specific offices to others (D&C 124:123). Only presiding priesthood officers (including General Authorities, stake presidents, mission presidents, temple presidents, bishops, branch presidents, and quorum presidents) hold keys pertaining to their respective offices. Latter-day Saints distinguish between holding the priesthood and holding keys to direct the work of the priesthood: one does not receive additional priesthood when one is given keys (Joseph F. Smith, IE 4 [Jan. 1901]:230).

The Prophet Joseph Smith taught that "the fundamental principles, government, and doctrine of the Church are vested in the keys of the kingdom" (TPJS, p. 21). "The keys have to be brought from heaven whenever the Gospel is sent"; they are revealed to man under the authority of Adam, for he was the first to be given them when he was given dominion over all things. They have come down through the dispensations of the gospel to prophets, including Noah, Abraham, Moses, Elijah; to Peter, James, and John; and to Joseph Smith and the designated prophets of the latter days (HC 3:385-87). Keys to perform or preside over various priesthood functions were bestowed upon Joseph Smith and Oliver Cowdery by John the Baptist (see Aaronic Priesthood: restoration of Aaronic Priesthood), by Peter, James, and John (see Melchizedek Priesthood: Restoration of Melchizedek Priesthood), and by Moses, Elias, and Elijah in the Kirtland Temple (see Doctrine and Covenants: Sections 109-110).

Many types of keys are mentioned in the scriptures of the Church (see MD, pp. 409-13). Jesus Christ holds all the keys. Joseph Smith received the keys pertaining to the restoration of the gospel of Jesus Christ (D&C 6:25-28; 28:7; 35:18), and through him **the First Presidency holds the "keys of the kingdom,"** including the sealing ordinances (D&C 81:1-2; 90:1-6; 110:16; 128:20; 132:19). Specific mention of certain keys and those who hold them include the following: The Quorum of the Twelve Apostles exercises the keys "to open the door by the proclamation of the gospel of Jesus Christ" in all the world (D&C 107:35; 112:16; 124:128). Adam holds "the keys of salvation under the counsel and direction of the Holy One," and "the keys of the universe" (D&C 78:16; TPJS, p. 157); Moses, "the keys of the gathering of Israel" (D&C 110:11); Elias, the keys to bring to pass "the restoration of all things" (D&C 27:6); and Elijah, "the keys of the power of turning the hearts of the fathers to the children, and the hearts of the children to the fathers" (D&C 27:9). **Holders of the Melchizedek Priesthood are said to have "the keys of the Church," "the key of knowledge," and "the keys of all the spiritual blessings of the church"** (D&C 42:69; 84:19; 107:18), while belonging to the Aaronic Priesthood are "the keys of the ministering of angels, and of the gospel of repentance, and of baptism by immersion for the remission of sins" (D&C 13:1; 84:26). All these stewardships will eventually be delivered back into the hands of Jesus Christ (TPJS, p. 157).[23] (emphasis added.)

It can be clearly seen through the quotes listed in this chapter that in Mormonism the Priesthood is everything; without its "Priesthood" concept, Mormonism would cease to exist. The Mormon Priesthood is the authority to act in God's name on earth. Also we see that the holder of Mormon Priesthood "Keys" is instrumental to the Mormon belief that only Mormons have the "authority" to act in God's name and therefore only they have the plan for His Church on earth. The holder of those various "Keys" is revered above any other living being and should not be confused with the rank and file Priesthood holder (every male twelve years old and above is a "Priesthood" holder in Mormonism). Specifically, the current Mormon "Prophet" holds all the "Keys" to exercise any "Priesthood" authority on earth – he is God's direct "oracle" on earth.

Mormonism believes that the earth will ultimately be ruled by and through the Mormon Priesthood. President J. Reuben Clark, 1st Counselor to the 8th Mormon Prophet, George Albert Smith, stated this principle at the General Priesthood Meeting of the General Conference of the Mormon Church in October 1948:

> **"Those of us who have been in the temple of course know of the obligations we take there. But there are obligations which are taken by every man who bears the priesthood, from the office of deacon up.** Do not dishonor your priesthood, brethren, and do not any of

you let your life so shape itself that you will lose the powers which the priesthood gives.

I return again to the theme that I have always mentioned in these priesthood meetings since I came into the Council, to the question of unity. Brethren, if we could act as united and in unison as we can sing and have sung in unison, there is no power that could withstand anything that we sought to do in righteousness.

May God give us the strength and the power and the will and the desire to honor our priesthood, to remember that we cannot lay it aside as a cloak; it is always with us to be dishonored and disgraced if we shall so act. May he give to us the will and the determination always so to honor our priesthood, that we may be indeed the agents of our Heavenly Father, to perform his will, — **to the end that ultimately righteousness may rule the earth, as it will ultimately through the priesthood**."[24] (emphasis added.)

Lest anyone feel that the quotes in this chapter are old and that the Mormon Church may have moved away from the expressed doctrinal positions, let me quote the current 1st counselor in the First Presidency (as of this writing, September 2007), Thomas S. Monson, in the 2007 General Conference, Priesthood Session, March 31, 2007:

"During the past several weeks, as I have contemplated what I might say to you tonight, **I have thought repeatedly of the blessing which is ours to be bearers of the sacred priesthood of God**. When we look at the world as a whole, with a population of over 6 ½ billion people, we realize that **we comprise a very small, select group**. We who hold the priesthood are, in the words of the Apostle Peter, "a chosen generation, a royal priesthood."

President Joseph F. Smith defined the priesthood as "the power of God delegated to man by which man can act in the earth for the salvation of the human family,...by which [men] may speak the will of God as if the angels were here to speak it themselves; by which men are empowered to bind on earth and it shall be bound in heaven, and to loose on earth and it shall be loosed in heaven." President Smith added, "[The priesthood] is sacred, and it must be held sacred by the people."

My brethren, the priesthood is a gift which brings with it not only special blessings but also solemn responsibilities. It is our responsibility to conduct our lives so that we are ever worthy of the priesthood we bear."[25] (emphasis added.)

Every Mormon, male or female, is fully indoctrinated to believe that the Mormon Church "alone," is the only church that has God's authority to function on earth. In an article in the weekly published Mormon Church periodical called, *Church News*, we find a simple, but all telling statement by a Mormon student attending Notre Dame to acquire his MBA:

"My testimony was strengthened by coming to understand that our Church is guided by priesthood power and revelation."[26]

This statement was made in an article titled "Two Faiths," which is about Mormon graduate students attending Notre Dame University. The context of the statement was in reference to Jeff Haddon, a Mormon graduate student, talking about how blessed he and his wife are for him to attend Notre Dame. His statement: "My testimony was strengthened by coming to understand that our Church is guided by priesthood power and revelation" is in contrast to the Catholic university he is attending, which Mormonism believes is not guided by priesthood power and revelation.

The continuous reinforcing that the Mormon Priesthood is everything, and without it a Mormon has nothing, lends itself to the molding of thought patterns that should reject obvious contradictions to rational thought, but are conditioned not too. Mormon Apostle Stephen L. Richards, who served as the 1st Counselor to the 9th Mormon Prophet, David O. McKay, perfectly elucidates this mental brain washing, defining it as "allegiance to the Priesthood":

"Knowing the attributes of the Priesthood as we do, **we do not fear it. <u>Our unanimity of thought and action in response to its suggestions or nominations is not constrained upon us by domination and coercion</u>**. It is but the natural product of our accord with the wisdom and the inspiration of our leaders and the persuasion of righteousness and truth. **<u>We who give our allegiance to the Priesthood are not slaves and puppets</u>, we are free, and the more perfectly <u>we yield to the doctrines and the dominion of the Priesthood, the more unanimous we become in its support</u>**."[27] (emphasis added.)

It is interesting that Mormon Apostle Richards should say: "Knowing the attributes of the Priesthood as we do, we do not fear it." This sentence is really setting up the follow-on sentence, "**<u>Our unanimity of thought and action in response to its suggestions or nominations is not constrained upon us by domination and coercion</u>**," which tries to disable the rational thinking man from objectively observing that the whole process of Mormon Priesthood allegiance is in fact: "domination and coercion."

The very thought of thinking for oneself is rejected in Mormonism:

"Any Latter-day Saint who denounces or opposes, whether actively or otherwise, any plan or doctrine advocated by the "prophets, seers, and revelators" of the Church is cultivating the spirit of apostasy. One cannot speak evil of the Lord's anointed and retain the Holy Spirit in his heart.

It should be remembered that Lucifer has a very cunning way of convincing unsuspecting souls that the General Authorities of the Church are as likely to be wrong as they are to be right. This sort of game is Satan's favorite pastime, and he has practiced it on believing souls since Adam. **He wins a great victory when he can get members of the Church to speak against their leaders and to "do their own thinking."** He specializes in suggesting that our leaders are in error while he plays the blinding rays of apostasy in the eyes of those whom he thus beguiles. What cunning! And to think that some of our members are deceived by this trickery."[28] (emphasis added.)

WHAT'S THE POINT?

The Mormon Church believes it is "the only true and living church upon the face of the whole earth,"[29] and, what truly sets it apart from all others is its "Priesthood." The Mormon "Priesthood" is all powerful—it is the power **"by which [men] may speak the will of God as if the angels were here to speak it themselves; by which men are empowered to bind on earth and it shall be bound in heaven, and to loose on earth and it shall be loosed in heaven**."[30] Bestowal of the Mormon "Priesthood" begins at age 12, and is solely a male institution.

"Covenants" are made when a Mormon male receives the "Priesthood." Specifically: Mormon males **covenant** to **"receiveth my servants"**[31]: Mormon Priesthood Leadership

100

(Priesthood Quorum Leader, Bishop, Stake President, Presiding Bishop, Quorum of Seventy, Apostles, Prophet). **If a Mormon male Priesthood holder fails to "receive my servants," then that Priesthood holder "shall not have forgiveness of sins in this world nor in the world to come."**[32] Belief in this covenant places Mormon males in a terrible predicament: if they fail to follow Mormon Priesthood authority, they could jeopardize their very eternity; failing to follow Mormon Priesthood leaders places a Mormon's very eternal life at risk. Spencer W. Kimball, the 12th Prophet of the Mormon Church made it very clear at the conclusion of the April 1978 General Conference:

"Now as we conclude this general conference, let us give heed to what was said to us. Let us assume the counsel given applies to *us*, to me. **Let us hearken to those we sustain as prophets and seers, as well as the other brethren, as if our eternal life depended on it, because it does!**"[33] (emphasis added.)

The Mormon "Church" is the only vehicle through which this "Priesthood" may be obtained and therefore exercised. One's standing within that organization then becomes of the utmost importance. To lose standing with the "Church" is to lose the ability to function in the power of its "Priesthood," and will ultimately control your eternal destiny. With the "Church" being everything, allegiance to it is "everything!" That being said, allegiance to the "Church" is inseparable with allegiance to the "Priesthood" and the "prophets, seers, and revelators" that hold the "Keys" and the power to direct that "Church" here on earth through that "Priesthood."

[1] *Religious Truths Defined*, Bookcraft, Salt Lake City, Utah, 1959, p. 235-236.

[2] *Ensign*, Published Monthly by The Church of Jesus Christ of Latter-day Saints, (Salt Lake City, Utah) May 2007, p. 57.

[3] *Encyclopedia of Mormonism*, 1-4 vols., edited by Daniel H. Ludlow (New York: Macmillan, 1992), pp.1133-1135, as found on the CD "LDS Library 2006" by Deseret Book.

[4] *Ensign*, July 1973, p. 108.

[5] Joseph Fielding Smith, Compiled by Bruce R. McConkie, *Doctrines of Salvation*, (Bookcraft, Salt Lake City, Utah 1956) 3:105-06.

[6] *Doctrine and Covenants*, 84:35-41.

[7] Smith, *Doctrines of Salvation*, 3:119-20.

[8] Jonathan Golden Kimball, Conference Report, April 1906, Afternoon Session., p. 19-20, as found on the CD "LDS Library 2006" by Deseret Book.

[9] *Church News*, week ending March 25, 2006, "Children of Lehi – Gospel is first loyalty", 6.

[10] *Ensign*, May 1998, p. 85.

[11] *Ensign*, May 1996, p.53.

[12] *Ensign,* May 1983, p. 29.

[13] *Ensign,* November 1984, p.64.

[14] *Ensign,* November 1981, p.64.

[15] *Ensign,* April 1970, p.20.

[16] Jerreld L. Newquist, *Prophets, Principles and National Survival* (Publishers Press, Salt Lake City, Utah, 1964) 44.

[17] John Taylor in Watt, ed., *Journal of Discourses*, 5:266.

[18] D. Michael Quinn, *The Mormon Hierarchy – Extentions of Power,* (Salt Lake City: Signature Books, 1997) 269.

[19] Ezra Taft Benson, Conference Report, October 1950, Afternoon Session., p. 147-148, as found on the CD "LDS Library 2006" by Deseret Book.

[20] Marion G. Romney, Conference Report, October 1949, Afternoon Meeting, p.43, as found on the CD "LDS Library 2006" by Deseret Book.

[21] Smith, *Doctrines of Salvation*, 3:295.

[22] Brigham Young in Watt, ed., *Journal of Discourses*, 2:183-184.

[23] *Encyclopedia of Mormonism*, pp. 780-781.

[24] *Immortality and Eternal Life, Melchizedek Priesthood Course of Study, 1968-69*, (Published by the First Presidency of The Church of Jesus Christ of Latter-day Saints, 1968) 177.

[25] *Ensign*, May 2007, p. 57.

[26] *Church News*, week ending June 9, 2007, "Two Faiths", 7.

[27] Stephen L. Richards, Conference Report, April 1937, Second Day—Morning Meeting, p. 50-51, as found on the CD "LDS Library 2006" by Deseret Book.

[28] *The Improvement Era*, "The Voice of the Church" Official Organ of the Priesthood Quorums, Mutual Improvement Associations, Department of Education, Music Committee, Ward Teachers, and Other Agencies of the Church of Jesus Christ of Latter-day Saints, June 1945, Vol. 8, NO. 6, pg 354.

[29] *Doctrine and Covenants*, 1:30.

[30] *Ensign*, May 2007, p. 57.

[31] *Doctrine and Covenants*, 84:36.

[32] Ibid., 84:41.

[33] *Search These Commandments, Melchizedek Priesthood Personal Study Guide*, (Published by The Church of Jesus Christ of Latter-day Saints, Salt Lake City, Utah, 1984) 276.

Chapter Four

THE MORMON/POLITICAL KINGDOM

It is very important for the American voter to really grasp what the word *kingdom* truly means in Mormonism. A Christian not familiar with the differences between Christianity and Mormonism may have a long, and perhaps very in-depth, discussion on various doctrinal positions with a Mormon and never realize they were not really communicating at all. Mormonism uses the Christian vocabulary, but brings along its own very unique dictionary. The word "*kingdom*," or the phrase "*Kingdom of God*," have a unique definition in that Mormon dictionary.

This chapter will be a very brief explanation of the Mormon Church doctrine that it, the Mormon Church, and it alone, is the "Kingdom of God" on earth. This chapter is just a short introduction so that the references to "the kingdom" in the various Mormon writings cited in this book can be understood within the context of Mormonism. There are several in-depth works on this subject that are listed at the end of this chapter for those who would like to look into this mixing of church and state. Mormon Apostle Bruce R. McConkie, in his epic work *Mormon Doctrine,* gives us insight into the Mormon Church's doctrinal position that it, the Mormon Church, is God's Kingdom:

KINGDOM OF GOD. *See* CELESTIAL KINGDOM, CHURCH OF JESUS CHRIST OF LATTER-DAY SAINTS, COMMON CONSENT, KEYS OF THE KINGDOM, KINGDOM OF HEAVEN, MILLENIUM.

1. **The Church of Jesus Christ of Latter-day Saints as it is now constituted is the *kingdom of God on earth*. Nothing more needs to be done to establish the kingdom.** (D. & C. 35:27; 38:9, 15; 50:35; 62:9; 65; 136:41.) The kingdom is here, and it is the same kingdom which Daniel said would be set up in the last days. (Dan. 2:44-45.) This same kingdom has been set up in past ages whenever the gospel has been on the earth, for the plan of salvation is the gospel of the kingdom. **The Church and kingdom are one and the same.**

Joseph Smith taught: "Some say the kingdom of God was not set up on the earth until the day of Pentecost, and that John did not preach the baptism of repentance for the remission of sins; **but I say, in the name of the Lord,** that the kingdom of God was set up on the earth from the days of Adam to the present time. **Whenever there has been a righteous man on earth unto whom God revealed his word and gave power and authority to administer in his name,** and where there is a priest of God — **a minister who has power and authority from God to administer in the ordinances of the gospel and officiate in the priesthood of God, there is the kingdom of God....** [Joseph Smith and all of his successors to the current Prophet of the Mormon Church are believed to be the "righteous man".]

"Where there is no kingdom of God there is no salvation. What constitutes the kingdom of God? ***Where there***

is a prophet, a priest, or a righteous man unto whom God gives his oracles, there is the kingdom of God; and where oracles of God are not, there the kingdom of God is not....

"Whenever men can find out the will of God and find an administrator legally authorized from God, there is the kingdom of God; but where these are not, the kingdom of God is not. All the ordinances, systems, and administrations on the earth are of no use to the children of men, unless they are ordained and authorized of God; for nothing will save a man but a legal administrator; for none others will be acknowledge(d) (sic) either by God or angels." (*Teachings*, pp. 271-274.)

The Church (or kingdom) is not a democracy; legislation is not enacted by the body of people composing the organization; they do not make the laws governing themselves. **The Church is a kingdom. The Lord Jesus Christ is the Eternal King, and the President of the Church, the mouthpiece of God on earth, is the earthly king. All things come to the Church from the King of the kingdom in heaven, through the king of the kingdom on earth. There is, of course, the democratic principle of common consent whereunder the people may accept or reject what the Lord offers to them. Acceptance brings salvation; rejection leads to damnation.**[1] (*italics* in the original, bracketed information and emphasis added.)

"On April 6, 1830 [the day the Mormon Church was organized], the *ecclesiastical kingdom of God* on earth was set up,..."[2] (*italics* in the original, bracketed information and emphasis added.)

The Mormon Church, unlike other churches in America, has from its inception, viewed itself not simply as a religious institution, but also as a melding of religion with political power. Mormonism views itself as "The Kingdom of God" on earth which will progress forward upon Jesus' return to earth.

In a letter addressed to the Queen [Victoria, Queen of Great Britain] in 1841, Mormon apostle Parley P. Pratt wrote: "Know assuredly, that the world in which we live is on the eve of a REVOLUTION, more powerful in its beginning—more rapid it its progress—more lasting in its influence—more important in its consequences—than any which man has yet witnessed upon the earth." The present political and religious establishments, the letter solemnly affirmed, were destined to vanish, and God was about to set up "a new and universal Kingdom, under the immediate administration of the Messiah and his Saints."[3] (bracketed information added.)
"all the political, and all the religious organizations that may previously exist, will be swallowed up into one entire union—one universal empire—having no laws but God's law, and Saints to administer them."[4]

The "Saints" referred to in the above quotes are members of "The Church of Jesus Christ of Latter-day Saints" – or the shortened version "Latter-day Saints," or "LDS," more commonly known as "Mormons." The above reference that "we live on the eve of a REVOLUTION," and the "political and religious establishments," "were destined to vanish," reflects the early Mormon doctrinal teachings of Jesus' immediate pending return in the, then, present generation of Joseph Smith. In the year 1835 Joseph Smith falsely prophesied of Jesus' immediate, imminent return:

"President Smith then stated...it was the will of God that those who went to Zion, with a determination to lay down their lives, if necessary, should be ordained to the ministry, and go forth to prune the vineyard for the last time, or the coming of the Lord, which was nigh-even fifty-six years should wind up the scene."[5]

Joseph Smith viewed himself as the "Prophet of the Restoration," endowed with power from on-high which often set him at odds with the American landscape and institutions of law:

Smith remained aloof from civil office, but in November 1835 he announced a doctrine I call "theocratic ethics." He used this theology to justify his violation of Ohio's marriage laws by performing a marriage for Newel Knight and the undivorced Lydia Goldthwaite without legal authority to do so:

"I have done it by the authority of the holy Priesthood and the Gentile law has no power to call me to an account for it. It is my religious priviledge [sic], and the congress of the United States has no power to make a law that would abridge the rights of my religion: I have done as I was commanded, and I know the Kingdom of God will prevail, and that the Saints will triumph over all their adversaries."

In addition to the bigamous character of this marriage, Smith had no license to perform marriages in Ohio.

Although that was the first statement of this concept, Smith and his associates put that theology into practice long before 1835, and long after. Two months later Smith performed marriage ceremonies for which neither he nor the couples had marriage licenses, and he issued marriage certificates "agreeable to the rules and regulations of the Church of Jesus Christ of Latter-day Saints." Theocratic ethics justified LDS leaders and (by extension) regular

Mormons in actions which were contrary to conventional ethics and sometimes in violation of criminal laws.

This ethical independence is essential for understanding certain seemingly inconsistent manifestations in Mormonism. Some had already occurred—the reversals in doctrine and divinely revealed procedures, and the publication of unannounced changes in written revelations and historical texts. The Knight marriage was a public example of Joseph Smith's violation of laws and cultural norms regarding marriage and sexual behavior—the performance of civil marriage ceremonies by legally unauthorized officiators, monogamous marriage ceremonies in which one or both partners were undivorced from legal spouses, polygamous marriage of a man with more than one living wife, his marriage proposals to females as young as twelve, his sexual relationships with polygamous wives as young as fourteen, polyandry of women with more than one husband, marriage and sexual cohabitation with foster daughters, and Mormon marriages of first cousins, brother-sister, and uncle-niece. Other manifestations of Mormonism's theocratic ethics would soon begin in Kirtland and continue intermittently for decades—the official denials of actual events, the alternating condemnation and tolerance for counterfeiting and stealing from non-Mormons, threats and physical attacks against dissenters or other alleged enemies, the killing and castration of sex offenders, the killing of anti-Mormons, the bribery of government officials, and business ethics at odds with church standards.[6]

The above quote from D. Michael Quinn spans the timeframe from Kirkland, Ohio, to Independence and Far West, Missouri, and on to Nauvoo, Illinois. The behavior by Mormon leadership clearly shows a continuous disregard for the laws of the United States which led to the Utah War of 1857/58 and the dissolution of the corporation of the Mormon Church by the Edmunds/Tucker Act of 1887. Quinn's coined term, "theocratic ethics," is quite accurate as Mormon leadership saw themselves as God's oracles and were therefore, only accountable to God and not to the government of the United States. This belief in Mormon leadership being accountable only to God is amply described by Brigham Young:

"The first principle of our cause and work is to understand that **there is a prophet in the church, and that he is at the head of the Church of Christ on earth**. Who called Joseph Smith to be a prophet? Did the people or God? God, and not the people, called him. Had the people gathered together and appointed one of their number to be a prophet, he would have been accountable to the people, but, inasmuch as he was called of God, and not by the people, **he is accountable to God only... and not to any man on earth**. **The twelve apostles are accountable to the prophet and not to the church for the course they pursue, and we have learned to go and do, as the prophet tells us**." – From sermon by Brigham Young, at Nauvoo, 1843, published in Millennial Star, Liverpool, England, Vol. XXI., page 741.[7] (emphasis added.)

Upon the Mormons' departure from Kirkland, Ohio and complete relocation to Missouri, the Mormons saw themselves as the current "Kingdom of God" on earth. They saw themselves as those who would usher in the fullness of the kingdom upon Christ's return. This belief is what generated the "extermination sermon" by Sydney Rigdon, 1st Counselor to Joseph Smith, on July 4th 1838. The belief that Mormonism was the "Kingdom of God" on earth, coupled with the problems generated by that belief, along with the radical sermons by Sydney Rigdon, were the catalyst that caused the Mormons to be expelled from the state by an order from Governor Boggs. In 1838, the difficulties the Church was experiencing in Missouri, with both non-Mormons and dissenters, fostered the beginning of a secret organization called the Danites. This secret "police force," removed "enemies" of the Church by violent means and was under the direct control of the Prophet of the Church, Joseph Smith:

> "In June 1838, Sampson Avard, who considered himself an ultra-loyal Mormon, proposed organizing the "Danites" among other ultra-loyal Mormons. The Danites were the first civil appendages of power since Zion's Camp. Some historians have claimed that Joseph Smith and the rest of the First Presidency were unaware of the Danite organization, but documentary evidence shows otherwise.
>
> Organized formally as the Daughters of Zion in June 1838 at Far West, they took their nickname from the prophecy of Daniel about the stone cut out of the mountain without hands (Dan. 2:44-45). Two weeks after the formation of a second group at Adam-ondi-Ahman, stake president and special counselor in the First Presidency John Smith called the organization "the Danites" in his diary which described the Danite meetings as routine events. Soon the group developed an infamous reputation for its intimidation of Mormon dissenters and its warfare against anti-Mormon militia units. Those two purposes were the explanation in Smith's diary for why "we have a company of Danites in these times." Rigdon later made a similar statement in the official church newspaper."[8]

The mixing of the political and theocratic became even more convoluted with the Mormon settlement of Nauvoo, Illinois. It was here that the Joseph Smith began another

112

secret organization: The "Council of Fifty." This council was an organization with a pure political agenda and was to plan and assist the "Church" to be in its rightful place for the imminent return of Jesus Christ.

"On 11 March 1844 Smith [Joseph Smith – 1ˢᵗ Mormon Prophet] organized into "a special council" twelve of those who had received the second anointing as "kings and priests of the most High God" plus ten other Mormons. A recent history officially published by the LDS church describes this as a meeting "to organize the political kingdom of God in preparation for the second coming of Christ." Contrasting with women's role in the Anointed Quorum, women were not part of this exclusively male theocratic body which, according to one author, 'came as the culmination of a long period of church political involvement in which the Saints sought to have the political balance of power.'"[9] (bracketed information added.)

This next quote from author Klaus J. Hansen brings some important points into focus with respect to the secret political organization called the "Council of Fifty."

"The Mormon church, in both its spiritual and temporal manifestations, thus existed to prepare its followers for the advent of the messianic kingdom. Ultimately, the earthly and spiritual kingdoms would be one; but, in the meantime, a dichotomy between reality and aspiration was inevitable. Yet, in their letter to Hedlock [leader of the Mormon mission to England in 1844], Young and Richards [Mormon Apostles: Brigham Young and Willard Richards] were referring to neither of these manifestations of the kingdom of God. Rather, the Lord revealed to Joseph Smith that still another manifestation of the "kingdom" was required to usher in the millennial reign of Christ. This was the political kingdom of God, destined to bring about the political transformation of the world, just as the church was intended to change the world religiously. Christ, at His coming, would usher in not only the ecclesiastical reign of a world church, but also of a political world government. And **in order to prepare the world for the reign of the Son of God, the Saints would have to establish a political government on earth prior to His coming.** As apostle George Q. Cannon admonished an audience of Mormon missionaries, the **time would come when the elders of the church would go out to the world not only as representatives of an ecclesiastical organization, but also as literal ambassadors of the Mormon kingdom of God, accredited to foreign governments. For the kingdom of God was "to become a political power, known and recognized by the powers of the earth,"** before the nations of the earth would have met with the ultimate destruction decreed by the Almighty, preparatory to the arrival of Christ the King Himself. The Mormon concept of the political kingdom of God, and the activities and aspirations of its governing body, the Council of Fifty, can only be understood, then, in the context of Mormon millennialism. In fact, the evolution and metamorphosis of the millenarian ideal in Mormon history was inextricably intertwined with the rise and fall of these two organizations."[10] (bracketed information and emphasis added.)

What Mr. Hansen clearly defines in the above quote is the fact that, within the bounds of Mormonism, the spiritual, temporal and political kingdoms of God are all wrapped up in one entity: The Mormon Church. The governing body that is to bring about the political kingdom of God is the secret "Council of Fifty."

When the Mormons left Nauvoo, Illinois and headed west, where they could find a place to live outside the laws of the United States so they could practice polygamy freely, the Council of Fifty went with them. From the Mormons' arrival in the Salt Lake Valley in 1847, to the establishment of statehood in 1896, Utah politics and government were dominated by the Council of Fifty.

Under the theocratic leadership of Brigham Young and the Council of Fifty, the Mormon Church defied the laws of the land until the United States could take it no longer:

"In 1887 the United States carried out an astonishing act. A nation founded upon the principle of religious freedom, which had enshrined that principle in its Constitution's Bill of Rights, passed a law that dissolved a church. The denomination involved, the LDS Church, was, as the historian Martin Marty has written, "safely describable as the most despised large group" of the day.

That year the Edmunds-Tucker Act added teeth to the 1862 Morrill Act, which had first raised the threat of suspending the church and limited its property holdings to $50,000. But that act was not enforced. The Edmunds Act of 1882 took direct aim at ending polygamy, and the Edmunds-Tucker Act of 1887 went far beyond authorizing "polyg hunts": it set out to destroy the church's temporal kingdom. The 1887 law provided for the dissolution of the corporation of the church under direction of the U.S. attorney general, with its property to be disposed of by the secretary of the Interior Department."[11]

This astonishing act was a direct result of the defiance by Mormon leadership to the laws of the United States. The Act was challenged by the Mormon Church and went all the way to the Supreme Court:

"In *Church of Jesus Christ of Latter-day Saints v. the United States*, the high court passed down a 5-4 decision on May 19, 1890, in support of the government action. The Majority opinion stated: "Congress had before it—a contumacious organization, wielding by its resources an immense power in the Territory of Utah, and employing those resources and that power in constantly attempting to oppose, thwart and subvert the legislation of Congress and the will of the government of the United States."[12]

The Edmunds-Tucker Act and the subsequent defeat of the challenge handed down by the highest court in the land, almost ended the Mormon Church as we know it. Seeing the handwriting on the wall for some time, the Church had been clandestinely transferring Church property over to private hands by having trusted leadership take possession under the auspices of returning it after the crisis was over. Polygamy was the vehicle which was used by the U.S. Congress to reign in this renegade church that wielded absolute power amongst its people. On the surface the issue appeared to be a moral concern; however, the real issue was political defiance. As fully quoted in Chapter One, Senator Frederick Dubois of Idaho, fully understood the issue, as did authors Richard and Joan Ostling, who expounded on the principle:

"**Those of us who understand the situation were not nearly so much opposed to polygamy as we were to the political domination of the Church.**"_[Senator Dubois] ...**The United States could not accept a quasi-independent nation-state in its midst, an independent theocratic kingdom, or a secular government on paper behind which stood a shadow church government that determined its laws and lawmakers, or a court system in which religious authority decided secular disputes**.... **Gentiles in the Intermountain West and**

across the country fought statehood, fearing that with a clear Mormon majority obediently following the church's direction, the church would control the secular affairs of Utah as well as those of nearby areas with a significant LDS population. Mormons, after all, had followed the commands of Joseph Smith and then Brigham Young in politics as well as belief, and it was not unreasonable to assume they would continue to obey their leaders' dictates."[13] (bracketed information and emphasis added.)

As stated in Chapter One, from 1894 to 1896 the Church received what was left of its properties back, after the dispersal. The Church's finances had taken a severe beating and it barely escaped a complete financial collapse. In the early 1890's the Church divested itself from the many corporate holdings it had accumulated in its drive for a theocratic state, prior to its achieving statehood. By 1907, however, once the Church was out of debt, it began again to reinvest in businesses.

As Mormons blurred into the multicultural American landscape, their kingdom paradigm shifted. In the nineteenth century the claims had been territorial, prescribing a geographic gathering to Zion. The Mormons had never been able to balance those territorial claims for the kingdom of God against the American secular society with its church-state separation. **The problem, writes Thomas O'Dea, was that "the Mormons never worked out consistently the political implications of their religious philosophy." The separatism of Smith's original nineteenth-century Mormonism, as in the O'Dea analysis, went beyond theocratic church government. It placed all areas of human activity within church**

control, under the all-encompassing authority of ecclesiastical leadership.

Joseph Smith's scriptures had taught that the U.S. Constitution is divinely inspired ("And for this purpose have I established the Constitution of this land, by the hands of wise men whom I raised up unto this very purpose"[D&C 101:80]). His kingdom of God claimed America for Zion, but Smith and Brigham Young never provided for the ambiguities and conflicts inherent in a theocratic kingdom that had to function somehow under a democratic umbrella.

Another major shift during this period was the waning of latter-day millennialism. Smith's predictions had inspired Second Coming expectations among the Saints around 1890. The LDS scriptures also teach that the final judgment and salvation will come in the 7,000[th] year of earth's "continuance, or its temporal existence" (D&C 77:6, 12). And Smith had told an 1843 General Conference that "there are those of the rising generation who shall not taste death till Christ comes."

More recently, that logically led Apostle Bruce R. McConkie to figure in the 1979 edition of his influential *Mormon Doctrine* that the Second Coming of Christ "is not far distant." But the millennial hope is muted among most of today's Mormons and no longer tied to an expectation of the Lord's return by a particular time. Former experiences like tongue-speaking are explained away and visions have become less frequent. The kingdom of God is the church, and before the Lord does return there will be chaos on earth and all earthly kingdoms will disintegrate. Then the church will be there, ready to provide order amid chaos. The survivalism in Mormon culture today—food storage and emergency kits—reflects the continued smoldering of some of the millennial embers.

Asked about this aspect of the faith, President Hinckley explains: "We've always been a practical people dealing with the issues of life. We've said that a religion that won't help people in this life won't do much for them in the life that comes. We believe that. And we don't spend a lot of time talking about or dreaming about the millennium to come. We don't know when it will happen. We're not spending a lot of time on it. We're doing today's job in the best way we know how to do it."

Still, millennial fascination survives into the twenty-first century, as evidenced by BYU professor Daniel C. Peterson's 1998 book *The Last Days*, with commentary on 550 end times teachings of the General Authorities. And devoutly Mormon Columbia University historian Richard Bushman remarked that Hinckley plays down the theme precisely because it is relevant, "not because it's dying. If the President were to blink an eye toward Jackson County, Missouri, people would flow there. The belief is still potent, but it's latent. That's still our view of history. All that nineteenth-century stuff is still in our culture. The church could, in a flash, constitute a complete society."[14] (emphasis added.)

The above quote by the Ostlings', "The Mormons had never been able to balance those territorial claims for the kingdom of God against the American secular society with its church-state separation," hits the nail directly on the head. Brigham Young could not separate the mixing of church and state:

"The business of the Latter-day Saints is to bring forth the kingdom of God in the last days, morally, religiously, and politically."[15] (emphasis added.)

The following two quotes by the 3rd Mormon Prophet, John Taylor, make the point that Mormons are to be led politically by their Priesthood:

> "This principle pervades all, whether in a civil or military capacity or in any other capacity. **We used to have a difference between Church and State, but it is all one now.** Thank God, we have no more temporal and spiritual! **We have got Church and State together**,.... We have no vague theories:... The time has come for decisive action; and **whether you were called to act in a religious, civil, or military capacity, it is all in the kingdom of God** and the will of God is to be done upon the earth as angels do it in heaven."[16] (emphasis added.)
>
> "In politics as in everything *else we want to know the will of God, and then do it*....Do we not believe in the voice of the people? Yes; but we believe in the voice of God first, in the middle, and in the end.... We do not think we have wisdom to manage our political affairs without the interposition of the Most High.... **I very much doubt the right of men to do as they please when they profess to be Latter-day Saints; because we have covenanted together to keep the commandments of God and obey the holy priesthood.** (John Taylor. 1867, JD-11:355-6)."[17] (emphasis added.)

These are very telling statements with respect to Church and State, politics, Mormon leadership, and control by covenant of the Mormon people. Mormon Prophet John Taylor clearly sees no problem with the mixing of Church and State when he says: "We used to have a difference between Church and State, but it is all one now.... We have got Church and State together.... whether you were called to act in a religious, civil, or military capacity, it is all in the kingdom of God..." He continues, "In politics as in everything *else we want to know the will of God, and then do it*." He qualifies this knowing the will of God in politics against the background of the "voice of the people" by stating "we believe in the voice of God first, in the middle, and in the end....We do not think we have wisdom to manage our political affairs without the interposition of the Most High." As previously documented in this book, the voice of God is believed in Mormonism to come through "The Brethren": The Prophet, his two Counselors and the Twelve Apostles. The last sentence is critical: "I very much doubt the right of men to do as they please when they profess to be Latter-day Saints; because we have covenanted together to keep the commandments of God and obey the holy priesthood." This Mormon Prophet makes it crystal clear: **As a Mormon, you do not have the right to do as you please. As a Mormon you have covenanted to** keep the commandments of God and **obey the holy priesthood. Politically, "as in everything," as a Mormon, you will obey the holy priesthood!**

THE CONSTITUTION WILL HANG BY A THREAD!

The Mormon Church can no longer openly defy the Federal Government; however, Mormonism teaches that the U.S. Constitution is going to hang by a thread and the "Elders of Israel [Mormons]" will step forward and save it. Mormon author Jerome Horowitz, in his book, "*The Elders of Israel and the Constitution*," details at length the belief that the Mormon Church will indeed save the Constitution:

"It is a belief of the Latter-day Saints that the Constitution of the United States is divinely inspired. In the *Doctrine and Covenants*, the Lord declared:

... I established the Constitution of this land, by the hands of wise men whom I raised up unto this very purpose.... [*D & C* 101:80]

It is also a Latter-day Saint belief, declared by Joseph Smith and reaffirmed by subsequent prophets, that the time would come when the Constitution of the United States would be all but destroyed. An expression used is that it would hang as by a single thread. [*Journal of Discourses*, 6:152].

These predictions continue to the effect that the Elders of Israel will be instrumental in saving the Constitution, if it is saved at all. [*Journal of Discourses*, 7:15]. The term "Elders of Israel," as used in this context, apparently refers to the Mormon people rather than to a specific priesthood group."[18] (bracketed information and emphasis added.)

The above bracketed quotes are hereby provided:

Orson Hyde, President of the Quorum of the Twelve Apostles, said that the "Elders of this Church," (the Mormon Church) would save the Constitution if it would be "saved at all":

"It is said that brother Joseph in his lifetime declared that the Elders of this Church should step forth at a particular time when the Constitution should be in danger, and rescue it, and to save it. This may be so; but I do not recollect that he said exactly so. I believe he said something like this—that the time would come when the Constitution and the country would be in danger of an overthrow; and said he, **If the Constitution be saved at all, it will be by the Elders of this Church.** I believe this is about the language, as nearly as I can recollect it."[19] (emphasis added.)

Brigham Young said the "destiny of the nation will hang upon a single thread," and the Mormons would step forward and save it:

> "Will the Constitution be destroyed? No: it will be held inviolate by this people; and, as Joseph Smith said, **"The time will come when the destiny of the nation will hang upon a single thread. At that critical juncture, this people will step forth and save it from the threatened destruction."** It will be so."[20] (emphasis added.)

More specifically, Brigham Young stated that the "Mormon" Elders would save the Constitution from utter destruction:

> "Brethren and sisters, our friends wish to know our feelings towards the Government. I answer, they are first-rate, and we will prove it too, as you will see if you only live long enough, for that we shall live to prove it is certain; and when **the Constitution of the United States hangs, as it were, upon a single thread, they will have to call for the "Mormon" Elders to save it from utter destruction; and they will step forward and do it."[21]** (emphasis added.)

John Taylor—the 3rd Mormon Prophet, and Brigham Young's successor—echoed these same sentiments:

> "The Prophet Joseph Smith said that "The Constitution of the United States was given by inspiration of God." But good, virtuous and holy principles may be perverted

by corrupt and wicked men. The Lord was opposed by Satan, Jesus had his Judas, and this nation abounds with traitors who ignore that sacred palladium of liberty and seek to trample it under foot. Joseph Smith said they would do so, and that when deserted by all, **the elders of Israel would rally around its shattered fragments and save and preserve it inviolate.**"[22] (emphasis added.)

WHAT'S THE POINT?

The mixing of Church and State are inseparable in Mormonism. The Mormon Church sees itself as "The Kingdom of God" on earth. Within Mormon doctrine and the prophecies of their leaders, Mormonism also says that a political kingdom must be ushered in prior to the Second Coming of Christ—and the Mormon Church will be the vehicle of that political kingdom. Nothing has changed in Mormon doctrine with respect to Mormonism claiming to be the "Kingdom of God" on earth and its belief that the King of Heaven, Jesus, rules that Kingdom by speaking His will directly through the earthly king, the Mormon Prophet. What has changed is the brash, unabashed pronouncement of those beliefs by Mormon leaders of the past. Mormon Church Headquarters in Salt Lake City, Utah, today is "Public Relations" conscience, and maintains a low-profile with respect to their doctrines of world political domination.

The belief that the "Mormon Elders" will save the Constitution when it is "hanging by a thread," is dismissed today by the Mormon Church Public Relations Machine as an old myth. The above quotes by two Mormon Prophets, Young and Taylor, and Orson Hyde, the President of the Quorum of the Twelve, however, clearly show that this attempt to dismiss this belief as an old myth is inaccurate. Those who have "the **right**, the **power**, and **authority to declare the mind and will of God** to his people…"[23], two Prophets and

---

one President of the Twelve, believed this would happen and instructed the Mormon people accordingly.

Growing up in the Mormon Church I heard this "myth" regularly, not only from Mormon family sources, but also from Mormon Church leaders and teachers. It is a commonly held belief in the Mormon fabric, and as documented above, preached by Mormon Prophets and Apostles. Chapter Five will clearly show, if this belief in saving the Constitution as it "hangs by a thread," should be advocated by "The Brethren" any Mormon would be under direct obligation to follow their direction in pursuing the course they dictate.

[1] Bruce R. McConkie, *Mormon Doctrine* (Bookcraft: Salt Lake City, Utah, 1966) 415-416.
[2] *Ibid.*, 418-419.
[3] Klaus J. Hansen, *Quest for Empire – The Political Kingdom of God and the Council of Fifty in Mormon History* (Michigan State University Press, 1967), 3-4.
[4] *Ibid.*, 10-11.
[5] Joseph Smith, *History of the Church of Jesus Christ of Latter-day Saints* (Salt Lake City: Deseret News, 1970), 2:182.
[6] D. Michael Quinn, *The Mormon Hierarchy – Origins of Power,* (Salt Lake City: Signature Books, 1994) 88.
[7] Josiah F. Gibbs, *Mountain Meadows Massacre*, (Salt Lake Tribune Publishing Company, 1910) online book at: http://www.utlm.org/onlinebooks/meadowscontents.htm
[8] Quinn, *Origins of Power*, 93.
[9] *Ibid.*, 120.
[10] Hansen, *Quest for Empire*, 11.
[11] Richard N. Ostling and Joan K. Ostling, *Mormon America: The Power and the Promise*, (HarperCollins Publishers Inc., San Francisco, 1999) 76.
[12] *Ibid.*, 77-78.

[13] *Ibid.*, 78-79.

[14] *Ibid.*, 91-93.

[15] Brigham Young in Watt, ed., *Journal of Discourses*, 9:316.

[16] John Taylor in Watt, ed., *Journal of Discourses*, 5:266.

[17] Jerreld L. Newquist, *Prophets, Principles and National Survival* (Publishers Press, Salt Lake City, Utah, 1964) 44.

[18] Jerome Horowitz, *The Elders of Israel and the Constitution*, (Parliament Publishers, Salt Lake City, Utah, 1970) 1-2.

[19] Orson Hyde in Watt, ed., *Journal of Discourses*, 6:152.

[20] Brigham Young in Watt, ed., *Journal of Discourses*, 7:15.

[21] Brigham Young in Watt, ed., *Journal of Discourses*, 2:182.

[22] John Taylor in Gibbs, ed., *Journal of Discourses*, 21:31.

[23] *Teachings of the Living Prophets*, Student Manual Religion 333, Published by The Church of Jesus Christ of Latter-day Saints (Salt Lake City, Utah, 1982) 9.

AUTHOR'S NOTE – See any of the following volumes for a much more in-depth treatise on the subject of the Mormon concept of their "Kingdom" on earth.

1. Klaus J. Hansen, *Quest for Empire – The Political Kingdom of God and the Council of Fifty in Mormon History* (Michigan State University Press, 1967).

2. D. Michael Quinn, *The Mormon Hierarchy – Origins of Power,* (Signature Books: Salt Lake City, 1994).

3. D. Michael Quinn, *The Mormon Hierarchy – Extensions of Power*, (Signature Books: Salt Lake City, 1997).

4. Jerald and Sandra Tanner, *Mormonism – Shadow or Reality?,* (Utah Lighthouse Ministry, Salt Lake City, 1982).

5. Richard Abanes, *One Nation Under Gods*, (Four Walls Eight Windows, New York, NY, 2002).

Chapter Five

FOLLOW THE PROPHETS, SEERS, AND REVELATORS – ORACLES – THE LORD'S ANOINTED!

Mormons hold an absolute allegiance to their Priesthood leadership and more specifically to, "The Brethren." The Mormon Prophet, his two Counselors, and the Twelve Apostles are commonly referred to as "The Brethren." These fifteen men are absolutely revered in Mormonism as God's literal "oracles" on earth. All of these men hold an absolute, elevated position in the Mormon hierarchy of "God's Kingdom on Earth." Mormon doctrine holds that the current President of the Mormon Church, the "Prophet," is God's direct, real time, representative on earth. There is no question in the Mormon mind that the "Prophet" speaks directly with, and for, God today.

Believing that the "Prophet" speaks expressly for God promotes a side of Mormonism which believes that it is the solemn 'duty' of a Mormon to "Follow the Prophet!" This idea, "Follow the Prophet," permeates the Mormon culture:

"In a setting where 14 of the 15 prophets of this dispensation have spoken in general conference over the years [the Mormon Tabernacle in Salt Lake City], Presiding Bishop H. David Burton counseled youth to follow the living prophets...But one of his favorite sermons, he said, was given by President Wilford Woodruff before the era of television. The point of the sermon was that the words of the living prophets are as important as the scriptures... The lesson for this evening, I hope, my young friends, is that we can keep our focus on the prophets of this dispensation. There are few guarantees in life, but one of those guarantees centers around following the words of the prophets."[1] (bracketed information added.)

This mantra to "Follow the Prophet" is a consistent doctrinal belief of Mormonism from its beginning. This doctrinal position stems from the belief that Joseph Smith was the "Prophet of the Restoration," and received hundreds — perhaps thousands — of "revelations" directly from God; thus, since God spoke directly to him, Mormons are to follow him. The "Doctrine and Covenants" is a book that Mormons revere as additional scripture which contains over 100 revelations purported to have been given to Joseph Smith by God. In Section 21 of "Doctrine and Covenants," Joseph Smith claims to have received a revelation on April 6, 1830, in which Mormons see the revealed Word of God directing them to receive what the "Prophet" says, as if it came from God Himself:

1. Behold, there shall be a record kept among you; and in it thou shalt be called a seer, a translator, a prophet, an apostle of Jesus Christ, an elder of the church through the will of God the Father, and the grace of your Lord Jesus Christ,
2. Being inspired of the Holy Ghost to lay the foundation thereof, and to build it up unto the most holy faith.

3. Which church was organized and established in the year of your Lord eighteen hundred and thirty, in the fourth month, and on the sixth day of the month which is called April.

4. **Wherefore, meaning the church, <u>thou shalt give heed unto all his words and commandments</u> which he shall give unto you as he receiveth them, walking in all holiness before me;**

5. **For <u>his word ye shall receive, as if from mine own mouth</u>, in all patience and faith.**

6. **<u>For by doing these things the gates of hell shall not prevail against you</u>; yea, and the Lord God will disperse the powers of darkness from before you, and cause the heavens to shake for your good, and his name's glory.**

7. For thus saith the Lord God: Him have I inspired to move the cause of Zion in mighty power for good, and his diligence I know, and his prayers I have heard.[2] (emphasis added.)

Notice in verse 4 that Joseph Smith is the subject, and God tells all Mormons that they are to "give heed unto all his words and commandments." In verse 5 God tells Mormons that "his word ye shall receive, as if from mine own mouth." So, Joseph Smith speaks for God. Verse 6 tells us: "For by doing these things the gates of hell shall not prevail against you." Here we see Mormons are told that by following Joseph Smith, who speaks directly for God, the gates of hell shall not prevail against them.

In a sermon preached by Brigham Young (2nd Prophet of the Mormon Church) at Nauvoo, Illinois in 1843, he said the first principle in the cause of Mormonism was to understand that Mormons have a Prophet and he is accountable to God only:

"The first principle of our cause and work is to understand that **there is a prophet in the church, and that he is at the head of the Church of Christ on earth.** Who called Joseph Smith to be a prophet? Did the people or God? God, and not the people, called him. Had the people gathered together and appointed one of their number to be a prophet, he would have been accountable to the people, but, inasmuch as he was called of God, and not by the people, **he is accountable to God only... and not to any man on earth. The twelve apostles are accountable to the prophet and not to the church for the course they pursue, and we have learned to go and do, as the prophet tells us.**" – From sermon by Brigham Young, at Nauvoo, 1843, published in Millennial Star, Liverpool, England, Vol. XXI., page 741.[3] (emphasis added.)

The above principle is of the utmost importance in understanding the mindset of Mormonism. The Mormon Prophet is accountable to no one on earth, the Mormon Apostles are accountable only to him and it is the job of all Mormons to do "as the prophet tells us." This principle is best explained by the 13th Mormon Prophet, Ezra Taft Benson who served as the Prophet from November 10, 1985, until his death May 30, 1994. In a speech given in 1980 to a Brigham Young Devotional Assembly titled "The Fourteen Fundamentals of a Prophet" Benson clearly laid out the Mormon Church doctrinal belief of "Following the Prophet." Read these fundamentals closely as they vividly show a belief system centered in a man, placing him above all accountability:

1. **The prophet is the only man who speaks for the Lord in everything.**
2. **The living prophet is more vital to us than the standard works** [the Mormon Standard Works are

the four books of the Mormon canon – Book of Mormon, Doctrine and Covenants, Pearl of Great Price, and the Bible].

3. **The living prophet is more important to us than a dead prophet.**
4. **The prophet will never lead the Church astray.**
5. **The prophet is not required to have any particular earthly training or credentials to speak on any subject or act on any matter at any time.**
6. **The prophet does not have to say "Thus saith the Lord," to give us scripture.**
7. **The prophet tells us what we need to know**, not always what we want to know.
8. **The prophet is not limited by men's reasoning.**
9. **The prophet can receive revelation on any matter—temporal or spiritual.**
10. **The prophet may be involved in civic matters.**
11. The two groups who have the greatest difficulty in following the prophet are the proud who are learned and the proud who are rich.
12. The prophet will not necessarily be popular with the world or the worldly.
13. The prophet and his counselors make up the First Presidency—the highest quorum in the Church.
14. **The prophet and the presidency—the living prophet and the First Presidency—follow them and be blessed; reject them and suffer.**[4] (bracketed information and emphasis added.)

Not to insult anyone's intelligence by restating the above listing, an honest review of these 14 fundamentals, when placed in the context of the Mormon people believing that one man on earth is God's direct representative, his living "oracle," is very dangerous. These fundamentals tell the Mormon people that their "Prophet" speaks for God "in

everything," is more vital than scripture, more important than any previous "prophet," can never lead the "Church" astray, needs no training or credentials to speak on any subject, does not need to say "Thus Saith the Lord" to give scripture, tells us exactly what we need to know, is not limited by men's reasoning, can receive revelation on any matter – temporal or spiritual, may be involved in civic matters, there are two kinds of people who won't listen to the Mormon Prophet – those who are too smart for their own good and those who have too much money for their own good, the Mormon Prophet won't be popular with those who aren't active members of the Mormon Church, the Prophet and his Counselors make up the "First Presidency" – the highest of the ruling bodies of the "Church", and **FOLLOW THE PROPHET AND HIS COUNSELORS, OR SUFFER!**
   Of particular note here are numbers 8 and 10:

> 8. The prophet is not limited by men's reasoning. There will be times when you will have to choose between the revelations of God and the reasoning of men— between the prophet and the politician or professor. Said the Prophet Joseph Smith, "Whatever God requires is right, no matter what it is, although we may not see the reason thereof until long after the events transpire" (*Scrapbook of Mormon Literature, vol. 2,* p. 173).[5]

   This principle places a Mormon in a blind obedience predicament. **If their Prophet tells them to do something, even though all reason and logic, fact or evidence, may be against the directive, they are to do it anyway.** Their Founding Prophet, Joseph Smith, gives the reason for this blind obedience: "Whatever God requires is right, no matter what it is, although we may not see the reason thereof until long after the events transpire." This doctrine of Mormonism is untenably against American democracy. **A Mormon who holds any Governmental position of authority, whether elected or appointed, may be forced by their religious beliefs to make a decision contrary to all logic, reason, facts or evidence because their Prophet has directed the request.**

10. The prophet may be involved in civic matters. When a people are righteous they want the best to lead them in government. Alma was the head of the Church and of the government in the Book of Mormon, Joseph Smith was mayor of Nauvoo, and Brigham Young was governor of Utah. Isaiah was deeply involved in giving counsel on political matters and of his words the Lord Himself said, "Great are the words of Isaiah" (3 Nephi 23:1). Those who would remove prophets from politics would take God out of government.[6]

This principle primes Mormons to have their Church leaders involved in the political arena. Don't misconstrue the point. I support people of faith, and church leaders speaking out on civic matters and morale issues. However, in Mormonism you have the belief that the "Church" leader is God's "oracle" on earth and speaks directly for God, with the admonition: "follow them and be blessed; reject them and suffer." That obligation and immediate judgment is not found in other faiths.

Those who accept Mormonism as their faith and therefore align themselves to the above "Fourteen Fundamentals of a Prophet," this author believes, are suspect when it comes to governmental service. Why? It is simply because their belief in a man who has no accountability on earth and has the right, in their eyes, to direct them in any matter on earth, places them outside the bounds of independent thought. Daniel H. Wells,

2nd Counselor to Brigham Young, gave a sermon in 1878, which amplifies the idea that Mormon Priesthood holders can and should direct Mormons in all matters, both spiritual and temporal, simply by virtue of the fact that they hold the Mormon Priesthood. Mormon Apostle Wells states that the kingdoms of the earth will become the kingdoms of "our God and his Christ" through the vehicle of the Mormon Priesthood:

> "Some persons in the Church think that an Apostle or a Bishop has no right to interfere in temporal things; that their business alone is to look after the spiritual affairs, and their temporal affairs they can attend to themselves. It is very possible some of these men understand financial matters better than the servants of the Lord; **but it should not be forgotten that the spirit of God and the Holy Priesthood will qualify men for all positions of life**. People can, through these agencies, acquire superior intelligence to administer in the things of this world, and it must be done before the eternal riches are conferred upon this people, because the light of heaven is superior to that of the world. The kingdoms of this earth are to become the kingdoms of our God and his Christ. I look for this government to come through the Holy Priesthood, and to exercise power in temporal, political and all other things,—a government that will extend to all men their rights and privileges."[7] (emphasis added.)

Mormons, by their "Church" doctrine, are obligated to follow their "Prophets, Seers, and Revelators." I will show in follow-on pages that, should a Mormon disagree with their Mormon Priesthood leadership and fail to accept their "counsel," these actions could have "eternal consequences." They could loose their ability in eternity to become "a God" themselves and could be relegated to a lower kingdom of heaven for eternity.

President J. Reuben Clark, 1st Counselor to the 8th Mormon Prophet, George Albert Smith, illuminated the principle of absolute obedience to Mormon leadership at the General Priesthood Meeting of the General Conference of the Mormon Church in April 1950:

> "Now, another point, brethren. Sometimes local presiding officers say, why, why should this be done, why should this course be followed? This does not apply to our local situation and that does not apply to somebody's else situation. Do you remember that after Adam was driven from the Garden of Eden he was offering sacrifice and an angel of the Lord came to him and said: "Why dost thou offer sacrifice unto the Lord?"
>
> He said: "I know not, save the Lord commanded me."
>
> And then the angel explained to Adam what the sacrifice meant, **and the point I want to make from that is that obedience must often precede knowledge.**
>
> We are prone to try to rationalize and to say that the things we cannot understand cannot be. Well how much is there in the physical world that we do not understand and that even the wisest of our scientific savants do not understand....The human mind cannot fully fathom the purposes of the Lord. We see them dimly. We see through a glass darkly, but that does not change the fact that the purposes are there, even though we do not understand them."[8] (emphasis added.)

The above bolded line is very important: **"obedience must often precede knowledge."** Add that to Daniel H. Wells statement that **"it should not be forgotten that the spirit of God and the Holy Priesthood will qualify men**

for all positions of life," plus the previous mentioned statement from Brigham Young, **"we have learned to go and do as the prophet tells us,"** and you have an ideology that should frighten most Americans (See Chapter Nine, Mountain Meadows Massacre). When you interfuse one last point, that all occupations, civil or military, are under the Mormon Priesthood, Americans should stand up and take notice. General Authority Albert P. Rockwood, one of the First Seven Presidents of the Quorum of the Seventy, made a statement of absolute control by the Mormon Church Priesthood to all occupations, both civil and military:

"all men holding the Priesthood employed in civil or military occupations were amenable to that priesthood for their acts."[9] (emphasis added.)

Mormon Apostle Neal A. Maxwell makes the point that no matter your earthly professional expertise, if the "Prophet" speaks, your professional knowledge and years of expertise mean nothing:

"Following the living prophets is something that must be done in all seasons and circumstances. We must be like President Marion G. Romney, who humbly said, **'...I have never hesitated to follow the counsel of the Authorities of the Church even though it crossed my social, professional, and political life'** (*Conference Report*, April 1941, p. 123). There are, or will be, moments when prophetic declarations collide with our pride or our seeming personal interests...Do I believe in the living prophet even when he speaks on matters affecting me and my specialty directly? Or do I stop sustaining the prophet when his words fall in my territory? if the latter, the prophet is without honor in *our* country!" (*Things As They Really Are*, p. 73).[10] (emphasis added.)

Couple this all together and you have the catalyst for blind obedience: Do as you are told, obey without knowledge, the Holy Priesthood qualifies men for all positions of life, all occupations, both civil and military are answerable to the Mormon Priesthood and believe in spite of your professional knowledge and accumulated expertise. All of these principles are part and parcel of Mormonism. These concepts are simply out of line with the American ideals of democracy. We as Americans trust our elected and appointed officials to act on our behalf without allegiance to an outside entity that may control those officials like a marionette dangling their eternal destiny on a string of absolute obedience. The above quote leaves no stone unturned: social, professional, and political life. It also makes quite clear the point: Do not let your pride or personal interests collide with "Following the Prophet!"

The 3rd Mormon Prophet, John Taylor, makes the point that unless Mormons submit and obey the law of God—which is delivered by their Priesthood leadership, specifically "The Brethren"—they "are not fit to occupy their places in the Kingdom":

> **"We are not fit to occupy our places in the kingdom**, either as High Priests, or as Seventies, or as Apostles, or as anything else, **except we are willing and obedient**: and the same thing applies to our families. **Then let us seek to submit ourselves to the law of God and do it.**"[11] (emphasis added.)

PROPHETS, SEERS, REVELATORS AND ORACLES

Key to understanding the conflict between Mormonism and holding governmental positions of power, is understanding the absolute belief in the position and authority of their leadership with respect to God Himself. The 11th

Prophet of the Mormon Church, Harold B. Lee, illustrates this point in a speech he presented at the General Priesthood Meeting, April 8, 1972, when he was 1st Counselor to Joseph F. Smith. The talk was reprinted in the July 1972 issue of the Mormon Church's magazine, *Ensign*:

"Now I want to impress this upon you. Someone has said it this way, and I believe it to be absolutely true: "That person is not truly converted until he sees the power of God resting upon the leaders of this church, and until it goes down into his heart like fire." Until the members of this church have that conviction that they are being led in the right way, and they have a conviction that these men of God are men who are inspired and have been properly appointed by the hand of God, they are not truly converted."[12]

To more fully comprehend the Mormon definition of these titles I will quote from a Mormon Church produced student text, intended for use in their College Educational System:

PROPHET:

A prophet is a teacher. That is the essential meaning of the word. He teaches the body of truth, the gospel, revealed by the Lord to man; and under inspiration explains it to the understanding of the people. He is an expounder of truth. Moreover, he shows that the way to human happiness is through obedience to God's law. He calls to repentance those who wander away from the truth. He becomes a warrior for the consummation of the Lord's purposes with respect to the human family. The purpose of his life is to uphold the Lord's plan of salvation. All this he does by close communion with the

Lord, until he is "full of power by the spirit of the Lord" (Micah 3:8; see also D. & C. 20:26, 34:10, 43:16)...

In the course of time the word "prophet" has come to mean, perhaps chiefly, a man who receives revelations, and directions from the Lord. The principle business of a prophet has mistakenly been thought to foretell coming events, to utter prophecies, which is only one of the several prophetic functions.

In the sense that a prophet is a man who receives revelations from the Lord, the titles "seer and revelator" merely amplify the larger and inclusive meaning of the title "prophet"...

A prophet also receives revelations from the Lord. These may be explanations of truths already received, or new truths not formerly possessed by man....

SEER:

A seer is one who sees with spiritual eyes. He perceives the meaning of that which seems obscure to others; therefore he is an interpreter and clarifier of eternal truth. He foresees the future from the past and the present. This he does by the power of the Lord operating through him directly, or indirectly with the aid of divine instruments such as the Urim and Thummim [Joseph Smith had a magic rock he called a "seer stone" that has been identified in Mormon writings as the Urim and Thummim]. In short, he is one who sees, who walks in the Lord's light with open eyes....

A seer is greater than a prophet.... One may be a prophet without being a seer; but a seer is essentially a prophet—if by "prophet" is meant not only a spokesman, but likewise a foreteller. Joseph Smith was both prophet and seer.

A seer is one who sees. But it is not the ordinary sight that is meant. The seeric gift is a supernatural endowment. Joseph was "like unto Moses;" and Moses, who saw God face to face, explains how he saw him in these words: "Now mine own eyes have beheld God; yet not my natural, but my spiritual eyes; for my natural eyes could not have beheld; for I should have withered and died in his presence; but his glory was upon me; and I beheld his face, for I was transfigured before him." (Moses 1:11.) Such is the testimony of the ancient Seer, as brought to light by the Seer of the Latter-days....

REVELATOR:

A revelator makes known, with the Lord's help, something before unknown. It may be new or forgotten truth, or a new or forgotten application of known truth to man's need. Always, the revelator deals with truth, certain truth (D. & C. 100:11) and always it comes with the divine stamp of approval. Revelation may be received in various ways, but it always presupposes that the revelator has so lived and conducted himself as to be in tune or harmony with the divine spirit of revelation, the spirit of truth, and therefore capable of receiving divine messages....[13] (bracketed information added.)

Not only are these men considered "Prophets, Seers, and Revelators," but they are also considered to be "oracles." Webster's Dictionary defines an oracle as: "1. among the ancient Greeks and Romans, *a*) the place where, or medium by which, deities were consulted *b*) the revelation of a medium or priest 2 *a*) a person of great knowledge *b*) statements of such a person." Mormonism believes that these men are "mediums" who have direct access to God and the right to speak for Him:

"Men who receive revelations or oracles for the people are themselves called *oracles*. (2 Sam. 16:23.) Members of the First Presidency, [and] Council of the Twelve ... – because they are appointed and sustained as prophets, seers, and revelators to the Church – are known as the *living oracles*."[14]

"Although the Church has many men who serve as "General Authorities," only the First Presidency and the members of the Quorum of the Twelve Apostles are sustained as prophets, seers, and revelators."[15]

"It should be in mind that some of the General Authorities have had assigned to them a special calling; they possess a special gift; they are sustained as prophets, seers, and revelators, which gives them a special spiritual endowment in connection with their teaching the people. They have the **right**, the **power**, and **authority to declare the mind and will of God** to his people..."[16] (emphasis added.)

The above quote makes it quite clear that the lofty position held by these men is believed by Mormons to give them the "**right**, the **power**, and **authority to declare the mind and will of God** to his people..." Within the context of a Mormon's religious experience, this is America, and as long as they abide by the laws of the land, they are free to believe what they will, and worship as they may. However, when this belief is leveraged upon a member of the Mormon Church, and they are functioning in a civic capacity, the "**right**, the **power**, and **authority to declare the mind and will of God** to his people..." is then placed upon the American public without their knowledge. Mormon leadership have, by the power by Mormon doctrinal beliefs, the ability to control their members "on any matter—temporal or spiritual." This is an imposition of a church upon the people that was never intended by our Founding Fathers who defined and wrote

143

our Constitution. We, as Americans, need to be aware this condition exists within the context of the Mormon Faith!

To those who may think I am reading into the these statements that which doesn't exist, let me quote the 10th Mormon Prophet, Joseph Fielding Smith, speaking in the General Priesthood Meeting of General Conference of The Church of Jesus Christ of Latter-day Saints, April 8, 1972:

> "Now, brethren, I think there is one thing which we should have exceedingly clear in our minds. Neither the President of the Church, nor the First Presidency, nor the united voice of the First Presidency and the Twelve will (n)ever (sic) lead the Saints astray or send forth counsel to the world that is contrary to the mind and will of the Lord."[17]

Note in the above quote that this 10th President/Prophet of the Mormon Church says that the First Presidency and the Twelve [Prophets, Seers, and Revelators] will (n)ever (sic) lead the Saints astray or send forth counsel to the world that is contrary to the mind and will of the Lord." (bracketed information added.) Not only does this quote say that Mormons believe these men's counsel is for them, but for the "world" as well, and can **never be contrary to "the mind and will of the Lord."**

Brigham Young expressed the same sentiments many years earlier:

> "The Lord Almighty leads this Church, and he will not suffer you to be led astray if you are found doing your duty. You may go home and sleep as sweetly as a babe in its mother's arms, as to any danger of your leaders leading you astray, for if they should try to do so the Lord would quickly sweep them from the earth."[18]

A Mormon confronted with pressure by their Church Hierarchy has been indoctrinated to believe that, contrary to any reservations or personal belief conflicts they may have with the pressure being applied, the position being imposed by the "Church" will never be "contrary to the mind and will of the Lord." So, the Mormon, who is in opposition to the pressure being applied by their Church, is in a religious doctrinal vice. The person may believe, and have evidence contrary to the position being advocated by the Mormon Church, however, they have been indoctrinated to believe that "The Brethren" can never lead them astray.

INDOCTRINATION

In Mormonism it is not just a mere belief that these men are "Living Oracles," it is an indoctrination process that continues year after year in the twice yearly General Conferences and through teaching manuals used in all general instruction (i.e., Sunday School, Priesthood meetings, Relief Society meetings [women's organization]). This concept of "Prophets, Seers, and Revelators" is voted on by the whole of the Mormon Church twice yearly in their General Conference as well as their local "Stake" Conferences. As of this writing, September 2007, the last sustaining vote in Conference was conducted by Thomas S. Monson, 1st Counselor in the First Presidency on March 31, 2007:

> "President Hinckley has asked that I now present the General Authorities, Area Seventies, and general auxiliary presidencies of the Church for a sustaining vote. May we all participate not only with our uplifted hand but with our pledged heart.
> It is proposed that we sustain Gordon Bitner Hinckley as prophet, seer, and revelator and President of The Church of Jesus Christ of Latter-day Saints;

Thomas Spencer Monson as First Counselor in the First Presidency; and James Esdras Faust as Second Counselor in the First Presidency.

Those in favor may manifest it by the uplifted hand.

Those opposed, if any, by the same sign.

It is proposed that we sustain Thomas Spencer Monson as President of the Quorum of the Twelve Apostles; Boyd Kenneth Packer as Acting President of the Quorum of the Twelve Apostles; and the following as members of that quorum: Boyd K. Packer, L. Tom Perry, Russell M. Nelson, Dallin H. Oaks, M. Russell Ballard, Joseph B. Wirthlin, Richard G. Scott, Robert D. Hales, Jeffrey R. Holland, Henry B. Eyring, Dieter F. Uchtdorf, and David A. Bednar.

Those in favor, please manifest it.

Any opposed.

It is proposed that we sustain the counselors in the First Presidency and the Twelve Apostles as prophets, seers, and revelators.

All in favor, please manifest it.

Contrary, if there be any, by the same sign."[19]

Bear with me for these next few pages. I am going to bombard you with quotes, with a little commentary injected, from the past and the present to show a consistent, ongoing, and unalterable belief in the divine position of the Mormon Church Hierarchy and the absolute indoctrination to unconditionally follow and adhere to their divine leadership.

To clarify the weight and the affect sermons from the Mormon Hierarchy have upon the Mormon people, I believe it is important to review the words of the 2nd Mormon Prophet, Brigham Young:

"I have never yet preached a sermon and sent it out to the children of men, that they may not call Scripture.

Let me have the privilege of correcting a sermon, and it is as good Scripture as they deserve. **The people have the oracles of God continually.**"[20] (emphasis added.)

To validate this delivery of "scripture" to Mormons through the speeches and "talks" given by their General Authorities in modern times, Apostle Bruce R. McConkie compiled the writings of Joseph Fielding Smith, 10th Prophet of the Mormon Church, into a three volume set of religious instruction titled *"Doctrines of Salvation."* In volume 1 under the heading "WHAT IS SCRIPTURE?" we read the following:

"When one of the brethren stands before a congregation of the people today, and the inspiration of the Lord is upon him, he speaks that which the Lord would have him speak. It is just as much scripture as anything you will find written in any of these records, and yet we call these the standard works of the Church. We depend, of course, upon the guidance of the brethren who are entitled to inspiration.

There is only one man in the Church at a time who has the right to give revelation for the Church, and that is the President of the Church. But that does not bar any other member in this Church from speaking the word of the Lord, as indicated here in this revelation, section 68, but a revelation that is to be given as these revelations are given in this book, to the Church, will come through the presiding officer of the Church; yet, the word of the Lord, as spoken by other servants at the general conferences and stake conferences, or wherever they may be when they speak that which the Lord has put into their mouths, *is just as much the word of the Lord as the writings and the words of other prophets in other dispensations."*[21] (*italics* in the original.)

This concept permeates Mormonism. Mormons believe their leaders are God's oracles and when they speak it is modern scripture; and, as we have clearly seen earlier in this chapter, laid out by former Mormon Prophet Ezra Taft Benson in his "Fourteen Fundamentals of a Prophet," number three says a living prophet overrules a dead prophet. That concept allows the Mormon Prophet total independence from anything that has ever been said or written. What the current Prophet says, trumps everything else, including their "Standard Works" (Book of Mormon, Doctrine and Covenants, Pearl of Great Price, and the Bible).

In 1994 President James E. Faust, former 2nd Counselor in the First Presidency said:

> **"I strongly counsel all who have membership in this church to follow the teachings and counsel of those who now have the keys as prophets, seers, and revelators.** They are the ones who will inspire us to deal with the vicissitudes of our time. **I plead with all not to try to selectively invoke gospel principles or scripture to wrongly justify spiritual disobedience, or to separate themselves from the responsibilities of covenants and ordinances contrary to the counsel of those who have the prophetic voice in the Church.** The scriptures and doctrines of the Church are not, as Peter warned, "of any private interpretation."
>
> **Great temporal and spiritual strength flows from following those who have the keys of the kingdom of God in our time. Personal strength and power result from obedience to eternal principles taught by the living legates of the Lord.** May the Spirit of God rest upon us as we **follow the living oracles.**"[22] (emphasis added.)

Webster's Dictionary defines "legates" as: an envoy or ambassador.

In the book, *Prophets, Principles and National Survival*, Mormon writer Jerreld L. Newquist, relates a story told by Wilford Woodruff, 4th Mormon Prophet, under a chapter subtitle of: **"Living Oracles More Important than Written Word."**

"I will refer to a certain meeting I attended in the town of Kirtland in my early days. At that meeting some remarks were made that have been made here today, with regard to the living oracles and with regard to the written word of God. The same principle was presented, although not as extensively as it has been here, when a leading man in the Church got up and talked upon the subject, and said: "You have got the word of God before you here in the Bible, Book of Mormon, and Doctrine and Covenants; you have the written word of God, and you who give revelations should give revelations according to those books, as what is written in those books is the word of God. We should confine ourselves to them."

When he concluded, Brother Joseph turned to Brother Brigham Young and said, "Brother Brigham I want you to take the stand and tell us your views with regard to the living oracles and the written word of God." Brother Brigham took the stand, and he took the Bible, and laid it down; he took the Book of Mormon, and laid it down; and he took the Book of Doctrine and Covenants, and laid it down before him, and he said: "There is the written word of God to us, concerning the work of God from the beginning of the world, almost, to our day." "And now," said he, "when compared with the living oracles those books are nothing to me; those books do not convey the word of God direct to us now, as do the words of a Prophet or a man bearing the Holy Priesthood in our day

149

and generation. **I would rather have the living oracles than all the writing in the books.**" That was the course he pursued. When he was through, Brother Joseph said to the congregation: **"Brother Brigham has told you the word of the Lord, and he has told you the truth."**
… the Bible is all right, the Book of Mormon is all right, the Doctrine and Covenants is all right, and they proclaim the work of God and the word of God in the earth in this day and generation until the coming of the Son of Man; **but the Holy Priesthood is not confined particularly to these books,** that is, it did not cease when those books were made. (President Wilford Woodruff, CR-10/97:18-9)"[23] (emphasis added.)

10th Prophet, Joseph Fielding Smith, compliments this last quote with the principle that the "living oracles," those who hold the "Keys" to all the Holy Priesthood functions, have "the revelations of his mind and will" and can only lead the people in truth:

"WISE LEADERSHIP OF BRETHREN. **I wish to testify that God has called these men, that he has appointed them, that he has given unto them the revelations of his mind and will, that they have the inspiration of his Spirit, that they are teaching and leading this people in truth. That is the conviction of every Latter-day Saint, who has the gospel at heart.**
What time, since the organization of the Church, have any of the brethren exercising the Spirit of the Lord, ever taught this people that which was false? What have they ever said unto you that you should do that which was not right; that which would not make you better citizens and better members of the kingdom of God?

You cannot, nor can any man, in righteousness, point to the time when any of them have wilfully stated anything that was contrary to the principles of righteousness, or that did not tend to make the people better in every way, that did not build them up in their salvation, temporally as well as spiritually...."[24] (emphasis added.)

Sometimes the quotes from the "The Brethren" are challenged by Mormons as **not being "official" canon;** or, sometimes we hear the statement: **"He was just speaking as a man;"** or, **"That was just his opinion."** Brigham Young, at a Special Conference held in the Tabernacle, Great Salt Lake City, August 29, 1852, specifically taught the Mormon people that when an Apostle speaks he is giving revelation or he is not magnifying his calling:

"Now, brethren, the calling of an Apostle is to build up the kingdom of God in all the world: it is the Apostle that holds the keys of his power, and nobody else. **If an Apostle magnifies his calling, he is the word of the Lord to this people all the time, or else he does not magnify his calling;—either one or the other.**

If he magnifies his calling, his words are the words of eternal life and salvation to those who hearken to them, just as much so as any written revelations contained in these three books (Bible, Book of Mormon, and Doctrine and Covenants). There is nothing contained in these three books that is any more revelation than the words of an Apostle that is magnifying his calling."[25] (emphasis added.)

Expounding on this same principle in a Conference talk, April 7, 1852, just a few months prior to the previous quote, Brigham Young said:

"If you know what the calling of an Apostle is, and if there were ten thousand of them on the earth at the same time, you must know that **the words of an Apostle who magnifies his calling are the words of the Almighty to the people all the time. He never need be called in question whether he revealed the mind of the Lord or not.**"[26] (emphasis added.)

What does the phrase, the expression, "magnifying his calling," mean? How do Mormons know that their leaders are "magnifying their calling?" Brigham Young gives us the answer:

"When I tell the truth, that is enough, and I care not whether those who hear it believe it or not, for that is their business. If you had lived in the days of Jesus, Peter, John, etc., and had seen men called to be Apostles of the Lord Jesus Christ; every time they taught the people, every time they preached, every time they prayed, and every time they administered in the house of God, if they did not do it by the Spirit of revelation and by the power of God, they did not magnify their calling. There are not many who know this. **If we do not speak to you by the Spirit of revelation and the power of God, we do not magnify our calling. I think that I tell you the words of the Lord Almighty every time I rise here to speak to you. ... If I do not speak here by the power of God, if it is not revelation to you every time I speak to you here, I do not magnify my calling.** What do you think about it? I neither know nor care. **If I do not magnify my calling, I shall be removed from the place I occupy. God does not suffer you to be deceived.** Here are my brethren and sisters pouring out their souls to God, and their prayers and faith are like one solid cloud ascending to the heavens. They want to be led right; they want the truth; they want to know how to serve God and prepare for a celestial kingdom. **Do you think the Lord will allow you to be fooled and led astray? No**.... **I want you to have faith enough concerning myself and my Counsellors for the Lord to remove us out of the way, if we do not magnify our calling, and put men in our places that will do right.** I had the promise, years ago, that I never should apostatize and bring an evil upon this people. God revealed that through Joseph, long before he died; and if I am not doing right, you may calculate that the Lord is going to take me home.... You must have faith in God that he will lead his people right, in a way to preserve them from every evil."[27] (emphasis added.)

The answer, according to Brigham Young, on "magnifying his calling," is: If a Mormon Leader speaks, he is "magnifying his calling." If they were to attempt to lead the Mormon People astray, God would remove them from their position and replace them with someone who would "magnify his calling." If a Mormon Leader has not been removed from office, then a Mormon is to have faith that their Leader indeed is "magnifying their calling." Mormon leaders have been removed from their Priesthood offices over the years; however, none of those removed were removed for any of the quotes used in this book. For all the quotes used in this book, those Mormon leaders quoted were "magnifying their calling."

This next quote defines an extremely important point: Those in the Mormon Church who are sustained as "Prophets, Seers, and Revelators," are no longer mere men; conditions have changed – they are now "the anointed ones — the chosen ones — chosen by Almighty God!" The author of this quote, Mormon Apostle Mark E. Petersen, was third in line to the office of "Prophet" when he made it; and, this quote was delivered at General Conference, a time Mormons believe their leadership provides real-time prophetic revelations to guide the people. Let's look at his real-time prophetic revelation for the people:

> "The First Presidency is a quorum of the Church and operates as such in beautiful harmony under the influence of the Holy Spirit, thus giving inspired guidance to the Saints.
>
> The First Presidency is the presiding council of the Church. These Brethren preside over all things. **They hold all the keys, powers, gifts, and blessings of this dispensation.**
>
> **The President is the presiding high priest. His counselors preside with him by delegation from him in carrying on the labors of this highest divinely organized quorum on earth.** All four in the presidency are Apostles of the Lord Jesus Christ; **all are prophets, seers, and revelators.** [At the time of this quote an additional Counselor was added to the First Presidency due to health problems within that Quorum, normally there are only three in this Quorum.]
>
> The Council of the Twelve comes next in line. These brethren also hold the divine keys, but only the President of the Church may exercise all of these keys in their fulness, for this privilege is given to but one man on earth at a time. The Twelve also work by delegation from the President of the Church. They receive assignments from him, and fulfill them with complete devotion.
>
> **It was the Lord himself who installed Apostles and prophets in this modern Church. It is, therefore, no idle gesture by which we sustain the First Presidency and the Twelve as prophets, seers, and revelators, for so they are, divinely chosen, duly ordained and set apart by the laying on of hands by those authorized to do so.**

They were called of God as was Aaron (see Heb. 5:4), according to the pattern described by the Apostle Paul in his epistle to the Hebrews. **They were appointed by revelation, ordained by other living prophets, and fully commissioned to act in the name of the Lord.**

God speaks through our great leaders and guides his people by their words. Did not the Lord himself say: "Whether by mine own voice or by the voice of my servants, it is the same"? (D&C 1:38; italics added.)

The President of the Church, who indeed is the living mouthpiece of God and the presiding high priest on earth, is given sacred endowments even as was the Prophet Joseph Smith, whom he succeeds in this high office.

By ordination he holds all of the keys, gifts, and powers in the priesthood that were bestowed upon the Prophet Joseph Smith by the holy angels as the Church arose again in these last days.

The President of the Church holds them all!"...

The people anciently were willing to accept the divine callings of their leaders, not regarding them any longer as mere fishermen or tentmakers, for those brethren were placed by the Lord into **a new category as his divinely chosen servants.** So we of today must look beyond the former occupations and personal activities of our modern leaders and see them as the servants of God that they are now.

They are inspired as were Peter and Paul. They have the same divine callings. They are the leaders whom God himself has given us. He raised them up specifically for the present day. **Then shall we not heed them?**...

I testify to you that they are men of God. I testify to you that our great leader, President Spencer W. Kimball personally is a seer and a revelator, a prophet in the same

155

sense as was Moses or Isaiah or Joseph Smith, and that he holds divine powers even as they did.

For our own sake, for the sake of our families, for the sake of this restored church of Jesus Christ to which we give our allegiance, but also to earn the blessing of heaven, let us serve the Lord and keep his commandments.

I have been on the Council of the Twelve now for nearly thirty-eight years. In that time I have labored under six Presidents of the Church. I have sat in their meetings as vital decisions were made. I have listened to their discussions and seen the flow of inspiration as it came to these six Presidents — **these six prophets, six revelators, six seers whom I have known and whom I have loved and in whom I have felt an hallowed presence over the years.**

I testify to you, by personal experience, that I have seen the power of God work upon them. I know that we live in a day of revelation. I know these brethren are divinely appointed servants of the Lord. I know that they speak for God.

If we follow them, do we not thereby follow Him who called them?

But conversely if we raise our hands or our voices against them, or if we ignore them, do we not in that manner resist the divine being who commissioned them as his servants? Can anyone afford to do that?

Is not our attitude toward these prophets an unerring reflection of our innermost feeling toward God? I mean our real, basic allegiance when it is divested of all outward show and stripped of all pretensions.

Can we truly love the Lord and at the same time reject his servants?

If we really do love God, then indeed we must and we will love and revere his anointed ones.

What if we did know them as boys in the neighborhood and saw no halos about them? What if we did mingle with them as they lived routine and ordinary lives in the past, meeting the world as it came, day by day? **We must realize that conditions have changed!**

God has now lifted them out of those familiar patterns and has given them a new status in life. He has summoned them to high callings in his ministry. **A sacred mantle has descended upon them, the mantle of their divine commission, the mantle of prophecy!**

They speak with new voices; they are guided by a heavenly light. **They are ordinary no longer! They are the anointed ones—the chosen ones—chosen by Almighty God!**...

The Lord will honor his prophets throughout eternity, for he will make them heirs of God and joint heirs with Christ. (Rom. 8:17.) The Lord expects us, his people, to honor them also, to sustain them and to follow them. **May we therefore always sing with deep sincerity this wonderful hymn, which in truth is a prayer, but also a covenant:**

We thank thee, O God, for a prophet
To guide us in these latter days.
We thank thee for sending the gospel
To lighten our minds with its rays.
We thank thee for every blessing
Bestowed by thy bounteous hand.
We feel it a pleasure to serve thee,
And love to obey thy command.
(Hymns, no. 196.)"[28] (bracketed information and emphasis added.)

There are many deep doctrinal concepts of Mormonism in the above quote that should greatly concern the American people. Read through the above quote from Mormon Apostle Mark E. Petersen again – realizing that as Brigham Young said, this sermon, given in General Conference is seen as scripture by Mormons. There are those who unequivocally call the Mormon Church a cult because of their undue allegiance to their leadership – reviewing the above quote, it is plain to see the foundation for this position. The song quoted by this Mormon Apostle, "We Thank Thee, O God For A Prophet," is memorized, known by heart and sung with reverence by every Mormon across the globe. Apostle Petersen, says **it's not just a song, it is a covenant and prayer** to be led by their "Prophet" in "these latter days."

Apostle Wilford Woodruff, who would later become the 4th Mormon Prophet, profoundly makes the point of being led by a "Prophet" in "these latter days":

"Now, whatever I might have obtained in the shape of learning, by searching and study respecting the arts and sciences of men – whatever principles I may have imbibed during my scientific researches, yet if the prophet of God should tell me that a certain principle or theory which I might have learned was not true, I do not care what my ideas might have been, I should consider it my duty, at the suggestion of my file leader, to abandon that principle or theory."[29]

Religion journalists, Richard and Joan Ostling, in their book *"Mormon America"* provide a fascinating quote about the absolute belief in Mormonism about following the Prophet. In a discussion about millennialism, where Mormonism teaches that Jesus will return to the earth at his second coming to the city of Independence, in Jackson County Missouri, Mormon historian Richard Bushman gives a glimpse of the limitless devotion factor of Mormons to their Prophet. He says that all the Prophet would have to do is blink towards Jackson County and Mormons would flow there:

> Still, millennial fascination survives into the twenty-first century, as evidenced by BYU professor Daniel C. Peterson's 1998 book *The Last Days*, with commentary on 550 end times teachings of the General Authorities. And devoutly Mormon Columbia University historian Richard Bushman remarked that Hinckley plays down the theme precisely because it is relevant, "not because it's dying. **If the President were to blink an eye toward Jackson County, Missouri, people would flow there.** The belief is still potent, but it's latent. That's still our view of history. **All that nineteenth-century stuff is still in our culture. The church could, in a flash, constitute a complete society.**"[30] (emphasis added.)

Nothing has changed since the days of Joseph Smith. Mormons today believe in their "Living Prophet," with the same fanaticism as their predecessors did of Joseph Smith in their day. In today's day and age, it is hard to fathom people that would drop everything for the nod of a head, or the blink of an eye. Actually, it's a bit frightening. This is the kind of power that led to the Mountain Meadows Massacre, and it's alive and well today!

Part and parcel of Mormonism is absolutely following their leadership; in fact it is essential for their salvation.

LOYALTY TO GOD'S SERVANTS

"Faithfulness to the Lord's servants is essential for salvation. So necessary is obedience to those who represent the Lord that he has revealed that if a person receives his servants, he receives him." (Doctrine and Covenants 84:35-38.)[31] To follow those whom the Lord has appointed will bring many blessings. The Lord said: And if my people will hearken unto my voice, and unto the voice of my servants whom I have appointed to lead my people, behold, verily I say unto you, they shall not be moved out of their place. But if they will not hearken to my voice, nor unto the voice of these men whom I have appointed, they shall not be blest, because they pollute mine holy grounds, and mine holy ordinances, and charters, and my holy words which I give unto them." (Doctrines & Covenants 124:45-46.)[32] (emphasis added.)

In his official capacity as the Mormon Prophet, Spencer W. Kimball, in the April 1978 General Conference, stated that for a Mormon, eternal life depends on following the "prophets and seers, as well as the other brethren":

"Now as we conclude this general conference, let us all give heed to what was said to us. Let us assume the counsel given applies to *us*, to me. **Let us hearken to those we sustain as prophets and seers, as well as the other brethren, as if our eternal life depended upon it, because it does!**"[33] (emphasis added.)

For a Mormon to have their "Prophet" tell them in "General Conference," which they believe is a time of direct instruction by those "appointed by God," that their eternal life is dependent upon them hearkening to those "we sustain as prophets and seers, as well as the other brethren," is the same as God Himself speaking this instruction to them. This allegiance supersedes everything else, including one's citizenship. To illustrate this point, let me quote Mormon General Authority B. H. Roberts, ordained as one of the

Seven Presidents of Seventy in 1888, and served as Mormon Church Historian from 1901 until his death in 1933. In General Conference, April 1907, Elder Roberts made the following statement:

> "It is sometimes urged that the permanent realization of such a desire is impossible, since the Latter-day Saints hold as a principle of their faith that God now reveals Himself to man, as in ancient times; that the priesthood of the Church constitute a body of men who have, each for himself, in the sphere in which he moves, special right to such revelation; that the President of the Church is recognized as the only person through whom divine communication will come as law and doctrine to the religious body; **that such revelation may come at any time, upon any subject, spiritual or temporal, as God wills; and finally that, in the mind of every faithful Latter-day Saint, such revelation, in whatsoever it counsels, advises or commands, is paramount.** Furthermore it is sometimes pointed out that the members of the Church are looking for the actual coming of a Kingdom of God on earth, that shall gather all the kingdoms of the world into one visible, divine empire, over which the risen Messiah shall reign. **All this, it is held, renders it impossible for a 'Mormon' to give true allegiance to his country, or to any earthly government.**"[34] (emphasis added.)

If that statement doesn't cause grave concern to the American voter, I'm not sure what will! This sermon lays out very clearly those principles which set Mormonism apart from the rest of Christianity: (1) that God now reveals Himself to man, as in ancient times; (2) that the priesthood of the Church constitute a body of men who have, each for himself, in the sphere in which he moves, special right to such revelation; (3) that the President of the Church is recog-

nized as the only person through whom divine communication will come as law and doctrine to the religious body;
(4) that such revelation may come at any time, upon any
subject, spiritual or temporal, as God wills; (5) that, in the
mind of every faithful Latter-day Saint, such revelation, in
whatsoever it counsels, advises or commands, is paramount;
(6) Christianity believes Jesus will return and set up His
kingdom on earth during a time called the "Millennium;"
however, in Mormonism the statement, "members of the
Church are looking for the actual coming of a Kingdom of
God on earth, that shall gather all the kingdoms of the world
into one visible, divine empire, over which the risen Messiah
shall reign," is believed by Mormons to be a kingdom that
will be administered by Jesus through the Mormon Church;
(7) The all encompassing statement of the above quote comes
in the last line: **"All this, it is held, renders it impossible
for a 'Mormon' to give true allegiance to his country, or
to any earthly government."** Yes, this sermon was delivered in 1907; but the principles upon which it was predicated
still exist today.

The Mormon Prophet of yesteryear, or the current
Mormon Prophet, are believed to have been and/or are now
God's direct oracles on earth, and through the Mormon
Priesthood, hold all keys and "have the **right**, the **power**,
and **authority to declare the mind and will of God** to his
people..."[35] Elder Earl C. Tingey, one of the Seven Presidents
of the Seventy, made this very comparison in the General
Conference of the Mormon Church in April 2007:

"How I love Brigham Young. His modern-day successor
is President Gordon B. Hinckley, also a beloved and
revered prophet....I bear humble witness that both
President Brigham Young and President Gordon B.
Hinckley are prophets who have led the Church by inspiration and revelation."[36]

Nothing has changed. The absolute fundamental belief of Mormonism is that the gospel of Jesus Christ was lost to the earth upon the death of the last apostle of Jesus Christ and therefore needed to be restored. This "restoration" was done through Joseph Smith and his successors. Joseph Smith received the "Priesthood", the power to act in God's name on earth, and that power and authority has passed lineally through his successors to this day and time. The "Church" is everything and absolute allegiance to the "prophets, seers, and revelators," that lead it and the "Mormon Priesthood," which is the power to administer it, is a requirement for exaltation in the next life.

Don't mistake what I am saying here. I am not advocating that a "Christian" cannot, nor should not, be trusted in any governmental capacity; quite the contrary. I believe that Christians make wonderful governmental servants as they bring to the table a strong moral background based on the fabric of the Ten Commandments and the teachings of the Bible as a whole. HOWEVER, Christians do not swear secret oaths of allegiance to a living male hierarchy on earth whom they are taught are always right – no matter what. Heber C. Kimball, 1ˢᵗ Counselor to Brigham Young was very blunt on this concept:

"WAKE UP, YE ELDERS OF ISRAEL, AND LIVE TO GOD and none else; and learn to do as you are told.... But if you are told by your leader to do a thing, do it. **NONE OF YOUR BUSINESS WHETHER IT IS RIGHT OR WRONG.**"[37] (emphasis added.)

I will offer one last quote on "Following the Prophet" from the Halls of Congress. I believe it encapsulates the principle defined in this Chapter. It was submitted as evidence in the "Proceedings Before The Committee On Privileges And Elections Of The United States Senate In The Matter Of The

Protests Against The Right Of Hon. Reed Smoot, A Senator From The State Of Utah, To Hold His Seat."

"Apostle George Q. Cannon said, in defining the course of the church authorities:

When I respect and honor Wilford Woodruff I bow to God; He has chosen him. * * * **If I listen to Wilford Woodruff, if I look to him to see how the spirit of God moves upon him; if I ask his counsel and take it, it is because God has commanded me. God has given him the keys of authority.** Let anybody try it and see what affect their action would have. When Joseph F. Smith obeys Wilford Woodruff he does it upon the same principle. **We reverence him as the prophet of God, and as our leader. We listen to him and are guided by his slightest wish.** It is because we know that he is the servant of God, chosen by the Almighty to fill that place, and that **he holds the keys of the priesthood to this generation on the earth at the present time.** I can say truthfully that **we strive to consult his slightest wish,** and honor him in his position, because we know that God has chosen him. And **who are we that we should withstand God? Who are we that we should question that which God reveals?** Does this sacrifice our independence? Not in the least. And these twelve apostles are in precisely the same position. When they accept the counsel of the first presidency they do it because they believe the first presidency to be chosen of God. They may have different views on many things; but **when the first presidency gives counsel every man that has the spirit of God accepts that counsel.** (Reported by the Deseret News, October 4, 1896.)"[38] (emphasis added.)

The views expressed by this Mormon Apostle over 100 years ago, are the views Mormonism still holds today.

MORMON PROPHETS AND APOSTLES WILL JUDGE WITH CHRIST ON JUDGMENT DAY!

This doctrinal belief of Mormonism cannot be underestimated in its controlling power. Mormonism believes that on resurrection morning Jesus will be standing as Judge; but also, each of the Prophets of Mormonism will be lined up by his side. Literally, Mormonism believes that standing next to Jesus on his right hand side at the Judgment will be Joseph Smith; next to him Brigham Young; next to him John Taylor; next to him Wilford Woodruff – etc., etc., down through the last Mormon Prophet before the Judgment begins. Along with these Mormon Prophets will be those who were their Apostles as well:

Those Who Will Judge

The Apostle John taught that "the father judgeth no man, but hath committed all judgment unto the Son" (John 5:22). The Son, in turn, will call upon others to assist in the Judgment. The Twelve who were with him in his ministry will judge the twelve tribes of Israel (see Matthew 19:28; Luke 22:30). The Nephite Twelve will judge the Nephite and Lamanite people (1 Nephi 12:9-10; Mormon 3:18-19). **President John Taylor said the First Presidency and the Twelve Apostles in our own dispensation will also judge us** (see The Mediation and Atonement, p. 157).[39] (emphasis added.)

This doctrinal principle places every Mormon in the position to be facing any of "The Brethren" who served as General Authorities in the Mormon Church while that Mormon was alive, on Judgment Day. If a Mormon was to have defied that Priesthood holder on this earth, that man will literally have direct input to Jesus Christ on the fate of that Mormon on Judgment Morning.

DO NOT "THINK FOR YOURSELF!"

Follow the Prophet, Follow the Prophet, Follow the Prophet! The quotes provided throughout this chapter very keenly point to the doctrinal concept within Mormonism that they have God's Divine Oracles on earth today to lead His "one and only true Church." These oracles cannot lead the Church astray, so it is the absolute duty to follow their direction, no matter what. With the mantra to follow Priesthood leadership being emphasized continuously, this next quote should not be a surprise to anyone:

> "Any Latter-day Saint who denounces or opposes, whether actively or otherwise, any plan or doctrine advocated by the "prophets, seers, and revelators" of the Church is cultivating the spirit of apostasy. One cannot speak evil of the Lord's anointed and retain the Holy Spirit in his heart.
>
> It should be remembered that Lucifer has a very cunning way of convincing unsuspecting souls that the General Authorities of the Church are as likely to be wrong as they are to be right. This sort of game is **Satan's** favorite pastime, and he has practiced it on believing souls since Adam. **He wins a great victory when he can get members of the Church to speak against their leaders and to "do their own thinking."** He specializes in suggesting that our leaders are in error while he plays the blinding rays of apostasy in the eyes of those whom he thus beguiles. What cunning! And to think that

some of our members are deceived by this trickery."[40] (emphasis added.)

If, a Mormon, beguiles themselves into believing that they can think on their own behalf, they are being deceived by the trickery of Satan! FOLLOW THE PROPHET AND HIS COUNSELORS, OR SUFFER!

In a speech given just four years before his death, Brigham Young challenges any Mormon to come forward and try and prove that he has ever given any "counsel" that is wrong:

> "Now I am going to tell you some more things, and how long will you remember them? Until you get home? Perhaps there are a few who will remember a few words of counsel that I shall give to you. **I am here to give this people, called Latter-day Saints, counsel to direct them in the paths of life.** I am here to answer; I shall be on hand to answer when I am called upon, for all the counsel and for all the instruction that I have given this people. **If there is an Elder here, or any member of this Church, called the Church of Jesus Christ of Latter-day Saints, who can bring up the first idea, the first sentence that I have delivered to the people as counsel that is wrong, I really wish they would do it; but they cannot do it, for the simple reason that I have never given counsel that is wrong; this is the reason.**"[41] (emphasis added.)

WHAT'S THE POINT?

The evidence is overwhelming that a Mormon must follow their "Prophet", "The Brethren," and the Mormon "Priesthood." THIS IS MORMON DOCTRINE! "The Brethren," those who are sustained as "prophets, seers, and revelators," by divine decree, "can never lead the Church astray." "The Brethren," "have the **right**, the **power**, and **authority to declare the mind and will of God** to his people..."[42] If a Mormon is given "counsel" by their leadership, they are to assume it is of divine origin, simply because that leader is in office. If the leaders were not "magnifying their calling" they would have been removed. Lastly, and of great concern, to the American voter, Mormons are placed in a "Doctrinal Vice" by believing "The Brethren" will have a direct input to Jesus Christ on "Resurrection Morning." If one of "The Brethren" was to give them counsel, directly or through their local leadership (Bishop, Stake President), and they chose not to obey that counsel, it could cost them their eternal standing before God on Judgment Day.

America, as a Republic, not a democracy, depends on elected representation in our Governmental halls. We elect politicians who are to represent us, "We the People." I believe the evidence presented in this Chapter should cause the American voter to question the independence of a Mormon in an elected or appointed public office to be free to represent "We the People," and not absolutely obligated to follow their Priesthood Leadership.

[1] *Church News,* week ending November 6, 2004, 7.

[2] *Doctrine and Covenants,* Section 21:1-7.

[3] Josiah F. Gibbs, *Mountain Meadows Massacre,* (Salt Lake Tribune Publishing Company, 1910) online book at: http://www.utlm.org/onlinebooks/meadowscontents.htm

[4] *Fourteen Fundamentals in Following the Prophet* by Ezra Taft Benson, http://www.lds-mormon.com/fourteen.shtml

[5] Ibid.

[6] Ibid.

[7] Daniel H. Wells, in Graham, ed., *Journal of Discourses,* 19:369.

8 *Immortality and Eternal Life, Melchizedek Priesthood Course of Study, 1968-69*, (Corporation of The President of The Church of Jesus Christ of Latter-day Saints, 1968) 164.

9 D. Michael Quinn, *The Mormon Hierarchy: Extensions of Power*, (Signature Books: Salt Lake City, 1997) 269.

10 *Search These Commandments, Melchizedek Priesthood Personal Study Guide*, (Published by The Church of Jesus Christ of Latter-day Saints, Salt Lake City, Utah, 1984) 275-276.

11 John Taylor in Watt, ed., *Journal of Discourses*, 5:266.

12 *Ensign*, July 1972, "The Strength of the Priesthood", (CR) as found on the CD "LDS Church Magazines 1971-1999" published by The Church of Jesus Christ of Latter-day Saints.

13 *Living Prophets for a Living Church*, (Published for the Use of College Students in the Church Educational System, 1974) 30.

14 *Teachings of the Living Prophets*, Student Manual Religion 333, Published by The Church of Jesus Christ of Latter-day Saints (Salt Lake City, Utah, 1982) 6.

15 *Ibid.*, 8.

16 *Ibid.*, 9.

17 *Ensign*, July 1972, "Eternal Keys and the Right to Preside", (CR) as found on the CD "LDS Church Magazines 1971-1999" published by The Church of Jesus Christ of Latter-day Saints.

18 Brigham Young, in Watt, ed., *Journal of Discourses*, 9:289.

19 *Ensign*, May 2007, 4.

20 Brigham Young, in Grimshaw, ed., *Journal of Discourses*, 13:95.

21 Joseph Fielding Smith, Compiled by Bruce R. McConkie, *Doctrines of Salvation*, (Bookcraft, Salt Lake City, Utah 1954) 1:186.

[22] *Ensign*, November 1994, "The Keys That Never Rust", (CR) as found on the CD "LDS Church Magazines 1971-1999" published by The Church of Jesus Christ of Latter-day Saints.

[23] Jerreld L. Newquist, *Prophets, Principles and National Survival* (Publishers Press, Salt Lake City, Utah, 1964) 9.

[24] Joseph Fielding Smith, *Doctrines of Salvation*, 3:297.

[25] Brigham Young, in Watt, ed., *Journal of Discourses*, 6:282.

[26] Brigham Young, in Watt, ed., *Journal of Discourses*, 6:319-320.

[27] Brigham Young, in Watt, ed., *Journal of Discourses*, 9:140-142.

[28] *Ensign*, November 1981, "Follow the Prophets", (CR) as found on the CD "LDS Church Magazines 1971-1999" published by The Church of Jesus Christ of Latter-day Saints.

[29] Wilford Woodruff, in Watt, ed., *Journal of Discourses*, 5:83

[30] Richard N. Ostling and Joan K. Ostling, *Mormon America: The Power and the Promise*, (HarperCollins Publishers Inc., San Francisco, 1999) 93.

[31] *Doctrine and Covenants* 84:35-38:
    35. And also all they who receive this priesthood receive me, saith the Lord;
    36. For he that receiveth my servants receiveth me;
    37. And he that receiveth me receiveth my Father;
    38. And he that receiveth my Father receiveth my Father's kingdom; therefore all that my Father hath shall be given unto him.

[32] *On Earth And In Heaven, A Course of Study for the Melchizedek Priesthood Quorums of The Church of Jesus Christ of Latter-day Saints*, (Published by the First Presidency of The Church of Jesus Christ of Latter-day Saints, 1966) 104-105.

[33] *Search These Commandments, Melchizedek Priesthood Personal Study Guide, 1984-85*, (Corporation of The President of The Church of Jesus Christ of Latter-day Saints, 1984) 276.

[34] Elder Brigham H. Roberts, *Conference Report*, April 1907, Afternoon Session., 46.

[35] *Teachings of the Living Prophets*, Student Manual Religion 333, 9.

[36] *Ensign*, May 2007, "Prophets—Pioneer and Modern Day," 30-31.

[37] Heber C. Kimball, in Hawkins, ed., *Journal of Discourses*, 6:32.

[38] 59th Congress, *1st Session*. SENATE. DOCUMENT No. 486, Proceedings Before The Committee On Privileges And Elections Of The United States Senate In The Matter Of The Protests Against The Right Of Hon. Reed Smoot, A Senator From The State Of Utah, To Hold His Seat., (VOLUME I, WASHINGTON: GOVERNMENT PRINTING OFFICE. 1906.) 4.

[39] *Gospel Principles*, (Published by The Church of Jesus Christ of Latter-day Saints, Salt Lake City, Utah, 1997) 296.

[40] *The Improvement Era*, "The Voice of the Church" Official Organ of the Priesthood Quorums, Mutual Improvement Associations, Department of Education, Music Committee, Ward Teachers, and Other Agencies of the Church of Jesus Christ of Latter-day Saints, June 1945, Vol. 8, NO. 6, pg 354.

[41] Brigham Young, in Cannon, ed., *Journal of Discourses*, 16:161.

[42] *Teachings of the Living Prophets*, Student Manual Religion 333, 9.

Chapter Six

COVENANTS AND ENDOWMENTS

An in-depth comprehension of Mormonism is impossible without an understanding of the covenants and endowments all Mormons are placed under. As discussed in Chapter Three, every Mormon male is placed under an oath and covenant when they accept ordination in any Priesthood Office. All Mormons are placed under covenant when they are baptized into the Mormon Church. Those who have gone through the Mormon "Temple Ceremony" have taken on supreme oaths and covenants that cannot even be talked about outside of the temple itself, or to anyone who has not gone through the secret ceremony.

Not to insult anyone's intelligence here, but let's review from Webster's Dictionary what the definition of "oath" and "covenant" are:

> oath – (1) a solemn affirmation or declaration, made with an appeal to God or some revered person or object for the truth of what is affirmed; (2) in law, that kind of solemn declaration which is necessary as a condition to the filling of some office more or less public, or giving evidence in a court of justice, being divided into

two classes: (a) assertory oaths, or those by which something is asserted as true; (b) promissory oaths, or those by which something is promised: as, the *oath* of office; the *oath* of witnesses, etc.

covenant – (1) a binding and solemn agreement by two or more persons, parties, etc. to do or keep from doing some specified thing; a compact. (2) in theology, the promises of God to man, usually carrying with them conditions to be fulfilled by man, as recorded in the Bible. (3) a solemn agreement between the members of a church, that they will hold to points of doctrine, faith, etc.[1]

BAPTISM

Let's look at the first covenant in Mormonism—Baptism:

We Make Covenants When We Are Baptized.

Many scriptures teach about baptism. In one of these scriptures, the prophet Alma taught that faith and repentance are steps that prepare us for baptism. He taught that **when we are baptized we make a covenant with the Lord. We promise to do certain things, and God promises to bless us in return**.

Alma explained that we must want to be called the people of God. We must be willing to help and comfort each other. **We must stand as witnesses of God at all times and in all things and in all places. As we do these things and are baptized, God will forgive our sins**. Alma told the people who believed his teachings about the gospel:

"Behold, here are the waters of Mormon....And now, as ye are desirous to come into the fold of God, and to be called his people,...what have you against being baptized in the name of the Lord, as a witness before him **that ye have entered into a covenant with him, that ye will serve him and keep his commandments,** that he may pour out his Spirit more abundantly upon you?" (Mosiah 18:8-10). The people clapped their hands for joy and said it was their desire to be baptized. Alma baptized them in the Waters of Mormon. (See Mosiah 18:7-17.) (emphasis added).

Alma taught that when we are baptized we make covenants with the Lord to—

1. Come into the fold of God.
2. Bear one another's burdens.
3. Stand as witnesses of God at all times and in all places.
4. Serve God and keep his commandments.

When we are baptized and keep the covenants of baptism, the Lord promises to—

1. Forgive our sins.
2. Pour out his Spirit more abundantly upon us.
3. Give us daily guidance and the help of the Holy Ghost.
4. Let us come forth in the First Resurrection.
5. Give us eternal life.[2]

There are some very key differences to understand between the Mormon Covenant of Baptism and Christian Baptism. As a Christian I have been baptized into Christ, buried with Christ and raised to live in Christ. In Mormonism people are baptized into the Mormon Church:

We Must Be Baptized to Become Members of the Church of Jesus Christ

"All those who humble themselves before God, and desire to be baptized...that...have truly repented of all their sins...shall be received by baptism into his church" (D&C 20:37).[3] (*italics* and emphasis in the original.)

Mormonism believes it is "*the only true and living church upon the face of the whole earth.*"[4] That point is significant in understanding the problem with Mormons serving in Government positions. As a Christian, my faith is in Jesus Christ and I learn about Him and his teachings through His Word, the Bible. In Mormonism, a person's allegiance is to the Mormon Church and its Priesthood, through its male hierarchy. As we have already seen in previous chapters, everything in Mormonism revolves around the Church and in following its leaders. Chapter 47 of "*Gospel Principles,*" is on "*Exaltation.*" Under the subtitle of, "**Requirements for Exaltation,**" we read number 17: "Listen to and obey the inspired words of the prophets of the Lord."[5] You cannot reach "Exaltation" in Mormonism unless you obey the living Prophet.

When we understand and apply the "Covenant of Baptism" as laid out in reference [2], from "*Gospel Principles,*" we can see the affect that these covenants have on Mormons. Remember what we learned in Chapter Five about following the Prophet—that he speaks directly for God in all things and to disobey him places one's eternity at stake. Along with the knowledge that "Exaltation" only comes through obeying the prophet, we conclude that Mormons have eternal consequences placed upon them with respect to their baptism covenants. As stated in the "*Gospel Principles*" quote, the Mormon **"must stand as witnesses of God at all times and in all things and in all places. As we do these things and are baptized, God will forgive our sins."** No matter the "time," the "thing," or the "place," if directed by Mormon Priesthood Leadership, a Mormon must obey the Priesthood

Leadership or else God will not forgive them of their sins. Only when Mormons keep the covenant of baptism (keep God's commandments), is God bound to forgive sins, pour out his Spirit, give daily guidance, let the Mormon come forth in the First Resurrection and give them eternal life.

TAKING THE SACRAMENT (COMMUNION)

When a Mormon partakes of their Sacrament (What Christians would call Communion, or the Lord's Supper), they renew the Covenant of Baptism:

> By partaking of the sacrament, worthy saints renew the covenant previously made by them in the waters of baptism (Mosiah 18:7-10); unbaptized children, being without sin, are entitled and expected to partake of the sacrament to prefigure the covenant they will take upon themselves when they arrive at the years of account-ability. Worthy partakers of the sacrament put them-selves in perfect harmony with the Lord. (3 Ne. 18.) As indicated by our Lord's statement they gain "the remis-sion of their sins." (*Inspired Version,* Matt. 26:24.)
>
> Those who partake of the sacrament worthily thereby put themselves under covenant with the Lord: 1. To always remember the broken body and spilled blood of Him who was crucified for the sins of the world; 2. To take upon themselves the name of Christ and always remember him; and 3. To keep the Commandments of God, that is, to "live by every word that proceedeth forth from the mouth of God." (D. & C. 84:44.)[6]

Taking the Sacrament is done twice on Sundays, at Sunday School and Sacrament Meetings. Each Sunday the Mormon is to renew the 'Covenant of Baptism.' Note number (3.) in the quote above: To keep the Commandments of God, that is, to "live by every word that proceedeth forth from the mouth of God. (D. & C. 84:44.)" Reflecting back on Chapter Five (Follow the Prophets, Seers, and Revelators – Oracles – The Lord's Anointed), Mormonism believes that its leaders, the Prophet, his two Counselors, and the Twelve: "have the **right**, the **power**, and **authority to declare the mind and will of God** to his people..."[7] (emphasis added). Every week, Mormons renew their covenant to follow the oracles of God.

PRIESTHOOD

Now let's look at the Priesthood oath. Specifically, the oath and covenant that Mormon males are placed under is a "promissory" oath in a "theology" covenant. Let's look at that oath and covenant that is listed as a "revelation of Jesus Christ unto his servant Joseph Smith,"[8] dated September 22 and 23, 1832, in Doctrine and Covenants Section 84:

35. And also all they who receive this priesthood receive me, saith the Lord;
36. For he that receiveth my servants receiveth me;
37. And he that receiveth me receiveth my Father;
38. And he that receiveth my Father receiveth my Father's kingdom; therefore all that my Father hath shall be given unto him.
39. And this is according to the oath and covenant which belongeth to the priesthood.
40. Therefore, all those who receive the priesthood, receive this oath and covenant of my Father, which he cannot break, neither can it be moved.
41. But whoso breaketh this covenant after he hath received it, and altogether turneth therefrom, shall not have forgiveness of sins in this world nor in the world to come.[9]

What is the covenant that Mormon males twelve years old and above are placed under when they are ordained into the "Priesthood"? The above verses clearly show that "they who receive this priesthood receive me," and "he that receiveth my servants receiveth me." The oath and covenant is to "receiveth my servants." The servants in Mormonism are specifically "prophets, seers, and revelators," as well as generally, all priesthood leadership. To validate this point, let me quote from Lesson 11 from "A Royal Priesthood, A Personal Study Guide for the Melchezidek Priesthood Quorums of The Church of Jesus Christ of Latter-day Saints, 1975-76":

Lesson 11 Sustaining God's Servants 2 Corinthians 5:20

What Does It Mean to Sustain the Lord's Servant's?

Men in the Priesthood Are Under Sacred Covenant to Receive the Servants of the Lord.

- ☐ Acts 3:22, 23.[10] Compare Joseph Smith 2:40.[11] What are some of the hazards in rejecting the counsel of Church leaders?
- ☐ D&C 1:14, 38.[12] How does the Lord feel about the inspired pronouncements of the leaders whom he has chosen?
- ☐ D&C 84:36, 37;[13] Luke 10:16.[14] How can we honor the Lord?
- ☐ It was as though the Lord by his own voice said… "I, the Lord, now call my servant President Spencer W. Kimball to lead my people and to continue the work of preparing them for that great day when I shall come to reign personally upon the earth. And I now say of him as I said of my servant Joseph Smith:

179

"...thou shalt give heed unto all his words and commandments which he shall give unto you as he receiveth them, walking in all holiness before me:

"For his word ye shall receive, as from mine own mouth, in all patience and faith.

"For thus saith the Lord God: Him have I inspired to move the cause of Zion in mighty power for good, and his diligence I know, and his prayers I have heard." (D&C 21:4, 5, 7.)

It seems easy to believe in the prophets who have passed on and to suppose that we believe and follow the counsel they gave under different circumstances and to other people. But the great test that confronts us, as in every age when the Lord has a people on earth, is whether we will give heed to the words of his living oracles and follow the counsel and direction they give for our day and time." (Bruce R. McConkie, *Ensign*, 4:41-72 [May 1974].)[15]

This study guide goes on to discuss what happens if a Mormon fails to follow their leadership:

Whenever there is a disposition manifested in any of the members of this Church to question the right of the President of the whole Church to direct in all things, you see manifested evidences of apostasy—of a spirit which, if encouraged, will lead to a separation from the Church and to final destruction; wherever there is a disposition to operate against any legally appointed officer of this Kingdom, no matter in what capacity he is called to act, if persisted in, it will be followed by the same results; they will "walk after the flesh in the lust of uncleanness, and despise government. Presumptuous are they, self-willed; they are not afraid to speak evil of dignities." (*Discourses of Brigham Young*, p. 83.)[16]

Continuing on page 39 of this study guide it discusses the **"Consequences of Disobedience."**

The moment a man says he will not submit to the legally constituted authority of the Church, whether it be the teachers, the bishopric, the high council, his quorum, or the First Presidency, and in his heart confirms it and carries it out, that moment he cuts himself off from the privileges and blessings of the Priesthood and Church, and severs himself from the people of God, for he ignores the authority that the Lord has instituted in his Church.... The Lord has established his church, organized his priesthood, and conferred authority upon certain individuals, councils and quorums, and it is the duty of the people of God to live so that they shall know that these are acceptable unto him. If we begin to cut off this one and that one, and set their authority aside, we may just as well at once set God aside, and say that he has no right to dictate." (Smith, *Gospel Doctrine*, p. 45)[17]

This last quote "Smith, Gospel Doctrine, p. 45," is from Joseph Fielding Smith the 6th Prophet of the Mormon Church. The Mormon Church using this quote in its Personal Priesthood Study Guide with respect to the Priesthood Oath and Covenant, is clearly making the association that the "oath and covenant" applies "to the legally constituted authority of the Church, whether it be the teachers, the bishopric, the high council, his quorum, or the First Presidency." This "oath and covenant" of the Mormon Priesthood clearly applies to the local level leadership as well as the corporate leadership in Salt Lake City.

Thomas S. Monson, 1st Counselor in the First Presidency, spoke in the Priesthood Session of the General Conference of the Church of Jesus Christ of Latter-day Saints, on March 31,

2007, quoting former 1ˢᵗ Counselor in the First Presidency, J. Reuben Clark Jr., saying:

> "Wherever we go, our priesthood goes with us. Are we standing in "holy places"? Said President J. Reuben Clark Jr., who served for many years as a counselor in the First Presidency: "The Priesthood is not like a suit of clothes that you can lay off and take back on....Depending upon ourselves [it is] an everlasting endowment."[18]

Here again is another term "endowment" that must be understood within the context of Mormonism in order to grasp the meaning of what is being conveyed here by the number two man in the Mormon Church, Thomas S. Monson.

TEMPLE ENDOWMENT

The *Encyclopedia of Mormonism* provides us with a Mormon definition of the "endowment":

Endowment

An Endowment generally is a gift, but in a specialized sense it is a course of instruction, ordinances, and covenants given only in dedicated temples of The Church of Jesus Christ of Latter-day Saints. The words "to endow" (from the Greek enduein), as used in the New Testament, mean to dress, clothe, put on garments, put on attributes, or receive virtue. Christ instructed his apostles to tarry at Jerusalem "until ye be endued with power from on high" (Luke 24:49), a promise fulfilled, at least in part, on the day of Pentecost (Acts 2). In modern times, a similar revelation was given: "I gave unto you a commandment that you should build a house, in the which house I design to endow those whom I have chosen with power on high; for this is the promise of the Father unto you; therefore I command you to tarry, even as mine apostles at Jerusalem" (D&C 95:8-9).

Though there had been preliminary and preparatory spiritual outpourings upon Latter-day Saints in Ohio and Missouri, the Endowment in its full sense was not received until the Nauvoo Temple era. As he introduced temple ordinances in 1842 at Nauvoo, the Prophet Joseph Smith taught that these were "of things spiritual, and to be received only by the spiritual minded" (TPJS, p. 237). The Endowment was necessary, he said, to organize the Church fully, that the Saints might be organized according to the laws of God, and, as the dedicatory prayer of the Kirtland Temple petitioned, that they would "be prepared to obtain every needful thing" (D&C 109:15). The Endowment was designed to give "a comprehensive view of our condition and true relation to God" (TPJS, p. 324), "to prepare the disciples for their missions in the world" (p. 274), to prevent being "overcome by evils" (p. 259), to enable them to "secure the fulness of those blessings which have been prepared for the Church of the Firstborn" (p. 237).

The Endowment of "power from on high" in modern temples has four main aspects. First is the preparatory ordinance, a ceremonial washing and anointing, after which the temple patron dons the sacred clothing of the temple.

Second is a course of instruction by lectures and representations. These include a recital of the most prominent events of the Creation, a figurative depiction of the advent of Adam and Eve and of every man and every woman, the entry of Adam and Eve into the Garden of Eden, the consequent expulsion from the garden, their condition in the world, and their receiving of the Plan of Salvation leading to the return to the presence of

God (Talmage, pp. 83-84). The Endowment instructions utilize every human faculty so that the meaning of the gospel may be clarified through art, drama, and symbols. All participants wear white temple robes symbolizing purity and the equality of all persons before God the Father and his Son Jesus Christ. The temple becomes a house of revelation whereby one is instructed more perfectly "in theory, in principle, and in doctrine" (D&C 97:14). "This completeness of survey and expounding of the gospel plan makes temple worship one of the most effective methods of refreshing the memory concerning the entire structure of the gospel" (Widtsoe, 1986, p. 5).

Third is making covenants. The temple Endowment is seen as the unfolding or **culmination of the covenants made at baptism. Temple covenants give "tests by which one's willingness and fitness for righteousness may be known"** (Widtsoe, p. 335). They include the **"covenant and promise** to observe the law of strict virtue and chastity, to be charitable, benevolent, tolerant and pure; **to devote both talent and material means to the spread of truth and the uplifting of the [human] race; to maintain devotion to the cause of truth; and to seek in every way to contribute to the great preparation that the earth may be made ready to receive... Jesus Christ" (Talmage, p. 84). One also promises to keep these covenants sacred and to "trifle not with sacred things"** (D&C 6:12).

Fourth is a sense of divine presence. In the dedicatory prayer of the temple at Kirtland, Ohio, the Prophet Joseph Smith pleaded "that all people who shall enter upon the threshold of the Lord's house may feel thy power, and feel constrained to acknowledge that thou hast sanctified it, and that it is thy house, a place of thy holiness" (D&C 109:13). Of temples built by sacrifice to the name of the Lord Jesus Christ, dedicated by his authority, and reverenced in his Spirit, the promise is given, "My name shall be here; and I will manifest myself to my people in mercy in this holy house" (D&C 110:8). In the temples there is an "aura of deity" manifest to the worthy (Kimball, pp. 534-35). Through the temple Endowment, one may seek "a fulness of the Holy Ghost" (D&C 109:15). Temple ordinances are seen as a means for receiving inspiration and instruction through the Holy Spirit, and for preparing to return to the presence of God.[19] (emphasis added.)

This "endowment" ceremony conducted only in Mormon temples, under the strictest code of secrecy is believed by Mormons to elevate them to "Exaltation" in the next life. "Exaltation" in Mormonism is achieving the status of "Godhood". Under the heading "EXALTATION" in the book *Mormon Doctrine*, written by Mormon Apostle Bruce R. McConkie, we read:

> *See* CALLING AND ELECTION SURE, CELESTIAL KINGDOM, CELESTIAL MARRIAGE, CHURCH OF THE FIRSTBORN, DAUGHTERS OF GOD, ENDOWMENTS, ETERNAL LIVES, ETERNAL PROGRESSION, FULNESS OF THE FATHER, GODHOOD, IMMORTALITY, JOINT-HEIRS WITH CHRIST, KINGS, PERFECTION, PLURALITY OF GODS, PLURAL MARRIAGE, PRIESTESSES, PRIESTHOOD, PRIESTS, QUEENS, REDEMPTION, SALVATION, SEALING POWER, SECOND COMFORTER, SERVANTS OF GOD, SONS OF GOD. Celestial marriage is the gate to *exaltation*, and exaltation consists in the continuation of the family unit in eternity. Exaltation is eternal life, the kind of life which God lives. Those who obtain it gain an inheritance in the highest of three heavens within the celestial kingdom. (D. & C. 131:1-4.)

They have eternal increase, a continuation of the seeds forever and ever, a continuation of the lives, eternal lives; that is, they have spirit children in the resurrection, in relation to which offspring **they stand in the same position that God our Father stands to us.** They inherit in due course the fullness of the glory of the Father, meaning that they have all power in heaven and on earth. (D. & C. 76:50-60; 93:1-40.) *"**Then shall they be gods**, because they have no end; therefore shall they be from everlasting to everlasting, because they continue; then shall they be above all, because all things are subject unto them. Then shall they be gods, because they have all power, and the angels are subject unto them."* (D. & C. 132:16-26; *Doctrines of Salvation*, vol. 2, pp. 35-79.)[20] (emphasis added.)

In the *Encyclopedia of Mormonism* under "Exaltation" we read:

Exaltation

To Latter-day Saints, exaltation is a state that a person can attain in becoming like God-salvation in the ultimate sense (D&C 132:17). Latter-day Saints believe that all mankind (except the sons of perdition) will receive varying degrees of glory in the afterlife. Exaltation is the greatest of all the gifts and attainments possible. It is available only in the highest degree of the Celestial Kingdom and is reserved for members of the Church of the Firstborn. This exalted status, called eternal life, is available to be received by a man and wife. It means not only living in God's presence, but **receiving power to do as God does,** including the power to bear children after the resurrection (TPJS, pp. 300-301; D&C 132:19). Blessings and privileges of exaltation require unwavering faith, repentance, and **complete obedience to the gospel of Jesus Christ.** [Mormonism].

In a revelation to the Prophet Joseph Smith, the Savior stated the following conditions: "Strait is the gate, and narrow the way that leadeth unto the exaltation and continuation of the lives, and few there be that find it, because ye receive me not in the world neither do ye know me" (D&C 132:22).

All Church ordinances lead to exaltation, and the essential crowning ordinances are the Endowment and the eternal marriage covenant of the temple (D&C 131:1-4, 132).[21] (bracketed information and emphasis added.)

As clearly seen, the "Endowment" is a secret, sacred ritual that is only administered in Mormon temples and carries with it the supreme achievement of man: Godhood. Thomas S. Monson, 1st Counselor to the current Prophet of the Mormon Church, as quoted above in the Priesthood Session of the General Conference of The Church of Jesus Christ of Latter-day Saints, on March 31, 2007, quotes former 1st Counselor in the First Presidency, J. Reuben Clark Jr., as saying:

"Wherever we go, our priesthood goes with us. Are we standing in "holy places"? Said President J. Reuben Clark Jr., who served for many years as a counselor in the First Presidency: "The Priesthood is not like a suit of clothes that you can lay off and take back on....Depending upon ourselves [it is] an everlasting endowment."[22]

This statement delivered in the "Priesthood Session of the General Conference of The Church of Jesus Christ of Latter-day Saints," makes the tie between "Priesthood" and the "Endowment" which is part and parcel of attaining "Godhood." The quote from President J. Reuben Clark, establishes the Mormon belief that holding the "Priesthood" is not an "on-again, off-again," proposition, it is "an ever-lasting endowment."

> "The priesthood, of course, must not be taken lightly, and as I have said to you before, the priesthood cannot be taken off and put back on at will as you would a coat. Once endowed by the priesthood it remains with you. You may forfeit its power, the power may go, but your priesthood is still there, and in the days to come God will judge us by the use we made of it, and we can no more escape that consequence than we can escape death. That fact should be with us always and never absent from us."[23]

This everlasting endowment, the Priesthood, is established in an oath and covenant to "receiveth my servants." This oath and covenant is just the beginning of the pledge of obedience to Priesthood leadership. This initial oath upon being ordained into the lower level, Aaronic, Priesthood is reinforced with each subsequent ordination to a higher office and culminates in ordination into the highest level of Mormon Priesthood, the "Melchizedek" Priesthood.

These oaths and covenants are then solemnized in secrecy in the Mormon temple ceremony known as the "endowment." <u>Four different times</u> during the "endowment" ceremony, <u>the Mormon participant is called to bind themselves in secret oaths</u>.

> "The apostle is under no greater commandment to be true to his covenant and membership in the Church than is the ordinary elder, or seventy, or any other individual holding the priesthood...Especially is this so, if the elder has received the ordinances of the house of the Lord."[24]

The "house of the Lord" in Mormonism is a common reference to one of their temples. The ultimate goal in Mormonism is to go to one of their temples and be married for "time and all eternity" (Celestial Marriage), and to receive one's "endowment." This goal is at the absolute center of the Mormon faith. This ceremony is believed to position a Mormon such that they can achieve Godhood in the next life. This ceremony also binds the participant by four different oaths. The following excerpts are quotes taken from the temple ceremony as conducted in 1984. For providing these quotes from the Mormon Temple Ceremony here in print, I am sure to draw extreme criticism from Mormons. Their common argument will be that I had no right to divulge their "sacred" ordinances. **I do not believe the Mormon right of "sacredness" overrules the American voters right to know what oaths and covenants their elected or appointed government officials have obligated themselves to in these various ceremonies!** The American voter needs to understand the absolute controlled position that individuals obligate themselves to when they submit to the "endowment ceremony" in a Mormon temple, with its secret oaths, or the oaths associated with receiving the Mormon Priesthood. These quotes on the Mormon Temple Ceremony cannot be found in Mormon literature as the participants are bound by solemn, secret oath to never divulge the secrets of the temple ceremony. The following quotes are taken from a volume titled: *"Evolution of the Mormon temple ceremony: 1842-1990"* from Utah Lighthouse Ministries in Salt Lake City. My commentary on various parts of the ceremony will be in brackets []. Excerpts from the ceremony:

SECOND LECTURER: If you proceed and receive your full endowment, you will be required to take upon yourselves sacred obligations, the violation of which will bring upon you the judgment of God;

for God will not be mocked. If any of you desire to withdraw rather than accept these obligations of your own free will and choice, you may now make it known by raising your hand. (Pause)

[Before an initiate can begin the ceremony they are warned that if they proceed with this ceremony, they are taking on "sacred obligations, the violation of which will bring upon you the judgment of God." An opportunity is given for a person to remove themselves from the ceremony if they are not willing to assume these "sacred obligations." I've never heard of anyone withdrawing – the embarrassment would be extreme.]

[Immediately after the Sixth Day of the Creation Scene, Elohim (the name given the Father God in Mormonism), is addressing Adam after Eve has eaten of the forbidden fruit. Participants in the ceremony are called patrons.]

THE LAW OF OBEDIENCE

ELOHIM: (condescendingly) Inasmuch as Eve was the first to eat of the forbidden fruit, if she will covenant that from this time forth she will obey your law in the Lord, and will hearken unto your counsel as you hearken unto mine, and if you will covenant that from this time forth you will obey the Law of Elohim, we will give unto you the Law of Obedience and Sacrifice, and we will provide a Savior for you, whereby you may come back into our presence, and with us partake of Eternal Life and exaltation.

EVE: (*humbly*) Adam, I now covenant to obey your law as you obey our Father.

ADAM: (humbly) Elohim, I now covenant with thee that from this time forth I will obey your law and keep your commandments.

ELOHIM: It is well, Adam. Jehovah, inasmuch as Adam and Eve have discovered their nakedness, make coats of skins as a covering for them.

JEHOVAH: It shall be done, Elohim.

The movie stops here, the lights come up, and the tape recording begins.

NARRATOR: Brethren and sisters, the garment which was placed upon you in the washing room is to cover your nakedness and represents the coat of skins spoken of. Anciently it was made of skins. You have received the garment, also your New Name. The officiator will represent Elohim at the Altar. A couple will now come to the altar.

A pre-selected "Witness Couple" seated front row, center-aisle comes forward and kneels at the altar facing forward. The Officiator stands behind the altar and gestures in pantomime with the tape.

NARRATOR: Brethren and sisters, this couple at the altar represent all of you as if at the altar. You must consider yourselves as if you were respectively Adam and Eve.

ELOHIM: We will put the sisters under covenant to obey the laws of their husbands. Sisters, arise. **(Women all stand up)** Each of you bring your right arm to the square. **(Women all raise right arms to the square)** [see Glossary for a definition of "right arms to the square"] You and each of you solemnly covenant and promise before God, angels, and these witnesses at this altar that you will each observe and keep the law of your husband, and abide by his counsel in righteousness. Each of you bow your head and say yes.

WOMEN: Yes.

ELOHIM: That will do. **(Women sit down)** Brethren, Arise. **(Men all stand up)** Bring your right arm to the square. **(Men all bring right arms to the square)** You and each of you solemnly covenant and promise before God, angels, and these witnesses at this altar that you will obey the law of God, and keep His commandments. Each of you bow your head and say yes.

MEN: Yes.

ELOHIM: That will do.

Men all sit down.

[This oath places all women under solemn oath to obey their husbands. This oath places all men under solemn oath to obey the law of God; how do Mormons receive the "law of God?" They receive it through their Priesthood leaders – the oracles of God on earth.]

THE LAW OF SACRIFICE

ELOHIM: You are now about to be put under covenant to obey and keep the Law of Sacrifice, as contained in the Old and New Testaments. This Law of Sacrifice was given to Adam in the Garden of Eden, who, when he was driven out of the Garden, built an altar on which he offered sacrifices. And after many days, an angel of the Lord appeared unto Adam, saying: "Why dost thou offer sacrifice unto the Lord?" And Adam said unto him: "I know not, save the Lord commanded me." And then the angel spake saying: "This thing is a similitude of the Sacrifice of the Only Begotten of the Father, who is full of grace and truth. Wherefore, thou shalt do all that thou doest in the name of the Son, and thou shalt repent and call upon God in the name of the Son forevermore." The posterity of Adam down to Moses, and from Moses to Jesus Christ offered up the first fruits of the field and the firstlings of the flock, which continued until the death of

Jesus Christ, which ended sacrifice by the shedding of blood.

And as Jesus Christ has laid down his life for the redemption of mankind, so **we should covenant to sacrifice all that we possess, even our own lives if necessary, in sustaining and defending the Kingdom of God** (**the Mormon Church**).

All arise. (**Patrons all stand up**) Each of you bring your right arm to the square. (**Patrons all raise right arms to the square**) You and each of you solemnly covenant and promise before God, angels, and these witnesses at this altar that you will observe and keep the Law of Sacrifice as contained in the Old and New Testaments, as it has been explained to you. Each of you bow your head and say yes.

ALL PATRONS: (each bowing head) Yes.

ELOHIM: That will do.

Patrons all sit down.

[**This oath of the "Law of Sacrifice" obligates Mormons that "we should covenant to sacrifice all that we possess, even our own lives if necessary, in sustaining and defending the Kingdom of God." Remember the "Kingdom of God" for them is Mormonism. They covenant to sacrifice all that they possess, even their own lives to sustain and defend Mormonism.**]

[As the patrons proceed through the seven phases of the Endowment Ceremony they are instructed in tokens, signs, and penalties of the Aaronic and Melchizedek Priesthood. These are a plagiarism from Masonic rituals. Patrons learn the four tokens and signs and three penalties:

-   The First Token/Sign and Penalty of the Aaronic Priesthood

- The Second Token/Sign and Penalty of the Aaronic Priesthood
- The First Token/Sign and Penalty of the Melchizedek Priesthood or Sign of the Nail
- The Second Token/Sign of the Melchezidek Priesthood or Sure Sign of the Nail

The tokens are various handshakes or hand gestures and each has a name. The signs are hand and arm gestures. The penalties are rather gruesome hand gestures of slitting one's throat, cutting open the chest and removing the heart, and disemboweling one's abdomen; these penalty actions are accompanied with an oath to never reveal these signs and tokens "Rather than do so I would suffer my life to be taken." This information was taken from a booklet titled "What's Going on in There?" by Chuck Sackett.]

[For the sake of brevity, I will only include here in the text one token and blood oath. A full review of the Mormon Temple Ceremony can be read on the website www.nauvoochristian.org click "Resources" on the left side menu and go to "Temple Endowments".]

THE FIRST TOKEN OF THE AARONIC PRIESTHOOD

ELOHIM: We now give unto you the First Token of the Aaronic Priesthood with its accompanying name, sign, and penalty. Before doing this, however, we desire to impress upon your minds the sacred character of the First Token of the Aaronic Priesthood, with its accompanying name, sign, and penalty, as well as that of all the other Tokens of the Holy Priesthood, with their names, signs, and penalties, which you will receive in the temple this day. They are most sacred, and are guarded by solemn covenants and obligations of secrecy to the effect that under no condition, even at the peril of your life, will you ever divulge them, except at a certain place that will be shown you hereafter. The representation of the execution of the penalties indicates different ways in which life may be taken.

[**This oath, covenant and penalty of death if the secret rituals are disclosed cannot be underestimated. This is a level of absolute obedience, control, and allegiance for which a Mormon believes they are under complete obligation, once they have become a "Temple Mormon."**]

The First Token of the Aaronic Priesthood is given by clasping the right hands and placing the joint of the thumb directly over the first knuckle of the hand, in this manner. (**The Officiator takes Adam** [male witness] **kneeling at the altar by the right hand and demonstrates the token to the audience.**) We give unto you the First Token of the Aaronic Priesthood. We desire all to receive it. All arise. (**The patrons all stand in place. The Witness Couple returns to their seats. Several temple workers circulate through the rows of patrons, giving each one the token. Each patron sits down after receiving it.**) If any of you did not receive this token, you will please raise your hands. (**Pause**)

The name of this token is the New Name that you received in the temple today. If any of you have forgotten the New Name, please stand. (**Pause**) The sign is made by bringing the right arm to the square, the palm of the hand to the front, the fingers close together, and the thumb extended. (**The Officiator demonstrates the sign to the audience**) This is the sign. **The Officiator continues to demonstrate the instructions.**

The execution of the Penalty is represented by placing the thumb under the left ear, the palm of the hand down, and by drawing the thumb quickly across the throat to the right ear, and dropping the hand to the side.

I will now explain the covenant and obligation of secrecy which are associated with this token, its name, sign, and penalty, and which you will be required to take upon yourselves. If I were receiving my own Endowment today, and had been given the name of "John" as my New Name, I would repeat in my mind these words, after making the sign **(Officiator makes the sign),** at the same time representing the execution of the penalty.

I, John, covenant that I will never reveal the First Token of the Aaronic Priesthood, with its accompanying name, sign, and penalty. Rather than do so, I would suffer **(pause — places right thumb under left ear)** my life **(pause — draws thumb quickly across the throat to the right ear)** to be taken **(drops hand to side).**

All arise.

Patrons all stand up.

Each of you make the sign of the First Token of the Aaronic Priesthood by bringing your right arm to the square, the palm of the hand to the front, the fingers together, and the thumb extended. **Patrons all make the sign.** This is the sign. Now, repeat in your mind after me the words of the covenant, at the same time representing the execution of the penalty.

I _____, think of the New Name, covenant that I will never reveal the First Token of the Aaronic Priesthood, with its accompanying name, sign and penalty. Rather than do so, I would suffer **(patrons all place right thumbs under left ears as described above)** my life **(patrons all draw thumbs across throats to right ears)** to be taken **(patrons all drop right hands down to sides).**

That will do.

Patrons all sit down. (If any of the brethren or sisters makes a mistake in the execution of the penalty, the execution of penalty is repeated by all of the patrons together as instructed.)

It is necessary to repeat the sign of the Execution of the Penalty. The Sign of the First Token of the Aaronic Priesthood is made by bringing the right arm to the square, the palm of the hand to the front, the fingers close together, and the thumb extended. This is the sign. **(Patrons all make sign)** It is not necessary to repeat again the words of the covenant in representing the execution of the penalty, but let the name of the token pass through your mind. Now represent the execution of the penalty. **(Patrons all draw their thumbs across their throats)**

That will do.

Patrons all sit down.

ELOHIM: Jehovah, see that Adam is driven out of this beautiful garden into the lone and dreary world, where he may learn from his own experience to distinguish good from evil.

JEHOVAH: It shall be done, Elohim.

The lights dim and extinguish, and the movie resumes.

THE LAW OF THE GOSPEL

VOICE OF PETER: A couple will now come to the altar. **(The Witness Couple comes forward and kneels at the altar)** Brethren and sisters, this couple at the altar represents all of you as if at the altar, and you will be under the same obligations that they will be. We are required to give unto you the Law of the Gospel as contained in the Book of Mormon and the Bible. To give unto you also a charge to avoid all lightmindedness, loud laughter, evil speaking of the Lord's anointed, the taking of the name of God in vain, and every other unholy and impure practice, and to cause you to receive these by covenant.

[Of particular note in this quote is the charge to avoid "evil speaking of the Lord's anointed." The Lord's anointed is specifically the Prophet, his Counselors, the Twelve, and all General Authorities, and this designation extends to all positions of leadership in the Mormon Church. To "evil speak" of the Lord's anointed would be to disagree with what Mormon Leadership says. They speak for God; so, if a Mormon does not follow their counsel, they are "evil speaking of the Lord's anointed." This obligation is not just "General Authorities," it pertains to local leadership as well.]

All arise. (**Patrons all stand up**) Each of you bring your right arm to the square. (**Patrons all raise right arms to the square**)

You and each of you covenant and promise before God, angels, and these witnesses at this altar, that you will observe and keep the Law of the Gospel and this charge as it has been explained to you. Each of you bow your head and say yes.

ALL PATRONS: (each bowing head) Yes.

PETER: That will do.

Patrons all sit down.

PETER: Jehovah, we have been down to the man Adam and his posterity in the Telestial World, and have cast Satan out of their midst. We have given unto them the Law of the Gospel as contained in the Book of Mormon and the Bible. Also a charge to avoid all lightmindedness, loud laughter, evil speaking of the Lord's anointed, the taking of the name of God in vain, and every other unholy and impure practice, and have caused them to receive these by covenant. We have also clothed them in the Robes of the Holy Priesthood and have given unto them the Second Token of the Aaronic Priesthood, with its accompanying name, sign, and penalty. This is our report.

THE LAW OF CONSECRATION

PETER: A couple will now come to the altar. (**The Witness Couple comes forward and they kneel at the altar as before.**) We are instructed to give unto you the Law of Consecration as contained in the book of Doctrine and Covenants (**Officiator picks up Doctrine and Covenants from the altar and holds it to the audience**), in connection with the Law of the Gospel and the Law of Sacrifice which you have already received. It is that you do consecrate yourselves, your time, talents, and everything with which the Lord has blessed you, or with which he may bless you, to the Church of Jesus Christ of Latter-day Saints, for the building up of the Kingdom of God on the earth and for the establishment of Zion.

[**Here a Mormon consecrates themselves and everything they own, or will ever own, to The Church of Jesus Christ of Latter-day Saints – The Mormon Church.**]

All arise. (**Patrons all stand up.**) Each of you bring your right arm to the square.

You and each of you covenant and promise before God, angels, and these witnesses at this altar that you will observe and keep the Law of Consecration as contained in this, the Book of Doctrine and Covenants. It is that you do consecrate yourselves, your time, talents, and everything with which the Lord has blessed you or with which he may bless you, to the Church of Jesus Christ of Latter-day Saints, for the building up of the Kingdom of God on the earth and for the establishment of Zion.

Each of you bow your head and say yes.

ALL PATRONS: (each bowing his head) Yes.

PETER: That will do.

(Patrons all sit down)[25] (bracketed information and emphasis added.)

THE FOLLOWING WAS TAKEN FROM *"Evolution of the Mormon Temple Ceremony 1842-1990."* (This "Lecture at the Veil" was removed from all temple ceremonies after 1990).

[The Lecture at the Veil is a good summation of the oaths and covenants that Mormons place themselves under in the temple ceremony. The "Veil" is the symbol of separation between earth life and the hereafter. After passing through the "Veil" in the temple ceremony, a Mormon enters the Celestial Kingdom where they will become Gods in the next life.]

LECTURE AT THE VEIL

(The following lecture is only given when there are patrons present who are receiving their own Endowments, or when the Endowment room is full, and additional time is needed to present the patrons at the Veil.)

PETER: A lecture will now be given which summarizes the instructions, ordinances and covenants, and also the tokens, with their key words, signs and penalties, pertaining to the Endowment, which you, have thus far received. You should try to remember and keep in mind all that you have heard and seen and may yet hear and see in this house. The purpose of this lecture is to assist you to remember that which has been taught you this day.

You must keep in mind that you are under a solemn obligation never to speak outside of the temple of the Lord of the things you see and hear in this sacred place.

NARRATOR: Brethren and sisters, the ordinances of the Endowment as here administered, long withheld from the children of men pertain to the Dispensation of the Fullness of Time and have been revealed to prepare the people for exaltation in the Celestial Kingdom, where God and Christ dwell. The deep meaning of the Eternal Truths constituting the Endowment, has been set forth in brief instructions, and by symbolic representation. If you give prayerful and earnest thought to the Holy Endowment, you will obtain the understanding and spirit of the work done in the temples of the Lord. The privilege of laboring here for the dead permits us to enter the temple frequently, and to refresh our memories, and to enlarge our understanding of the Endowment.

You were first washed and anointed, a Garment was placed upon you, and a New Name was given you. This name you should always remember; but you must never reveal it to any person, except at the Veil. You then entered this room. Here you heard voices of persons representing a council of the Gods, Elohim, Jehovah, and Michael. Elohim said: "See, yonder is matter unorganized, go ye down and organize it into a world, like unto the other worlds that we have heretofore formed." As the creation of the earth progressed, you heard the commands and the reports of the persons representing the Gods.

If we are faithful, we shall enter the Celestial Kingdom, and there hear and know the Gods of heaven. They are perfect, we are imperfect, They are exalted, we may attain exaltation.

Our spirits at one time lived with the Gods, but each of us was given the privilege of coming upon this earth to take upon himself a body, so that the spirit might have a house, in which to dwell.

Michael, one of the council of the Gods, became the man Adam, to whom was given the woman Eve. However, as Adam, he did not remember his life and labors in the council. It is so with us all. We came into the world with no memory of our previous existence.

We then followed Adam and Eve into the garden, where Elohim provided that they might eat freely of all kinds of fruit of the garden, except the fruit of the Tree of Knowledge of Good and Evil. He forbade them to partake of this fruit, saying that in the day they did so, they should surely die. When Adam and Eve were left alone in the garden, Satan appeared, and tempted them. Eve yielded to the temptation, partook of the fruit, and offered it to Adam. Adam had resisted the temptation of Satan, but when Eve offered him the forbidden fruit he partook of it, that they might continue together, and perpetuate the human race. Adam and Eve now understood that it was Lucifer who had tempted them. They became self-conscious. Discovering their nakedness, and hearing the voice of the Lord, they made aprons of fig leaves and hid themselves. They had learned that everything has its opposite, such as good and evil, light and darkness, pleasure and pain. The Lord again entered the garden, Adam and Eve confessed their disobedience. The Lord cursed Satan, and cast him out of the Garden of Eden, and the Lord commanded: "Let cherubim, and a flaming sword be placed to guard the way of the Tree of Life, lest Adam put forth his hand, and partake of the fruit thereof, and live forever in his sins."

Before their departure however, instructions were given them. Addressing Eve, the Lord said: "Because thou hast hearkened to the voice of Satan, and hast partaken of the forbidden fruit, and given unto Adam, I will greatly multiply thy sorrow and thy conception. In sorrow shalt thou bring forth children, nevertheless, thou mayest be preserved in childbearing. Thy desire shall be to thy husband, and he shall rule over thee, in righteousness." To Adam, the Lord said: "Because thou hast hearkened to the voice of thy wife, and hast partaken of the forbidden fruit, the earth shall be cursed for thy sake. Instead of producing fruits and flowers spontaneously, it shall bring forth thorns, thistles, briars, and noxious weeds, to afflict and torment man. And by the sweat of thy face shalt thou eat thy bread all the days of thy life, for dust thou art, and unto dust shalt thou return."

Having been commanded, Jehovah provided Adam and Eve with coats of skins for a covering. The Garment which was placed upon you after you had been washed and anointed, represents the coat of skins or covering of Adam and Eve. They were also promised that further light and knowledge would be given them.

The Law of Obedience was then taught Adam and Eve, and accepted by them. Eve covenanted with Adam that thenceforth she would obey the law of her husband, and abide by his counsel in righteousness; and Adam covenanted with the Lord that he would obey the Lord, and keep his commandments. You, likewise covenanted to comply with the Law of Obedience. The Law of Sacrifice, accompanying the Law of Obedience, as contained in the Old and New Testaments of the Bible, was next presented to Adam; and you were all placed under covenant to observe it. The Law of Obedience and Sacrifice includes the promise of the Savior, the Only Begotten of the Father, who is full of grace and truth, and who by His sacrifice has become the Redeemer of Mankind. All things should be done in the Name of the Son. An angel of the Lord explained this to Adam, who was given the privilege of showing his Obedience by offering sacrifices to the Lord, in similitude of the sacrifice of Jesus Christ. Later, the people of Israel lived under this law, which continued in force until the death of Jesus Christ.

The First Token of the Aaronic Priesthood, with its accompanying name, sign, and penalty was given you; and you were told that the name of this token is your New Name or the New Name of the dead, if officiating for the dead. The sacred nature of the tokens of the Priesthood was carefully explained at this time. **<u>You were placed under solemn covenant never to reveal these tokens, with their accompanying names, signs, and penalties, even at the peril of your life. You were told that the execution of the penalties indicate different ways in which life may be taken;</u>** then, Adam and Eve were driven out of the garden into the Telestial Kingdom, or the lone and dreary world, the world in which we are now living. There, Adam offered a prayer saying "Oh God, hear the words of my mouth!", repeating it three times. Satan entered, and claiming to be the god of this world, asked Adam what he desired. Adam replied that he was waiting for messengers from his Father. **Satan declared that a preacher would soon arrive. A man representing a sectarian minister entered and preached doctrine which Adam did not accept.**

Peter, James and John were sent down by the Lord, to learn, without disclosing their identity, if the man Adam had been faithful to his covenants. They found that he had been faithful and so reported. They were sent down again, this time in their true character as Apostles of the Lord Jesus Christ, to visit and to instruct Adam and his posterity in the Telestial World. Before so teaching the people, they cast Satan out. **<u>The Law of the Gospel, as contained in the Book of Mormon and the Bible was then given Adam and his posterity. You were placed</u>**

under covenant to obey the Law of the Gospel, and to avoid all lightmindedness, loud laughter, evil speaking of the Lord's anointed, and taking the name of the Lord in vain. The Robe of the Holy Priesthood was placed upon your left shoulder, according to the order of the Aaronic Priesthood. The Second Token of the Aaronic Priesthood was given you, with its name, sign, and penalty; and you were informed that the name of this token is your first given name, or the first given name of the person for whom you are officiating. The Robe of the Holy Priesthood was then changed to the right shoulder, as was done anciently, when officiating in the ordinances of the Melchizedek Priesthood. With the robe on the right shoulder, you have authority also if called to the Bishopric, to act in the Aaronic Priesthood. You were then introduced with the Robe of the Holy Priesthood on the right shoulder into the Terrestrial Kingdom. The Law of Chastity was there explained to you in plainness, and you were placed under covenant to obey this law. The First Token of the Melchizedek Priesthood, or Sign of the Nail, with its accompanying name, sign, and penalty was next given you. You were told that the name of the First Token of the Melchizedek Priesthood is "the Son" meaning the Son of God.

The Book of Doctrine and Covenants, in connection with the Book of Mormon and the Bible was presented to you; and the Law of Consecration as contained in the book of Doctrine and Covenants was explained to you, and you received this law by covenant.

The Second Token of the Melchizedek Priesthood, the Patriarchal Grip, or Sure Sign of the Nail, or the Nail in the Sure Place was given you, together with its sign. The name of this token will be given you at the veil. This token has reference to the crucifixion of the Savior.

When he was placed upon the cross, the crucifiers drove nails through the palms of his hands, then fearing that the weight of his body would cause the nails to tear through the flesh of his hands, they drove nails through his wrists. Hence, in the palm is the Sign of the Nail, and in the wrist is the Sure Sign of the Nail, or the Nail in the Sure Place. You have now progressed so far in the Endowment that you are ready to receive the name of the Second Token of the Melchizedek Priesthood, and to pass through the Veil, into the Celestial Kingdom.

The sisters in this company who are to be married and sealed for time and eternity should be taken through the Veil by their intended husband. Others will be taken through the Veil by the regular temple workers.

Brethren and sisters, you will have received this day, the sacred ordinances of the Endowment, the Eternal Plan of Salvation for man as he journeys from his pre-existent state, to his future high place in the Celestial Kingdom, has been presented to you. **You have covenanted to obey all the laws of the gospel, including the laws of Obedience, Sacrifice, Chastity, and Consecration, which make possible an exaltation with the Gods;** and you have received the First and Second Tokens of the Aaronic Priesthood, and the First and Second Tokens of the Melchizedek Priesthood, with the names, signs, and penalties of these tokens, except the name of the Second Token of the Melchizedek Priesthood, which will be given you at the Veil. All this is done for the glory, honor and endowment of the children of Zion.

Brethren and sisters, strive to comprehend the glorious things presented to you this day. No other people on earth have ever had this privilege, except as they have received the keys of the Priesthood, given in the Endowment.

These are what are termed "the Mysteries of Godliness," that which will enable you to understand the expression of the Savior, made just prior to his betrayal: "This is life Eternal, that they might know the Only True God, and Jesus Christ, whom thou has sent." May God bless you all, amen.[26] (emphasis added.)

There is no more important ceremony in all of Mormonism than the "Temple Endowment Ceremony." When the important role of the temple endowment is understood within the doctrine of Mormonism, coupled with the secrecy and solemnity of the ritual, it becomes easier to understand the ironhanded obligation a Mormon that has participated in these required, binding oaths and rituals is placed under. As an American voter it is imperative to comprehend the level of influence and control that the Mormon Church has over its members because of these oaths, covenants, and rituals.

As of 1990, the Mormon Temple Ceremony was altered to remove the blood oaths. A patron no longer has to act out the slitting of their throat, the cutting open of the chest or the disemboweling as a penalty for revealing the secret temple rituals. Patrons still swear never to reveal the Mormon Temple Ceremony; however, they no longer have to act out the penalty of what will happen to them if they do. It should be remembered that as of this writing in 2007, any Mormon 36 years of age or older that went through the ceremony prior to the changes in 1990 swore these blood oath penalties as part of the ceremony; that image is forever embedded in their mind, and reinforces the penalties for breaking the oaths that were sworn in those ceremonies.

THE "OATH OF VENGEANCE"

There is another serious "oath" in Mormon history: "The Oath of Vengeance." This was an oath that was so serious and repulsive in nature it was removed from the Mormon Temple Ceremony in 1927. This oath swore vengeance against the United States of America, to "avenge the blood of the prophets upon this nation," and the participant was to "teach this to my children and to my children's children unto the third and fourth generation."[27] Most Mormons today disavow any knowledge of it. Studying this oath, especially in the sworn testimony before the United States Senate, as found in "*U. S. Senate Document No. 486*" gives a clear understanding of how Mormons are sworn to secrecy with respect to what transpires inside a Mormon Temple. Many Mormons refused to testify, or would not answer when called before the United States Senate in the Reed Smoot Committee Hearings. The obligations that caused Mormons to refuse to testify then, are in place today. How can we as Americans trust those whom we elect, or those whom are appointed to serve us in positions of power within the Government, if they will not tell us what oaths and obligations they have sworn, which may compromise their ability to freely and independently represent "WE the People?" See Appendix Four for more details.

WHAT'S THE POINT?

As noted in Chapter Four, "The Political Kingdom," the Mormon Church believes it is "*The Kingdom of God on Earth.*" Through oaths and covenants of obedience it sets forth a faith system that requires absolute obedience to the faith system, in order for one to reach exaltation after death. Beginning with Baptism, which is required to become a member of the Mormon Church, covenants of obedience to serve God and keep his commandments begin. As a Christian, I believe I am to strive to keep the Commandments that God has given in the Bible—If the whole world kept the 10 Commandments, wouldn't it be a different place—however,

in Mormonism serving God and keeping his commandments means to follow the Prophet and the Priesthood of
Mormonism.

Chapter Three, "The Mormon Priesthood," laid out the
prominent position of the Priesthood, in Mormonism—
without the "Priesthood," there is no Mormon Church.
Entry into and each successive office in the Priesthood is
centered on covenants to receive the Leaders of the Church,
"my servants." To reject that covenant means you will "not
have forgiveness of sins in this world nor in the world to
come."[28]

The ultimate ordinance for Godhood in Mormonism is
the Temple Endowment Ceremony. In this ceremony four
oaths are sworn: (1) The Law of Obedience; (2) The Law
of Sacrifice; (3) The Law of the Gospel; and (4) The Law of
Consecration. In the Mormon Temple Ceremony the Mormon
Patron covenants everything to the Mormon Church: "you
do consecrate yourselves, your time, your talents, and everything with which the Lord has blessed you or with which he
may bless you, to the Church of Jesus Christ of Latter-day
Saints, for the building up of the Kingdom of God on the
earth and for the establishment of Zion."[29]

These oaths of absolute obedience to Mormon Church
Leadership, impose upon a member of the Mormon Church
absolute allegiance. Within the belief system of Mormonism,
if a Mormon breaks these oaths, their eternal destiny is
at stake. Remember from Chapter Five, on Resurrection
Morning, the Mormon will be facing not only Jesus, but
all Mormon Prophets and Apostles as well. These doctrinal
concepts place a Mormon in utter and complete bondage or
servitude to the Mormon Church.

Mormon Apostle Boyd K. Packer makes the point
perfectly: "When you receive an ordinance, whether it be
baptism, the sacrament, an ordination or setting apart, an
endowment or a sealing, you receive an obligation."[30] I

cannot stress this point enough, the obligation is to obey all of the commandments; first and foremost of which is, obeying your Priesthood Leadership, which is obeying God Himself: "For he that receiveth my servants receiveth me."[31]

[1] *Webster's New Twentieth Century Dictionary*, Second Edition, 1983, Simon and Schuster, New York.

[2] *Gospel Principles*, Published by The Church of Jesus Christ of Latter-day Saints (Salt Lake City, Utah, 1997) 133-134.

[3] Ibid., 131.

[4] *Doctrine and Covenants*, 1:30.

[5] *Gospel Principles*, 304.

[6] Bruce R. McConkie, *Mormon Doctrine* (Bookcraft: Salt Lake City, Utah, 1966) 660.

[7] *Teachings of the Living Prophets*, Student Manual Religion 333, Published by The Church of Jesus Christ of Latter-day Saints (Salt Lake City, Utah, 1982) 9.

[8] *Doctrine and Covenants*, 84:1.

[9] *Ibid.*, 84:35-41.

[10] *Acts* 3: 22-23:
> 22. For Moses truly said unto the fathers, A prophet shall the Lord your God raise up unto you of your brethren, like unto me,; him shall ye hear in all things whatsoever he shall say unto you.
> 23. And is shall come to pass, *that* every soul, which will not hear that prophet, shall be destroyed from among the people.

[11] *Joseph Smith* 2:40:
> 40. In addition to these, he quoted the eleventh chapter of Isaiah, saying that it was about to be fulfilled. He quoted also the third chapter of Acts, twenty-second and twenty-third verses, precisely as they stand in our New Testament. He said that that prophet was Christ: but the day had not yet come when "they who would

not hear his voice should be cut off from among the people," but soon would come.

[12] *Doctrine and Covenants* 1:14, 38:

    14. And the arm of the Lord shall be revealed; and the day cometh that they who will not hear the voice of the Lord, neither the voice of his servants, neither give heed to the words of the prophets and apostles, shall be cut off from among the people:

    38. What I the Lord have spoken, I have spoken, and I excuse not myself; and though the heavens and the earth pass away, my word shall not pass away, but shall be fulfilled, whether by mine own voice or by the voice of my servants, it is the same.

[13] *Doctrine and Covenants* 84:36, 37:

    36. For he that receiveth my servants receiveth me;

    37. And he that receiveth me receiveth my Father;

[14] *Luke* 10:16:

    16. He that heareth you heareth me; and he that despiseth you despiseth me; and he that despiseth me despiseth him that sent me.

[15] *A Royal Priesthood, A Personal Study Guide for the Melchizedek Priesthood Quorums of The Church of Jesus Christ of Latter-day Saints, 1975-1976*, (Corporation of The President of The Church of Jesus Christ of Latter-day Saints, 1975) 37.

[16] *Ibid*, 38.

[17] *Ibid*, 39.

[18] *Ensign*, Published monthly by The Church of Jesus Christ of Latter-day Saints (Salt Lake City, Utah) May 2007, 57.

[19] *Encyclopedia of Mormonism*, 1-4 vols., edited by Daniel H. Ludlow (New York: Macmillan, 1992) 454-455.

[20] Bruce R. McConkie, *Mormon Doctrine*, (Bookcraft, Salt Lake City, Utah, 1966) 256-257.

[21] *Encyclopedia of Mormonism*, 479.

[21] *Ensign*, May 2007, 57.

[23] *Immortality and Eternal Life, Melchizedek Priesthood Course of Study, 1968-69*, (Published by the First Presidency of The Church of Jesus Christ of Latter-day Saints, 1968) 162.

[24] Joseph Fielding Smith, Compiled by Bruce R. McConkie, *Doctrines of Salvation*, (Bookcraft, Salt Lake City, Utah 1956) 3:119-20.

[25] Chuck Sackett, *What's Going On In There?*, (Sword of the Shepherd Ministries, Inc., Thousand Oaks, California, 1982) excerpts from pages 22-45.

[26] Jerald and Sandra Tanner, *Evolution of the Mormon Temple Ceremony: 1842-1990*, (Utah Lighthouse Ministry, Salt Lake City, Utah, 1990) 98-101.

[27] Will Bagley, *Blood of the Prophets*, (University of Oklahoma Press: Norman, 2002) 21.

[28] *Doctrine and* Covenants, 84:41.

[29] *Evolution of the Mormon Temple Ceremony: 1842-1990*, 91.

[30] *Search These Commandments, Melchizedek Priesthood Personal Study Guide*, (Published by The Church of Jesus Christ of Latter-day Saints, Salt Lake City, Utah, 1984) 284.

[31] *Doctrine and Covenants*, 84:36.

AUTHORS NOTE:

A complete review of Mormon Temple Ceremonies can be done at: http://www.nauvoochristian.org/temple_endowments.php

Chapter Seven

IT'S NOT JUST FEDERAL OR STATE – IT'S LOCAL AND FEMALE AS WELL

The possibility of Mormon Church manipulation in all layers of Government is quite real. That exploitation is not just conceivable at the Federal or the State level, but the likelihood at the local level is just as certain. Don't be disillusioned into thinking this is only a Mormon male problem because of the all male Priesthood membership. All women fall under the mantle of Mormon male Priesthood leadership, no matter what their position in the Mormon Church is. In all positions of leadership in Women's (Relief Society) or Children's (Primary) programs, the woman always has a male Priesthood holder whom she is subservient to, and reports to.

The principle of absolute obedience and allegiance to Mormon Priesthood authority, as part of keeping God's commandments, is gender neutral in Mormonism. Yes, Mormon males twelve years old and above are ordained into the Aaronic, lower level, Priesthood, and males nineteen years and older are ordained into the Melchizedek, or higher level, Priesthood. But, obedience to Mormon Priesthood authority is not just a male requirement. All Mormons, male or female, are taught this "allegiance" to their Priesthood and Mormon leadership line of authority:

> Among Latter-day Saints the injunction to "follow the Brethren" derives from this requirement of obedience to Jesus and to prophetic instruction. In this context, "the Brethren" are the General Authorities, particularly the First Presidency and the Quorum of the Twelve Apostles, who are formally sustained as prophets, seers, and revelators. The principle involved can be extended to include local priesthood leaders such as priesthood quorum presidencies, bishops and stake presidents, and the presidencies of the women's auxiliary organizations-Relief Society, young women, and primary-within their respective jurisdictions. This extension of the principle to all Church leaders at every level is based on the recognition that all officers in the Church are entitled to revelation in their callings and on the assumption that they are in harmony with the Brethren. Referring specifically to the prophet who is currently President of the Church, the Lord has instructed members to "give heed unto all his words and commandments which he shall give unto you as he receiveth them, walking in all holiness before me; For his word ye shall receive, as if from mine own mouth, in all patience and faith" (D&C 21:4-5).[1]

As you can see by the above quote, the principle of "following the Brethren" continues from the General Authorities to the local hometown authorities as well.

Males take specific covenants of obedience when ordained into the Priesthood as we have already seen in Chapter Three; however, all Mormons make covenants when they are baptized and renew these covenants each week when they partake of the sacrament. Those who have gone through the "Endowment Ceremony" at a Mormon Temple have sworn specific oaths of obedience there as explained in Chapter Six.

Given the documentation in the previous chapters of this book, there should be no question in anyone's mind of the doctrine to "Follow the Prophet," and of those who are sustained as "prophets, seers, and revelators." The expansion of the "Follow the Prophet" doctrine, as I've begun to layout, beginning with the last quote, goes to the local level and is a principle of the utmost importance. Certainly at the highest levels of the Mormon Church, but also taught at the local level is the doctrine: not to "speak against the Lord's Anointed."

Brigham Young taught that at the local level the Bishop is not to be questioned. If he is doing wrong, he will be removed from office; however, a Mormon is not to find fault with him. Those who are in a position of leadership over a Mormon are deemed to be a "presiding officer," or "file leader," and are considered "The Lord's Anointed:"

"Brother Kimball said, today, when he was speaking, if you suffer yourselves to find fault with your Bishop, you condescend to the spirit of apostasy. Do any of you do this? If you do, you do not realize that you expose yourself to the power of the Enemy. What should your faith and position be before God? Such that, if a Bishop does not do right, the Lord will remove him out of your Ward. You are not to find fault. As brother Wells has said, **speak not lightly of the anointed of the Lord.** But you say they are out of the way. Who has made any of my brethren a judge over their Bishop? You read in the Book of Doctrine and Covenants, in a revelation to Joseph Smith, (brother Kimball and myself were present,) that it takes twelve High Priests to sit in council upon the head of a Bishop. Can they judge him? No; for they must then have the Presidency of the High Priesthood to sit at their head and preside over them. Yet many rise up and coudemn their Bishop.... **One of the first steps to apostacy is to find fault with your Bishop;** and when that is done, unless repented of, a second step is soon taken, and by-and-by the person is cut off from the Church, and that is the end of it. Will you allow yourselves to find fault with your Bishop? No; but come to me, go to the High Council, or to the President of the Stake, and ascertain whether your Bishop is doing wrong, **before you find fault and suffer yourselves to speak against a presiding officer.**"[2] (emphasis added.)

10th Mormon Prophet, Joseph Fielding Smith, in his three volume doctrinal series, *Doctrines of Salvation*, addressed the issue of "Speaking against the Lord's Anointed":

"EVIL SPEAKING AGAINST LORD'S ANOINTED

UNGODLY MEN DEFAME AUTHORITIES OF CHURCH. **It is a serious thing for any member of this Church to raise his voice against the priesthood, or to hold the priesthood in disrespect; for the Lord will not hold such guiltless; so he has promised, and he will fulfil....**

It seems to be **the *heritage of the ungodly*,** of the ***bigoted*,** and of **those who *love iniquity*,** to **sit in judgment** and to place themselves as dictators, saying what shall be done and what shall be said by **the authorities of the Church.** They accuse the brethren of all manner of iniquity, dissimulation, falsehood, and try to cause a division between them and the people over whom they preside. They take unto themselves the prerogative of saying what shall and what shall not be the doctrine of the Church, what shall and what shall not be the government of the Church, when it concerns them not at all.

JUDGMENT AWAITS CHURCH MEMBERS WHO CRITICIZE BRETHREN. But it is not of this class particularly that I desire to refer, but to **those members of the Church who have entered into the waters of baptism and have made covenants before the Lord that they will observe his laws and respect his priesthood,** who have been persuaded, or who are in danger of being persuaded, by such characters.

Occasionally, when a man has himself committed sin and has lost the spirit of the gospel, he will raise his voice against the actions of the authorities who preside over the Church; he will call them in question, sit in judgment upon them and condemn them. **I wish to raise a warning voice to all such who hold membership in the Church, and say unto them, that they had better repent and turn unto the Lord, lest his judgments come upon them,** lest they lose the faith and be turned from the truth....

It is a serious thing for a man holding membership in this Church to say in his heart, or openly, that these men holding the keys of the kingdom have sinned, when they have not sinned, and cause dissension, if it is in his power to do so among his brethren. ***The judgments of the Lord will overtake him.*** He will be brought in question before the Lord, and shall be cast out and find his place among the unbelievers; and those who flattered him and encouraged him to raise up his heel against his brethren will turn from him and leave him to his shame."[3] (*italics* in the original, emphasis added.)

The 6th Prophet of the Church, Joseph F. Smith, was very adamant with respect to following the Priesthood authority of all levels of the Church:

The moment a man says he will not submit to the legally constituted authority of the Church, whether it be the teachers, the bishopric, the high council, his quorum, or the First Presidency, and in his heart confirms it and carries it out, that moment he cuts himself off from the privileges and blessings of the Priesthood and Church, and severs himself from the people of God, for he ignores the authority that the Lord has instituted in his Church.... **The pith of the matter is: the Lord has established his church, organized his priesthood, and conferred authority upon certain individuals, councils and quorums, and it is the duty of the people of God to live so that they shall know that these are acceptable unto him. If we begin to cut off this one and that one, and set their authority aside, we may just as well at once set God aside, and say that he has no right to dictate"** (Smith, Gospel Doctrine, p. 45).[4] (emphasis added.)

This last quote, "Smith, Gospel Doctrine, p. 45," is from Joseph Fielding Smith the 6th Prophet of the Mormon Church. The Mormon Church, using this quote in its Personal Priesthood Study Guide with respect to the Priesthood Oath and Covenant, is clearly making the association that the "oath and covenant" applies "to the legally constituted authority of the Church, whether it be the teachers, the bishopric, the high council, his quorum, or the First Presidency." This "oath and covenant" of the Mormon Priesthood clearly applies to the local level leadership as well as the corporate leadership in Salt Lake City. All women are under the cloak of male Priesthood leadership and submission to the legally constituted authority of the Church equally applies to them.

Spencer W. Kimball, the 12th Prophet of the Mormon Church made it very clear at the conclusion of the April 1978 General Conference that eternal life is dependent upon following all Church leadership:

"Now as we conclude this general conference, let us give heed to what was said to us. Let us assume the counsel given applies to *us*, to me. **Let us hearken to those we sustain as prophets and seers, as well as the other brethren, as if our eternal life depended on it, because it does!**"[5] (emphasis added.)

The "brethren" in the above quote is not "The Brethren" which are identified as the Prophet, his two Counselors, and The Twelve, as they are clearly associated with the phrase "prophets, seers, and revelators." Since this phrase was used prior to the wording "other brethren," it is clear that Kimball is referring to all Priesthood leadership. He is also explicit in his Prophetic Calling, stating that "eternal life" is dependent upon following the Priesthood.

We learned in Chapter Three that the "Mormon Priesthood" is the foundation upon which the Mormon Church is built. The 10th Mormon Prophet, Joseph Fielding Smith, said that all Church authority and offices are but an appendage to the Mormon Priesthood:

ALL OFFICES ARE APPENDAGES TO PRIESTHOOD. When an elder is ordained, he receives the Melchizedek Priesthood and then the office of elder, seventy, or high priest, as the case may be, and the *office* which he receives designates the *nature* of his duties. Not only is the office of bishop and elder an *appendage* to the priesthood but so is every other office, for they all grow out of the priesthood. *The apostle, high priest, seventy, and every other office is an appendage to the priesthood.*

The Lord has, himself, declared that *all authorities or offices in the Church are appendages to the priesthood.* That is to say, *they are circumscribed by priesthood and grow out of it.*[6] (*italics* in the original.)

The complete focus of the Mormon Church, with respect to its organization and leadership, is that it is all held together by the one all encompassing ingredient: the Priesthood. Think of the Priesthood as the electricity being supplied by wire to your house (if you were a Mormon). As long as that wire is in place, electricity is provided to the house. Cut that wire and the lights go out. That electrical wire goes from your house all the way to the power plant that generates the electricity. "The Brethren" are the power plant in Mormonism, and the various levels of Mormon Church organization are the substations in between the power plant and your house. The transformer on the power pole that leads to your house would be the Priesthood leader just above you in your Ward. Thus, following the top leadership positions in Mormonism is a given, but also, following the local "Lord's Anointed," is just as important. Ezra Taft Benson, 13th Mormon Prophet makes this point:

> "What increases our favor with God? One of the purposes of life is to be proved to see if we "will do all things whatsoever the Lord [our] God shall command [us]" (Abraham 3:25). In short, we are to learn the will of the Lord and do it. We are to follow the model of Jesus Christ and be like Him. God's will for you can be determined from three sources: (1) The scriptures-particularly the Book of Mormon. (2) Inspired words from the Lord's anointed-counsel from prophets, seers, and revelators. (3) Local Church leaders likewise are also entitled to give inspired direction for those over whom they preside."[7] (brackets in original.)

As previously discussed in this book, the culmination of all earthly goals in Mormonism is to go to a Mormon Temple and have one's endowment performed. In order to go into a Temple a Mormon must obtain a Temple Recommend.

This process begins by getting an appointment with one's local Bishop to be interviewed. The interview consists of the Bishop asking a list of questions that must all be answered correctly in accordance with Mormon Church standards or the interviewee cannot advance to the next level of questioning with the Stake President. Question number 4, of the 15 questions, specifically pertains to "Following the Brethren" down to the "local authorities":

"4. Do you sustain the President of the Church of Jesus Christ of Latter-day Saints as the Prophet, Seer, and Revelator and as the only person on the earth who possesses and is authorized to exercise all priesthood keys? Do you sustain members of the First Presidency and the Quorum of the Twelve Apostles as prophets, seers, and revelators? **Do you sustain the other General Authorities and local authorities of the Church?**"[8] (emphasis added.)

The reinforcement of this principle is ever ongoing in the Mormon Church. In the June 2007 issue of *"Ensign"* we find an article titled "Supporting Your Bishop." Mormon author, Joseph Staples, repeats this principle under the sub-heading, "Accept His Challenges and Follow His Counsel":

"The Bishop is a representative of the Lord Jesus Christ. He may challenge us. He may ask us to serve in positions that might be out of our comfort zone. He may ask us to stretch and give. For our benefit, for his benefit, and as a means of building the Lord's kingdom here on earth, **we should follow the bishop's counsel and accept and magnify the callings he or his counselors extend to us.**"[9]

As a side-bar to this article is a quote from the current Mormon Prophet, Gordon B. Hinckley: "Everyone…is accountable to a bishop or a branch president."[10] Male or female, all must "follow The Brethren," right down to the local level. An excellent amplifying point to this principle can be found in *"The Latter-day Saint Woman."* In the "Introduction" to this manual it reads: "This manual for women and girls is for new members of the Church. Its purpose is to teach gospel principles and doctrines and to motivate the sisters to love the gospel and to want to live by its teachings."[11] In Lesson 13 "Follow the Brethren," under the heading "Our Local Priesthood Leaders Are Called of God," we read:

> *Through what servants, other than the prophet, would the Lord speak to us today? (Through worthy Church members who have been set apart to lead us)*
>
> The prophet and other General Authorities preside over all units of the Church. However, since they cannot personally conduct the affairs of all units, they have delegated the right to preside, and to conduct, to others. The Lord calls worthy priesthood bearers to act under the leadership of the General Authorities in our local areas. These local leaders are called by revelation to lead in righteousness. Although they may not feel they are fully prepared or trained for their leadership calls, the Lord has chosen them to lead at this time, and he will magnify their abilities to perform their callings.
>
> After local leaders are chosen, they are presented for our sustaining vote. When we raise our hands to sustain them, we are promising to follow them and help them in their callings.
>
> Elder S. Dilworth Young commented about the relationship between obedience and recognizing the authority of local leaders:

"We acknowledge that in order to obey *all things* whatsoever we are commanded, we must obey the leaders through whom the commands come" (Conference Report, Apr. 1967, p. 40; "The Principle of Obedience," *Improvement Era*, June 1967, p. 49).

What might a local priesthood leader ask us to do? How can we show that we believe he is called of God?

Mothers have a responsibility to teach their children to sustain and support their local priesthood leaders. They should never criticize priesthood leaders or say unkind things about them. **Criticizing our leaders endangers our own salvation.** We should be careful to speak highly of priesthood leaders in front of our children. We should teach them to be loyal to the offices of the Lord's kingdom. Our children will then learn by example to be loyal to both the offices and those called to serve as our priesthood leaders in these offices.

"The men who hold the priesthood are but mortal men; they are fallible men....

"Nevertheless, God has chosen these men. He has singled them out. They have not done it themselves; but He has selected them, and He has placed upon them the authority of the Holy Priesthood, and they have become His representatives in the earth.

"... And those who lift their voices... against the authority of the Holy Priesthood... will go down to hell, unless they repent." (George Q. Cannon, *Gospel Truth*, vol. 1, p. 276)

What can we do to support our local priesthood leaders?(Pray for them, avoid criticizing them, show respect for them, teach our children to respect them, follow their counsel, and accept and fulfill assignments received from them.)[12] (*italics* in the original.)

Previous chapters have very clearly documented the males obligation/covenant to follow his Priesthood authority, or to put it in military terms, follow his "Chain of Command." As can be seen by this women's training manual, females in the Church have a bounden duty as well.

WHAT'S THE POINT?

This book is about a principle - absolute allegiance/obedience to the Mormon Church, through its governing agent, the Priesthood. As has been amply chronicled in previous chapters, the dogma to "Follow the Prophet," is the primary tenet of Mormonism. However, under the agent of the Priesthood, the local level Priesthood leaders are to be followed as well or the Mormon could be "endangering their own salvation." This brings the conflict between Mormonism and the political arena to the local level. The conflict between a Mormon's responsibility to represent the people and not their Church, through doctrinal allegiance to their Priesthood leadership, crosses the complete gamut of the political spectrum. The principle is the same from the President of the United States to the local City Council or School Board.

[1] *Encyclopedia of Mormonism*, 1-4 vols., edited by Daniel H. Ludlow (New York: Macmillan, 1992) 520.

[2] Brigham Young, in Watt, ed., *Journal of Discourses*, 9:141.

[3] Joseph Fielding Smith, Compiled by Bruce R. McConkie, *Doctrines of Salvation*, (Bookcraft, Salt Lake City, Utah 1956) 3:295-297.

[4] *A Royal Priesthood, A Personal Study Guide for the Melchizedek Priesthood Quorums of The Church of Jesus Christ of Latter-day Saints, 1975-1976*, (Corporation of The President of The Church of Jesus Christ of Latter-day Saints, 1975) 39.

[5] *Search These Commandments, Melchizedek Priesthood Personal Study Guide,* (Published by The Church of Jesus Christ of Latter-day Saints, Salt Lake City, Utah, 1984) 276.

[6] Smith, *Doctrines of Salvation,* 3:105-06.

[7] Ezra Taft Benson, *The Teachings of Ezra Taft Benson,* p.343

[8] http://www.lds-mormon.com/new_temple_questions.shtml

[9] *Ensign,* Published monthly by The Church of Jesus Christ of Latter-day Saints (Salt Lake City, Utah) June 2007, 59.

[10] Ibid., 59.

[11] *The Latter-day Saint Woman, Basic Manual for Women, Part B,* Published by The Church of Jesus Christ of Latter-day Saints (Salt Lake City, Utah, 1993) (Introduction) v.

[12] Ibid., 109-111.

Chapter Eight

ISN'T THIS THE JACK KENNEDY ARGUMENT?

To answer the legitimate question, "Isn't this the Jack Kennedy argument?", I have provided the speech that Candidate Kennedy gave to the Southern Baptist Leaders on September 12, 1960 and printed in the *New York Times* on September 13, 1960. At the end of the speech I have provided commentary on the differences between Jack Kennedy's position and the condition that exists in Mormonism through its doctrinal position of covenants, oaths and obligations.

ADDRESS TO SOUTHERN BAPTIST LEADERS
(1960) John F. Kennedy

The Protestant immigrants to the New World brought many things in their baggage, including a deep-seated distrust of Roman Catholicism. Although Catholics had been among the early settlers of the New World, they had been a minority in the thirteen colonies that eventually became the United States. Not until significant numbers of Catholics began migrating to the United States in the mid-nineteenth century did anti-Catholicism emerge as a potent, and ugly, political and social phenomenon.

Although Irish Catholics began to play a major role in local and state politics in the latter nineteenth century, the first Catholic to seek a national office was the popular governor of New York, Alfred Emanuel Smith, who was the Democratic nominee for president in 1928. Anti-Catholic prejudice, the fear that a Catholic president would "take orders" from the Pope, insured Smith's defeat. Methodist Bishop Adna Leonard declared: "No Governor can kiss the papal ring and get within gunshot of the White House." Even liberal Protestants were concerned. The Christian Century declared it could not "look with unconcern upon the seating of a representative of an alien culture, of a medieval, Latin mentality, of an undemocratic hierarchy and of a foreign potentate in the great office of the President of the United States."

Smith's defeat at the polls seemed to foreclose a Catholic from seeking the White House, until John F. Kennedy captured the Democratic nomination in 1960. Much to his dismay, he discovered that many southern Protestant groups still believed in old canards about every Catholic having to obey the Pope's commands unquestioningly. He finally decided to try to defeat the issue by meeting it head-on, and on September 12, 1960, he delivered the following statement before the Greater Houston Ministerial Association.

There, according to one of his biographers, "he knocked religion out of the campaign as an intellectually respectable issue." Anti-Catholicism, of course, could not be eradicated that easily, but Kennedy's meeting the issue forthrightly limited the damage to those whose prejudices would never respond to reason. And with his election that November, barriers to Catholics in American politics melted away.

For further reading: T. H. White, The Making of the President 1960 (1961).

THE SPEECH

ADDRESS TO SOUTHERN BAPTIST LEADERS

I am grateful for your generous invitation to state my views.

While the so-called religious issue is necessarily and properly the chief topic here tonight, I want to emphasize from the outset that I believe that we have far more critical issues in the 1960 election: the spread of Communist influence, until it now festers only ninety miles off the coast of Florida — the humiliating treatment of our President and Vice President by those who no longer respect our power — the hungry children I saw in West Virginia, the old people who cannot pay their doctor's bills, the families forced to give up their farms — an America with too many slums, with too few schools, and too late to the moon and outer space.

These are the real issues which should decide this campaign. And they are not religious issues — for war and hunger and ignorance and despair know no religious barrier.

But because I am a Catholic and no Catholic has ever been elected President, the real issues in this campaign have been obscured — perhaps deliberately, in some quarters less responsible than this. So it is apparently necessary for me to state once again — not what kind of church I believe in for that should be important only to me, but what kind of America I believe in.

I believe in an America where the separation of church and state is absolute — where no Catholic prelate would tell the President (should he be a Catholic) how to act and no Protestant minister would tell his parishioners for whom to vote — where no church or church school is granted any public funds or political preference — and where no man is denied public office merely because his religion differs from the President who might appoint him or the people who might elect him.

I believe in an America that is officially neither Catholic, Protestant nor Jewish — **where no public official either requests or accepts instructions on public policy from the Pope, the National Council of Churches or any other ecclesiastical source — <u>where no religious body seeks to impose its will directly or indirectly upon the general populace or the public acts of its officials</u>** — and where religious liberty is so indivisible that an act against one church is treated as an act against all.

For, while this year it may be a Catholic against whom the finger of suspicion is pointed, in other years it has been, and may someday be again, a Jew — or a Quaker — or a Unitarian — or a Baptist. It was Virginia's harassment of Baptist preachers, for example, that led to Jefferson's statute of religious freedom. Today, I may be the victim — but tomorrow it may be you — until the whole fabric of our harmonious society is ripped apart at a time of great national peril.

Finally, I believe in an America where religious intolerance will someday end — where all men and all churches are treated as equal — where every man has the same right to attend or not to attend the church of his choice — where there is no Catholic vote, no anti-Catholic vote, no bloc voting of any kind — and where Catholics, Protestants and Jews, both the lay and the pastoral level, will refrain from those attitudes of disdain and division which have so often marred their works in the past, and promote instead the American ideal of brotherhood.

That is the kind of America in which I believe. And it represents the kind of Presidency in which I believe — a great office that must be neither humbled by making it the instrument of any religious group, nor tarnished by arbitrarily withholding it, its occupancy from the members of any religious group. I believe in a President whose views on religion are his own private affair, neither imposed upon him by the nation or imposed by the nation upon him as a condition to holding that office.

I would not look with favor upon a President working to subvert the First Amendment's guarantees of religious liberty (nor would our system of checks and balances permit him to do so). And neither do I look with favor upon those who would work to subvert Article VI of the Constitution by requiring a religious test — even by indirection — for if they disagree with that safeguard, they should be openly working to repeal it.

I want a chief executive whose public acts are responsible to all and obligated to none — who can attend any ceremony, service or dinner his office may appropriately require him to fulfill — and whose fulfillment of his Presidential office is not limited or conditioned by any religious oath, ritual or obligation.

This is the kind of America I believe in — and this is the kind of America I fought for in the South Pacific and the kind my brother died for in Europe. No one suggested then that we might have a "divided loyalty," that we did "not believe in liberty or that we belonged to a disloyal group that threatened "the freedoms for which our forefathers died."

And in fact this is the kind of America for which our forefathers did die when they fled here to escape religious test oaths, that denied office to members of less favored churches, when they fought for the Constitution, the Bill of Rights, the Virginia Statute of Religious Freedom — and when they fought at the shrine I visited today — the Alamo. For side by side with Bowie and Crockett died Fuentes and McCafferty and Bailey and Bedillio and Carey — but no one knows whether they were Catholics or not. For there was no religious test there.

I ask you tonight to follow in that tradition, to judge me on the basis of fourteen years in the Congress — on my declared stands against an ambassador to the Vatican, against unconstitutional aid to parochial schools, and against any boycott of the public schools (which I attended myself) — and instead of doing this do not judge me on the basis of these pamphlets and publications we have all seen that carefully select quotations out of context from the statements of Catholic Church leaders, usually in other countries, frequently in other centuries, and rarely relevant to any situation here — and always omitting of course, that statement of the American bishops in 1948 which strongly endorsed church-state separation.

I do not consider these other quotations binding upon my public acts — why should you? But let me say, with respect to other countries, that I am wholly opposed to the state being used by any religious group, Catholic or Protestant, to compel, prohibit or prosecute the free exercise of any other religion. And that goes for any persecution at any time, by anyone, in any country.

And I hope that you and I condemn with equal fervor those nations which deny it to Catholics. And rather than cite the misdeeds of those who differ, I would also cite the record of the Catholic Church in such nations as France and Ireland — and the independence of such statesmen as de Gaulle and Adenauer.

But let me stress again that these are my views — for, contrary to common newspaper usage, I am not the

Catholic candidate for President [but the candidate] who happens also to be a Catholic.

I do not speak for my church on public matters — and the church does not speak for me.

Whatever issue may come before me as President, if I should be elected — on birth control, divorce, censorship, gambling, or any other subject — I will make my decision in accordance with these views, in accordance with what my conscience tells me to be in the national interest, and without regard to outside religious pressure or dictate. And no power or threat of punishment could cause me to decide otherwise.

But if the time should ever come — and I do not concede any conflict to be remotely possible — when my office would require me to either violate my conscience, or violate the national interest, then I would resign the office, and I hope any other conscientious public servant would do likewise.

But I do not intend to apologize for these views to my critics of either Catholic or Protestant faith, nor do I intend to disavow either my views or my church in order to win this election. If I should lose on the real issues, I shall return to my seat in the Senate satisfied that I tried my best and was fairly judged.

But if this election is decided on the basis that 40,000,000 Americans lost their chance of being President on the day they were baptized, then it is the whole nation that will be the loser in the eyes of Catholics and non-Catholics around the world, in the eyes of history, and in the eyes of our own people.

But if, on the other hand, I should win this election, I shall devote every effort of mind and spirit to fulfilling the oath of the Presidency — practically identical, I might add with the oath I have taken for fourteen years in the Congress. For, without reservation, I can, and I quote "solemnly swear that I will faithfully execute the office of President of the United States and will preserve, protect, and defend the Constitution so help me God."[1] (emphasis added.)

THE DIFFERENCES

Let me address the sections I emphasized of Jack Kennedy's speech to clearly discriminate between the principle he was espousing, separation of church and state, and the contradiction that is displayed in Mormon Doctrine.

1. **I believe in an America where the separation of church and state is absolute — where no Catholic prelate would tell the President (should he be a Catholic) how to act;"** and "**where no public official either requests or accepts instructions on public policy from the Pope, the National Council of Churches or any other ecclesiastical source — where no religious body seeks to impose its will directly or indirectly upon the general populace or the public acts of its officials.**" As listed in Chapter Five, 13th Mormon Prophet, Ezra Taft Benson, delivered a speech at BYU titled, "The Fourteen Fundamentals of a Prophet." Some of these 14 points specifically show contradictions between President Kennedy's speech and Mormon Doctrine: (1) The prophet is the only man who speaks for the Lord in everything; (5) The prophet is not required to have any particular earthly training or credentials to speak on any subject or act on any matter at any time; (8) The prophet is not limited by men's reasoning; (9) The prophet can receive revelation on any matter—temporal or spiritual; (10) The prophet may be involved in civic matters; (11) The two groups who have the greatest difficulty in following the prophet are the proud who are learned and

the proud who are rich; (14) The prophet and the presidency—the living prophet and the First Presidency—follow them and be blessed; reject them and suffer.[2]

President Kennedy is making the point that he believes in the separation of church and state so that no Catholic prelate would tell the President "how to act," or would try to impose "their will" upon the President. Fundamentals 1, 5, 8, 9, 10, 11, and 14, leave no doubt that Mormonism believes it has the divine right, via God through His earthly mouthpiece, the Prophet, to tell any Mormon "how to act" and "what to do," on any matter, religious or civic. The Prophet speaks for God, as do "The Brethren." Any issue, public, personal, religious, or political, is within the purview of the "mouthpiece of God."

2. I want a chief executive whose public acts are responsible to all and obligated to none — who can attend any ceremony, service or dinner his office may appropriately require him to fulfill — and whose fulfillment of his Presidential office is not limited or conditioned by any religious oath, ritual or obligation.

The above quote by Jack Kennedy couldn't be a more stark contrast between the ideals of a free American electorate and the rigidly controlled Mormon populace. As thoroughly outlined in Chapters Three-Seven, Mormons are under complete domination by their religious doctrinal beliefs. Their belief in the divine right of their Priesthood to absolutely control all aspects of their lives, from the Prophet to local level leaders, culminates in the battery of oaths that they swear and are held in bondage to from baptism to the Temple Ceremony oaths. These oaths, along with the belief that "The Brethren" will be standing next to Jesus and acting as their judges on "Judgment Morning," are an incredibly powerful obstacle that a Mormon must set aside in order to be unencumbered and objective. If the Priesthood, from the local level to Church Headquarters in Salt Lake City, "counsels" a Mormon to follow a certain political path, agenda, or to act in a particular way, the pressure to act as directed is in exact opposition to the pervading attitude—responsible to all and obligated to none—that Jack Kennedy is demanding of in his candid speech.

D. Michael Quinn wrote an exhaustive two part series on the Mormon Power Pyramid: *The Mormon Hierarchy, Origins of Power* and, *The Mormon Hierarchy, Extensions of Power*. In *Extensions of Power*, Quinn takes four chapters (Chapters 7-10) and almost 200 pages of fully documented text to discuss the Mormon Church's intrusive involvement in local, state and national politics. When it comes to politics, the Mormon Church acts like a massive corporation trying to protect its equally massive financial holdings, rather than an ecclesiastical body trying to follow the teachings of Christ.

WHAT'S THE POINT?

Mormons being controlled by the leadership of their Church cannot be compared to the Jack Kennedy argument. The doctrinal positions of Mormonism are directly at odds with a free and unencumbered politician, political appointee or any governmental position of power. The Mormon belief in "Following the Prophet," with its carry-over to "The Brethren" and all the way down to local level Priesthood authority, places a Mormon in literal subjection to Mormon Priesthood leaders. The obligations of numerous oaths, some sworn in absolute secrecy in the Temple rituals, place a Mormon in compulsory servitude to the Church and its Priesthood line of authority. Couple this with the stated belief that the Mormon Prophet has the divine right to involve himself in civic matters, is divinely endowed to speak on any earthly subject, is the earthly king proclaiming the Kingdom of God through the Mormon Church, and you have all the ingredients required for direct meddling by an outside force into all levels of American Government, from the Oval Office to the local School Board.

[1] John F. Kennedy, Address to the Southern Baptist Leaders, http://usinfo.state.gov/usa/infousa/facts/democrac/66.htm

[2] *Fourteen Fundamentals in Following the Prophet* by Ezra Taft Benson, http://www.lds-mormon.com/fourteen.shtml

Chapter Nine

MOUNTAIN MEADOWS MASSACRE

Chapters Nine and Ten of this book are application chapters. There will be a profound effort by Mormon apologists to rationalize away the documentation provided in this book to support each of the preceding chapters and the distinct Mormon doctrines that run counter to the acceptable ideology of the American voter with respect to the political landscape. These unique Mormon doctrines which show a clear and distinct aberration from the acceptable standards of participation in the American political arena will take on a new light when contrasted with the real events they helped to shape and influence.

Two terribly tragic events have happened to this country on September the 11th. Americans will never forget the horror of seeing the news channel replays of the planes striking the Twin Towers in New York, the Pentagon in flames, and the reports of a fourth plane going down in a field in Pennsylvania. We should never forget that frightful day in United States History. September 11, 2001, was the second tragedy our country suffered on September 11th. The first was a brutal massacre in a remote meadow in Southwestern Utah called Mountain Meadows on September 11, 1857.

On that awful day, 150 years ago, 120 unarmed non-Mormon, men, women and children were brutally murdered in cold blood by Mormons and Indians on the trail to Tulare, California. This ghastly event is known in American history as the "Mountain Meadows Massacre." This brutal act of domestic terrorism is only surpassed in the annals of American history by the Oklahoma City Bombing, where 168 Americans lost their lives. The Oklahoma City Bombing was planned and conducted by two men. Mountain Meadows was planned and executed by Mormon Church Priesthood Leadership and at least 60, possibly as many as 100, Mormon men and an unknown number of Indian accomplices.

Why is this event so important in relation to the Mormon Church? It is difficult to understand how at least 60 Mormon men, who believed they were doing God's will, could lure 120 men, women and children, out into the open under a white truce flag and then turn and brutally murder them. A study of the Mountain Meadows Massacre takes one on a walk through the morass of blasphemous Mormon doctrines and unquestioning allegiance to Mormon Priesthood leadership that would steer these Mormon men to commit the most despicable crime in American history. The Mormon doctrines that have been detailed in the previous chapters will be played out here in the telling of this gruesome, horrid act of religious fanaticism that simply must be told.

HOW IT BEGAN

In April of 1857 a wealthy wagon train, known as the Fancher-Baker Train, left Beller Spring, Arkansas with as many as 1,000 head of cattle. After traveling the Cherokee Trail, they arrived in Salt Lake City on August 3rd where they were met with a very chilly reception.

Two important events happened in Salt Lake City just prior to their arrival: (1) News had come that a popular

Mormon Apostle, Parley P. Pratt, had been murdered "as he attempted to escape from one Hector McLean, the angry husband of a woman he had taken as his tenth wife. But to overheated emotions in Utah, the apostle was killed for his religious beliefs. Like Joseph and Hyrum Smith, he was a martyr whose blood cried for vengeance."[1] The wagon train members' only crime was having come from the state of Arkansas where Parley P. Pratt had been killed. Completely false rumors circulated among the Mormons that members of the wagon train had been involved in Apostle Pratt's murder as well as having been in the mob which killed Joseph and Hyrum Smith. (2) Utah was in a state of rebellion. The Mormons left Illinois to get away from the laws of the United States. When they arrived in Utah it was a Mexican territory. With the United States winning the War with Mexico, Utah become a Territory of the United States and the Mormons were once again under U.S. law. Brigham Young ran Utah as a theocratic state and refused to be governed under United States Law. Then President James Buchanan, dispatched Colonel Johnson of the Second U.S. Calvary to bring Utah back under control. This news arrived in Salt Lake City, just one week prior to the train's arrival.

PREPARE THE PEOPLE FOR WAR!

The day the train arrived in Salt Lake City, Brigham Young dispatched his 2nd Counselor in the First Presidency, George A. Smith, to prepare the people for war.

"Traveling fast, Smith averaged nearly forty miles a day over the 250 miles or so from the territorial capital to Iron County. Even so, he found time at each settlement along the southern trail to California to instruct local leaders to sell no grain or other supplies to "gentile" emigrants, to harvest and hide up their wheat early, and to drill and outfit their military forces for active operations to repel the approaching U.S. Army expedition. Wherever he went, the apostle fanned the militant spirit of the reformation. According to legend, Smith told Parowan settlers that bones make a good fertilizer for fruit trees. As for American soldiers coming to Utah, he went on, he could "think of nothing better that they could do than to feed a fruit tree in Zion." He later said, "in spite of all I could do, I found myself preaching a military discourse." At Harmony, a few miles south of Cedar City, Rachel Lee said Smith "delivered a discourse on the spirit that actuated the United States toward this people—full of hostility and virulence."[2]

On August the 5th the Fancher-Baker train headed south continuing its trek to Tulare, California. The train met much hostility, as no one would sell provisions to them, and the Mormons would not allow them to stop and graze their cattle along the way where they could prevent it. They arrived at Mountain Meadows on September 5th and encamped, intending to allow their cattle to graze on the luscious grass of the meadow.

"George A. Smith arrived in Great Salt Lake City at 4:00 P.M. on August 31, "having traveled about seven hundred miles of rough roads and preached in all the Settlements of Iron, Washington, and Beaver Counties." The next day Jacob Hamblin [Indian Agent] brought ten or twelve Indians "to See Brigham the great Morman chief."...

As the Fancher train made camp some seventy miles north of Mountain Meadows on the evening of September 1, 1857, Young met for about an hour with the southern chiefs to implement his plan to stop overland emigration on the southern road....

Describing his meeting with the Paiutes in his journal, Young claimed he could "hardly restrain them from exterminating the 'Americans.'" In truth, that Tuesday night Young encouraged the Indians to seize the stock of the wagon trains on the southern route. Jaunita Brooks [author, The Mountain Meadows Massacre, 1950] recognized the importance of this crucial meeting but could only speculate on its purpose. Historians have long assumed no detailed eyewitness account of the interview existed, but the diary of Young's brother-in-law and interpreter, Dimick Huntington, has survived in the LDS Archives since 1859. Describing the September 1 parlay, Huntington wrote:

"I gave them all the cattle that had gone to Cal the south rout it made them open their eyes they sayed that you told us not to steal so I have but now they have come to fight us & you for when they kill us they kill you they sayd the[y] was afraid to fight the Americans & so would raise [allies] and we fight"

The language of Huntington's critical journal entry is archaic, but its meaning is clear. Even a devout Mormon historian has identified the "I" in this entry as Brigham Young."[3]

DIRECT LEADERSHIP INVOLVEMENT!

The above quote from *Blood of the Prophets*, published in August 2002, the first book on this tragedy since Mormon author Juanita Brooks' book in 1950, provides the 'smoking gun' diary entry of Dimick Huntington, which directly ties Brigham Young to this event. This link has been assumed since the incident, but no direct tie has been uncovered until author Will Bagley's printing of Dimick Huntington's diary account.

On Sunday the 6th of September, the day before the first attack, a council was held in Parowan to discus the fate of the wagon train. The Mormon historian B. H. Roberts admits that such a meeting was held:

> "It was customary for the local leading men at Cedar and from the smaller settlements in its vicinity to gather in a **council meeting** after the close of the regular Sunday services of the church, to consider the questions of local community interest. At such a meeting on the 6th of September the question concerning the conduct of, and **what ought to be done with,** the Arkansas emigrants was brought up and debated. Some in the council **were in favor of destroying them,** and others were not."[4] (emphasis added.)

It is plain to see by the diary entry of Dimick Huntington that Brigham Young had declared the emigrants to be enemies and Apostle Smith had met with local church leaders on his trip to Southern Utah defining Brigham's position and intentions. On the morning of September 7th, under direction of Mormon Bishop, John D. Lee, as ordered by Mormon Stake President, Isaac C. Haight, the Indians surprise attacked the wagon train killing and wounding many. The emigrants quickly returned fire, killing several Indians, and fortified the train for battle. The Indians, not expecting such resistance, quickly lost their taste for this battle and a state of siege set in which lasted until September 11th.

News of the failed Indian attempt to wipe out the train reached the Mormon authorities in Iron County. They met, decided, and dispatched militia to the Meadows to deal with the emigrants. The decision to take action was delivered by John M. Higbee, who was not only the 1st Counselor to Stake

President Haight, but also a Major in the Iron County Militia (a remnant of the Nauvoo Legion). The plan was to have John D. Lee, a Mormon Bishop, **lure the emigrants under a white truce flag** to surrender and lay down their arms in exchange for safe passage to Cedar City. Once the emigrants were lured out on the meadow away from the wagons and their firearms, they were to be massacred leaving "**none who could tell the tale**" alive.

On the morning of September 11, 1857, John D. Lee and William Bateman approached the train with a **white truce flag** and laid out the diabolical offer. The emigrants agreed, believing the Mormon militia awaiting escort duties on the meadow were their deliverers. The women and children **eight years old and older** were led out in single file first, followed by the men. Each man had an armed militia member at his side. **The wounded and children seven years of age and under were loaded into two separate wagons.** Upon the command of Major Higbee "**Do your duty,**" the Mormon militia turned and killed the men and then the Indians, having laid in wait in ambush, joined by Mormons disguised as Indians brutally murdered the women and children. The militia on the wagons turned, and at point blank range, executed the wounded. In spite of the claims by the Mormon Church for years that the Indians did most of the killing and only a few whites participated, "Nephi Johnson later maintained that his fellow militiamen did most of the killing."[5] In just a matter of minutes the horrific, unthinkable act was done. The seventeen children under the age of eight who were spared were then distributed to various Mormon homes.

HOW COULD THIS HAPPEN?

This atrocity defies rationality. How do you get between 60 and 100 men to brutally murder unarmed men women and children? "Two facts made the case even more difficult to fathom. First, nothing that any of the emigrants purportedly did or said, even if *all* of it were true, came close to justifying their deaths. Second, the large majority of perpetrators led decent, nonviolent lives before and after the massacre."[6]

A study of Mormon doctrines uncovers the answer to the question: How could such a dastardly deed such as this ever happen? Unfortunately for these emigrants they were in the wrong place at the wrong time. The news of the murder of Mormon Apostle Parley P. Pratt, and the subsequent false claim that these emigrants were accomplices to that death as well as the death of Joseph and Hyrum Smith, placed them under the **'Law of Vengeance'**: "You and each of you do solemnly promise and vow that you will pray, and never cease to pray, and never cease to importune high heaven **to avenge the blood of the prophets on this nation,** and that you will teach this to your children and your children's children unto the third and fourth generation." "All bow your heads and say yes."[7] **This oath was sworn by every Mormon who participated in the Temple Ceremony** until it was finally removed February 15, 1927.

Not only were these emigrants worthy of death under the 'Law of Vengeance,' but also under the **Mormon doctrine of 'Blood Atonement.'** This Mormon doctrine states that there are certain sins that a person can commit that are outside the cleansing blood of Jesus Christ and can only be atoned for **by shedding one's own blood.** The following list details Mormon crimes requiring the blood of the person committing them to cleanse them from these sins:

(1) Murder
(2) Adultery and Immorality
(3) Stealing
(4) Using the name of the Lord in vain
(5) For not receiving the gospel

(6) For marriage to an African
(7) For covenant breaking
(8) For apostasy
(9) For lying
(10) For counterfeiting
(11) For condemning Joseph Smith or consenting to his death[8]

ABSOLUTE AUTHORITY!

The Mormon men, who carried out this terrible heinous crime, believed they were following the orders of the Mormon Priesthood as well as their Military Superiors. As developed in Chapter Three, the Mormon Priesthood has absolute authority and as detailed in Chapter Five, "Following the Prophet," is a requirement for salvation and exaltation. The following quotes emphasize that point:

Brigham Young said "...it is reported that I have said that whoever the President appoints, I am still the Governor. I repeat it, all hell cannot remove me. (cries of 'amen') I am still your Governor. (cries of 'glory to God.') I will still rule this people until God himself permits another to take my place. I wish I could say as much for the other officers of the government. The greater part of them are a gambling, drinking, whoring set....Do you think I'll obey or respect them? No! I'll say as I did the other day, when the flag was hauled down from before the Military Quarters — **'Let them take down the American Flag; we can do without it.'** (great applause, stamping of feet and yells.)"[9] (emphasis added.)

Joseph Smith said the following: "God made Aaron to be the mouthpiece of the children of Israel, and **he will make me to be God to you in his stead,** and the elders to be mouth for me; and if you don't like it you must lump it."[10] (emphasis added.)

Brigham Young said: "The first principle of our cause and work is to understand that there is a prophet in the church, and that he is at the head of the Church of Christ on earth. **Who called Joseph Smith to be a prophet?** Did the people or God? **God, and not the people,** called him. Had the people gathered together and appointed one of their number to be a prophet, he would be accountable to the people, but, inasmuch as **he was called of God, and not by the people, he is accountable to God only**…and not to any man on earth. The twelve apostles are accountable to the prophet and not to the church for the course they pursue, and **we have learned to go and do as the prophet tells us**." – From sermon by Brigham Young, at Nauvoo, 1843, published in Millennial Star, Liverpool, England, Vol. XXI., page 741.[11] (emphasis added.)

Heber C. Kimball, 1st Counselor to Brigham Young said: "Did you actually know Joseph Smith? No. Do you know brother Brigham? No. Do you know brother Heber? No, you do not. Do you know the Twelve? You do not, if you did, you would begin to know God, and **learn that those men who are chosen to direct and counsel you are near kindred to God and to Jesus Christ, for the keys, power, and authority of the kingdom of God are in that lineage**."[12] (emphasis added.)

Heber C. Kimball delivered the following intense sermon: "In regard to our situation and circumstances in these valleys, brethren, WAKE UP! WAKE UP, YE ELDERS OF ISRAEL, AND LIVE TO GOD and none else; and **learn to do as you are told,** both old and young: learn to do as you are told for the future…. **But if you are told by your leader to do a thing, do it. None of your business whether it is right or wrong**….They do not know that by believing on any man's testimony they increase in knowledge, wisdom, and the power of God. They forget that. Do you not see that I can learn more to be led than I can to lead, if I have the right man to lead me? **Brother Brigham is my leader; he is my Prophet, my Seer, and my Revelator; and whatever he says, that is for me to do; and it is not for me to question him one word, nor to question God a minute. Do you not see?** I will tell you what is right for me to do. If there is time, (and that there is not, it is not necessary) go along and bow down before the Lord God. Say I, "Father, help me to be faithful and do the words of brother Brigham, my leader, that I may see glory in it, and that I may see immortality and eternal lives in it."[13] (emphasis added.)

We think these Mormon missionaries are laboring under a mistake in one particular. **It is not so much the particular doctrines, which Smith upholds and practices, however abominable they may be in themselves, that our citizens care about—as it is the anti-republican nature of the organization, over which he has almost supreme control—and which is trained and disciplined to act in accordance with his selfish will. The spectacle presented in Smith's case of a civil, ecclesiastical and military leader, united in one and the same person, with power over life and liberty, can never find favor in the minds of sound and thinking Republicans.** The day has gone by when the precepts of Divine Truth, could be propagated at the point of the sword—or the Bible made the medium of corrupt men to gratify their lustful appetites and sordid desires—[*Quincy Whig*.[14] (emphasis added.)

All of the above quotes are disturbing. When you look at these quotes and understand that the Mormon people absolutely believed them, it becomes easier to understand what is not understandable: how every day men could commit such an unthinkably brutal and heinous crime as the Mountain Meadows Massacre.

The last quote above from the *Nauvoo Expositor* (the newspaper that Joseph Smith ordered destroyed and landed him in the Carthage Jail where he was killed in a gun battle with a mob) was a reprint from the *Quincy Whig*. This quote is very telling. Mormons constantly promote the image of their being persecuted solely on the premise of their religious beliefs. The reprinted article from the *Quincy Whig* counters the "religious persecution syndrome" with the fact that the local opposition was due to the concern by the area citizenry that Mormonism's civil, ecclesiastical, and military power was being vested in one person. The United States Constitution correctly separates powers to prevent abuses by any one person or group. This very idea of preventing uncontrolled and unchecked power was the foundation upon which the Constitution was written. The citizens of Quincy were justly concerned. This concentration of power did not die with Joseph Smith in a jail in Carthage, Illinois. Unfortunately this ideology went West and found its place in the Mormonism of Territorial Utah. This concentration of power led to the tragedy of the Mountain Meadows Massacre. See Appendix One for more information.

The mentality of the above quotes should frighten any thinking person. The absolute control exuded in the above quotes is alarming. Joseph Smith said he was God to the people. Brigham Young said Joseph and all subsequent prophets were/are called of God and therefore answer only to God. Mormons are to "go and do as the prophet tells us." These quotes tally up to one supreme idea: total, utter, blind obedience. When you top this all off with the statement "learn to do as you are told…none of your business whether it is right or wrong," by Heber C. Kimball, in conjunction with all the other listed absolute control statements of the Mormon Priesthood, it is a train wreck just waiting to happen. The demonstration of this combined authority and power over the Mormon people was evident when we realize that the Mormon Militia issuing the orders on that fateful day were also the senior Mormon Priesthood holders in Southern Utah. In accordance with Mormon doctrine, they were speaking for the prophet since they had been given direction by the Mormon Apostle George A. Smith who had just left Southern Utah on his "prepare for war" trip. Here you have the recipe for the massacre that followed.

DENIAL. BRIGHAM KNEW!

The Mormon Church then, and today, denies direct involvement with the massacre. In official Mormon writings the Mormons involved are dismissed as "other white men" and are not identified as Senior Mormon Leadership. When pressed, the Mormon Church admits Mormons were involved but describes them as 'fanatics of the worst stamp.' Here is a short laundry list of the 'fanatics of the worst stamp': 2 Stake Presidents (one was the mayor of Cedar City) and a 1st and 2nd Counselor in a Stake Presidency (one was the Marshall of Cedar City), 4 Stake High Councilmen, 4 Bishops and one 1st Counselor in a Bishopric, 2 City Councilmen, and 1 Attorney at Law. This tally is 27% of the 60 known perpetrators and 16% of the possibly 100 Mormons involved. These men could hardly be classified as 'fanatics of the worst stamp'; not to escape attention here is the fact that these men were not only the senior leadership of the Church in Southern Utah, but also, the senior Militia Officers and senior leaders in Civil Government and law enforcement. To insinuate that these men who were the senior ecclesiastical, military, civil, and law enforcement leaders in Southern Utah, and no one noticed that they were "fanatics of the worst stamp," and removed them from their collective offices, is a deliberate act of deception on the part of the Mormon Church. This many evil men in a multitude of leadership positions that escapes everyone's notice, is simply not possible. The Mormon Church's denial of involvement is "deception of the worst stamp!"

The Church also tries to allude that Brigham Young never knew about the details of the massacre until years later. Ridiculous! Mormon Bishop, John D. Lee, stated in his court trial, that he gave Brigham Young a full report immediately after the event. This is corroborated by Mormon Apostle Wilford Woodruff's Diary entry for Sept 29th, 1857: "John D. Lee also arrived from Harmony with an express and an awful tale of Blood."[15]

Jacob Hamblin, the Indian Agent who brought the Indian Chiefs to meet with Brigham on September 1, 1857, and on whose land Mountain Meadows lay, also told Brigham: "Jacob Hamblin, a reputable witness, testified at the second Lee trial that 'soon after it [the massacre] happened, 'he reported to Brigham Young and George A. Smith what Lee had told him of the affair; of the part that white men had taken in it; and that in greater detail than he had given it, or was able to give in his testimony in court,'...**Brigham Young said to him that 'as soon as we can get a court of justice we will ferret this thing out, but till then, don't say anything about it.'"**[16] (emphasis added.)

A year and a half after the tragedy, when the Federal Government heard of the massacre, Army Brevet Major Carleton, of the First Dragoons, was ordered to conduct an investigation. He was horrified at what he and his men found. Upon arrival at the Meadows, **the bones were scattered across the plain, with evidence of coyote and wolf gnawing.** The Mormons had dragged the bodies into a ravine and thrown some bush over them, leaving them easily accessible to wild animals. Major Carleton directed, the bones be gathered, buried, and a twelve-foot high conical shaped rock cairn be erected with a twelve foot cross placed atop it facing Salt Lake City. The cedar cross had the words etched upon it **"Vengeance is mine. I will repay saith the Lord."**

Joseph Fielding Smith, 10th Mormon prophet, in 1950 wrote "Lee also reported in person, laying the blame solely to the Indians. Governor Young wept bitterly and was horrified at the recital of the tale."[17] Quite a different story is related by the diaries of the era. Shortly after the Army had left the Meadows, Brigham Young visited the site and upon reading the inscription on the cross he reacted with an attitude quite different than that reported by Joseph Fielding Smith: **"It should be vengeance is mine and I have taken a little."** One of Young's escorts lassoed the cross with a rope, turned his horse, and pulled it down. **Brigham Young "didn't say a word,"** recalled Dudley Leavitt. "He didn't give an order. He just lifted his right arm to the square, and in five minutes there wasn't one stone left upon another. **He didn't have to tell us what needed to be done. We understood."**[18] (emphasis added.)

Part of Major Carleton's investigation revealed that the spoils (livestock, wagons, rifles, clothing and household goods) were delivered to the Church's Tithing Office and sold, with the Church retaining the money: "...a party of armed men under the command of a man named John D. Lee, who was then a Bishop in the Church, but who has since (as Brigham Young says) been deposed, left the settlements of Beaver City (north of Parowan), Parowan City, and Cedar City on what was called "a secret expedition," and after an absence of a few days returned, bringing back strange wagons, cattle, horses, mules, and other household property. **There is legal proof that this property was sold at the Official Tithing Office of the Church**...."[19] (emphasis added.)

THE SEVENTEEN CHILDREN

During his investigation, Major Carleton learned about what became of the 17 children who survived the massacre. A year and a half after the massacre, the children were recovered by Federal Indian Superintendent, Jacob Forney. In the same document cited above, we read that Major Carleton learned that the Mormons had billed the Federal Government for the children's room and board and lied that they had to purchase the children from the Indians. Carleton then made the following statement: **"Has there ever been an act which at all equaled this in devilish hardihood, in more than devilish effrontery? Never, but one: and even then the price was but '30 pieces of silver.'"**[20]

The Mormons reported that they had to purchase the children from the Indians. However, when the children were recovered and asked about this, they stated that **they had never been in the custody of the Indians**. These spared children bring up another bizarre piece of the Mormon doctrine puzzle.

Why were these children "seven years of age and under" spared? The answer was to ensure none of the Temple Mormons involved "shed innocent blood." In Mormon doctrine, once a person has gone through the Mormon Temple Ceremony and received their "endowments," they may commit any sin, except the "shedding of innocent blood," and will still become a God in the next life: "Verily, verily, I say unto you, if a man marry a wife according to my word, and they are sealed by the Holy Spirit of promise, according to mine appointment, and he or she shall commit any sin or transgression of the new and everlasting covenant whatever, and all manner of blasphemies, and **if they commit no murder wherein they shed innocent blood, yet they shall come forth in the first resurrection, and enter into their exaltation;**..."[21] (emphasis added.)

The following quotes define the Mormon definition of "innocence": (1) In the gospel sense, innocence is the state of purity and freedom from sin which men must possess to gain salvation in the kingdom of God. (Alma 11:37.) **Little children live in a state of perfect innocence and consequently are saved without works on their part.**[22] (emphasis added.) (2) Attainment of the age and state of accountability is a gradual process. Thus the Lord says "power is not given unto Satan to tempt little children, until they begin to become accountable before me." (D. & C. 29:47.) Children who develop normally become accountable **"when eight years old"** (D. & C. 68:27)...[23] (emphasis added.)

As previously partially quoted, Mormon Apostle Wilford Woodruff's Diary entry for Sept 29th, 1857 tells of John D. Lee's initial report of the incident to Brigham Young: "John D. Lee also arrived from Harmony with an express and an awful tale of Blood. A company of California emigrants, of about 150 men, women and children, many of them belonging to the mob in Missouri and Illinois, had been massacred.... **Brother Lee said that he did not think there was a drop of innocent blood in their camp."**[24] (emphasis added.) **This statement has no bearing to anyone involved in this crime except Temple Mormons.** If Temple Mormons were not involved in this crime, the doctrine of "innocent blood" would never have been mentioned by this Mormon Apostle who would become their 4th Prophet. It is clear all of the information about this massacre was relayed to Brigham Young, including the involvement of Mormons who had been through the Temple Endowment Ceremony. Brigham's many statements that the Indians were the perpetrators of this crime was a lie.

MURDERERS REWARDED!

Not only did Brigham Young know the details of this cold blooded murder, he rewarded the two major players: **"In his private sealing room, Brigham Young married Emma Batchelor to John D. Lee** on January 7, 1858. To celebrate, Lee provided a treat of cherry brandy, sugar, and liquors, while Mrs. Ezra Taft Benson "made the bride a cake & a good dinner." Lee's guests, including Isaac Haight, ate "drank & made merry & had a firstrate good time." **The prophet married Isaac Haight to Elizabeth Summers** on January 24, the day before Lee, Haight and their new wives left Salt Lake. Lee gave Haight a brace of Colt Revolvers, perhaps as a wedding gift. Lee had taken the initiative in contracting his marriage to Emma, but the timing of the two weddings led to charges that the new brides were the men's reward for their work at Mountain Meadows."[25] (emphasis added.)

There is no question that Brigham Young knew that Isaac Haight as the Stake President was the senior Mormon Priesthood Leader in the area that had direct control over the execution of the Mountain Meadows Massacre. He also knew of John D. Lee's (his adopted son) involvement as well. Where is the outrage? Where is the justice? Where are the disciplinary actions of the Church and the Government? Instead, we find rewards given of additional wives to the two most culpable on scene perpetrators of this horrible crime, by the man who ordered the Indians to initiate the attack.

BRIGHAM LIED!

Six years after the fact, Brigham Young had no qualms of standing in the pulpit and lying about the massacre: "...A company of emigrants were traveling on the route to California. **Nearly all of that company were destroyed**

by Indians. That unfortunate affair has been laid to the charge of the whites. A certain judge that was then in the territory wanted the whole army to accompany him to Iron County to try the **whites** for the murder of that company of emigrants.... **but to this day they have not touched the matter, for fear the Mormons would be acquitted from the charge of having any hand in it, and our enemies would thus be deprived of a favorite topic to talk about, when urging hostility against us.** 'The Mountain Meadows Massacre! Only think of the Mountain Meadows Massacre!!' Is their cry from one end of the land to the other."[26] (emphasis added.) When Brigham Young delivered this sermon he knew full well that the Indians did not act alone. However, such is the rewriting of Mormon history, and in this case, the falsifying of American history.

TRIAL AND EXECUTION

The uproar across the Nation would not allow this crime to go unpunished, no matter how much Brigham Young and the rest of the Church hierarchy tried to obstruct justice. It was decided to blame the entire event on John D. Lee, and even though at least 60 Mormon men were involved, possibly as many as 100, he alone was tried and excommunicated in 1870: "John D. Lee was excommunicated from the Church with the injunction from President Young that under no circumstances should he ever be admitted as a member again."[27]

John D. Lee was eventually arrested, brought to trial, and acquitted in May 1876. The jury was made up of 8 Mormons and 4 Gentiles (non-Mormons) and, you guessed it, the vote for conviction was exactly 8 against, and 4 to convict, perfectly splitting between Mormons and Gentiles. The outrage across the country was too much for the Mormon Church to bear. A second trial was convened and this time the jury was all Mormons; however, Brigham had given the nod to subdue the outrage of the first trial and the verdict was unanimous for conviction. What had changed from the first trial to the second? Nothing had changed, except the head nod from Church Leadership. In March of 1877, Lee was pronounced guilty and sentenced to die on the spot of the crime, Mountain Meadows, where he was executed by firing squad March 23, 1877.

Just before he was shot, he made this statement: "It seems I have to be made a victim—a victim must be had, and I am the victim. I am sacrificed to satisfy the feelings—the vindictive feelings, or in other words to gratify parties.... I am a true believer in the gospel of Jesus Christ. I do not believe everything that is now being taught and practiced by Brigham Young. I do not care who hears it.... I studied to make this man's will my pleasure for thirty years. See, now, what I have come to this day! **I have been sacrificed in a cowardly, dastardly manner.** I cannot help it. It is my last word—it is so...Sacrifice a man that has waited upon them, that has wandered and endured with them in the days of adversity, true from the beginnings of the Church! And I am now singled out and I am sacrificed in this manner! What confidence can I have in such a man! I have none, and I don't think my father in heaven has any."[28] (emphasis added.)

Why was John D. Lee shot by firing squad? Reading thus far, you should know the answer: **Blood Atonement.** Death by firing squad allowed him to "shed his own blood" to cover his sin. Utah allowed capital punishment by firing squad to allow Mormons "to shed their own blood," until March 24, 2004. In his book, *Mormon Doctrine*, Mormon Apostle Bruce R. McConkie makes the following statement under the heading of Hanging: "Hanging. *See* BLOOD ATONEMENT DOCTRINE, CAPITAL PUNISHMENT, MURDERERS. As a mode of capital punishment, ***hanging*** or execution on a gallows **does not comply** with the law of blood atonement,

for the blood is not shed."[29] (emphasis added.) John D. Lee was executed by firing squad so his blood could be spilled, and under the Mormon doctrine of "Blood Atonement," he could atone for his own sins.

LEE RESTORED TO GODHOOD!

His atonement in the eyes of the Mormon Church must have been accepted by their god, since after years of petitions by his ancestors The First Presidency and the Quorum of the Twelve restored his Church blessings: "Temple worker Merrit L. Norton had presented the family's request, and **on April 20, 1961, The First Presidency and the Quorum of the Twelve authorized the restoration of Lee's Membership and Temple Blessings.** Norton was baptized for his dead grandfather, and on May 9 Apostle Ezra Taft Benson officiated in the endowment and sealing ceremonies at the Salt Lake Temple."[30] (emphasis added.)

As stated in footnote [27] above, Brigham Young said "that under no circumstances should he [John D. Lee] be admitted as a member again." As noted in the *"Fourteen Fundamentals in Following the Prophet"* by the 13th Mormon Prophet, Ezra Taft Benson, listed in Chapter Five, Fundamental Number 3 says: The living prophet is more important to us than a dead prophet. So, David O. McKay, the living prophet in 1961, trumped Brigham Young the dead prophet, who according to Fundamental Number 1: ...speaks for the Lord in everything. One or the other of these Prophets must not have been listening to the right lord. And so goes this whole horrific tale.

WHAT'S THE POINT?

This unthinkable act in the annals of American History was orchestrated by the very dogmas that set Mormonism apart from Christianity: Unquestionable allegiance to Follow the Prophet; The Prophet is God's direct mouthpiece on earth; Absolute authority to act in God's name through their Priesthood; Mormonism is God's Kingdom on earth; and, Mormons are sworn to secret oaths and covenants. These points of Mormon doctrine, as explained in the previous chapters, were the driving factors for this massacre. These doctrines may be looked at with skepticism or rationalized away as simply odd beliefs that no one would really adhere to, yet when the evidence is analyzed, they are shown to be the recipe for this devilish deed.

Mountain Meadows Massacre cannot be honestly dismissed as just a group of out of control radicals who acted on their own. It is simply not rational to believe that at least 60 men would brutally murder unarmed men, women, and children—especially men who claimed to have a foundational belief system based on revelations from God. What motivated these men to commit this massacre? The answer: They believed that God's mouthpiece on earth, Brigham Young, had ordered this massacre to be done. What force could control these men to act in such a brutal manner and then to remain silent about such a hideous crime? The answer: The Mormon Priesthood and the secret oaths that were/are sworn in the Temple Endowment Ceremony:

> "After the burial detail completed its grisly chore, Nephi Johnson said the men formed a circle to hear "a great many speeches." According to Lee, he, Dame, Haight, Klingensmith, Higbee, and Charles Hopkins spoke, praising God for delivering their enemies into their hands and "thanking the brethren for their zeal in God's cause." **The officers stressed "the necessity of always saying the Indians did it alone, and that the Mormons had nothing to do with it."**

"At Dame's request Haight told the men "<u>they had been privileged to keep a part of their covenant to avenge the blood of the prophets</u>." The men closed the circle, each putting his left hand on the shoulder of the man next to him and <u>raising his right arm to the square</u>. Higbee, Haight, Lee, and Dame stood at the center, facing the four points of the compass. <u>Stake president Haight led the men in a solemn oath never to discuss the matter, even among themselves, to keep the whole matter secret from every human being, and "to help kill all who proved to be traitors to the Church or people in this matter." Lee recalled the men voted unanimously to kill anyone who divulged the secret. It would be treason to the men who killed the emigrants and "treason to the Church." They were forbidden to tell their wives or even to talk of it among themselves</u>. "The orders to lay it all to the Indians, were just as positive as they were to keep it all secret," Lee wrote. "This was the counsel from all in authority." <u>Exhortations and commands directed the men "to keep the whole matter secret from every one but Brigham Young</u>." The meeting ended after Colonel Dame blessed the men. In the afternoon, they broke camp and left for their homes."[31] (emphasis added.)

Notice in the above quote the numerous doctrinal points of Mormonism that have been discussed in the previous chapters of this book. This isn't a coincidence—it's Mormon doctrine and its alive and well today!

What could possibly justify the killing of 120 innocent people? The answer: Stories were circulated that some of these people were accomplices in the murder of Joseph Smith and Hyrum Smith, and Mormon Apostle Parley P. Pratt; along with the news that the President of the United States had dispatched troops to Utah to regain control. These people were Gentiles and not part of God's chosen people who were establishing the "Kingdom" on earth—they were the enemy.

The absolute blind obedience factor to "Follow the Brethren," caused good men to do unthinkable things. Author Will Bagley writes of Mormon Bishop John D. Lee: "Lee later said he knew that he was doing a damnable deed, but his faith in the godliness of his leaders convinced him he was simply not worthy of the "important part [he] was commanded to perform."[32]

The Mountain Meadows Massacre is an atrocity too evil to even begin to comprehend; yet, it happened. The only explanation that this author can conceive for this dreadful event, is the religious fanaticism driven by the dogmatic doctrines of Mormonism that have been covered in the previous chapters of this book.

AUTHORS NOTE: THE HORROR CONTINUES!!

As of this writing, September of 2007, the horror of the Mountain Meadows Massacre lives on. The remains of the 120 innocent victims still lie underneath piles of stones on the meadow where they were brutally murdered. They lie in four mass graves where Brevet Major Carleton's Dragoons placed them after arriving at the meadows and finding their remains scattered across the landscape. The Mormon Church has purchased the killing fields where this despicable event happened and the land where the four mass graves are located. The graves are now on the Mormon Church's private property, and they strictly control who has access.

The descendants of the Massacre have petitioned the Mormon Church to turn the killing field over to a neutral third party: The Federal Government. This initiative is called: Federal Stewardship. By placing the area into Federal Stewardship, the descendants would have free access to the mass graves and could properly bury and honor their murdered relatives.

The Mormon Church refused this attempt in 1999, and again in the spring of 2007. In an Associated Press article by Jennifer Dobner, printed in the *Ogden Standard Examiner* on Tuesday, June 19, 2007, we read the explanation of Mormon spokesman Elder Marlin Jensen for the reason the Mormon Church declined Federal Stewardship, "He told us that President (Gordon B.) Hinckley had turned us down. He doesn't think it's in the best interests of the church to allow federal stewardship of the meadows," said Bolinger, the foundation president who is related to 30 of those killed. "That really bit me bad."[33]

Phil Bolinger is the President of the Mountain Meadows Monument Foundation, a group dedicated to preserving the history and honoring those who were so viciously slain on that September day. As reported in the previously mentioned Associated Press article, Phil Bolinger stated in the meeting with the Mormon representative, Marlin Jensen on April 25, 2007: **"It's not right for the people who had complicity to the killings to be the grave owner."** He followed up with a sage question, **"I asked him, 'How do you think the Kennedy family would feel if the Lee Harvey Oswald family had control of the Kennedy tomb?"[34]** That question says it all—would we Americans allow such a thing? NEVER!! This holdout by the Mormon Church, refusing to allow the descendants of the innocent victims to properly bury their dead, is outrageous. These aren't the actions of a religious organization—a religious organization would have compassion for such a tragedy. These are the actions of a large corporation trying to protect its assets—it's all about business, plain old dollars and cents!

I thought the Mormon Church was all about families? Their actions have certainly proven they are not. This most despicable act in American history lives on while the

Mormon Church thumbs its nose at the descendants of those its Priesthood killed.

I interviewed four of the descendants of this massacre on our TV show "Truth Outreach." Those shows were very hard to film—I could hardly keep my emotions in check. This brutal, senseless, religious fanatical killing, done by order of the Mormon Priesthood, just makes my blood boil. I hope it makes yours boil as well! The only thing that will make the Mormon Church budge one inch on this issue is **NEGATIVE PUBLIC OPINION!!**

If you want to right one of the **WORST WRONGS** in American history, then get involved. The Mountain Meadows Monument Foundation (MMMF) has started a petition campaign to collect signatures demanding the Mormon Church to turn this killing field over to the Federal Government so the families can properly inter their dead. Visit the Mountain Meadows Monument Foundation (MMMF) website (just Google Mountain Meadows Monument Foundation and click on the 1857massacre website). The main page has a link to download a PDF.file of the petition. Or you may write to the Nauvoo Christian Visitors Center, P.O. Box 93, Nauvoo, IL 62354 and we'll send you a couple petitions. Pass them around your church, work, and your neighborhood. Hundreds of thousands of signatures, letters and phone calls are the only thing that will get the Mormon Church's attention. Only the angry outcry of the American public will force the Mormon Church to do the right thing. Tell everyone you know about this!

If you wish to write a letter demanding release of Mountain Meadows, send it to:

Elder Marlin Jensen, LDS CHURCH, 35 North West Temple St., Salt Lake City, UT 84150. You may call and complain to the LDS Church: Tom Owen 801-240-1000. Call the Switchboard in Washington D.C. to be connected to your US Senator or Congressman: (202) 224-3121. Get involved, you can make a difference to right this ugly wrong!! Let your voice be heard!!

MMMF needs strength in numbers—if you're interested in joining a just cause send your $20.00 yearly member-ship fee to: Membership Application, Mountain Meadows Monument Foundation, Inc., 8002 Wind Rock Lane, Harrison, AR 72601—Helen and I did!!

[1] David L. Bigler, *Forgotten Kingdom, The Mormon Theocracy in the West 1847-1896*, (Utah State University Press, Logan, Utah, 1998) 146.

[2] Ibid., 162.

[3] Will Bagley, *Blood of the Prophets, Brigham Young and the Massacre at Mountain Meadows*, (University of Oklahoma Press, Norman, 2002) 113-114.

[4] *A Comprehensive History of the Church of Jesus Christ of Latter-day Saints*, (Published by the Church, Deseret News Press, Salt Lake City, Utah, 1930) Vol. 4, 149.

[5] *Ensign*, September 2007, 19.

[6] Ibid., 14.

[7] Jerald and Sandra Tanner, *Evolution of the Mormon Temple Ceremony: 1842-1990*, (Utah Lighthouse Ministry, Salt Lake City, Utah, 1990) 182.

[8] Jerald & Sandra Tanner, *Mormonism-Shadow or Reality?*, (Modern Microfilm Company, Salt Lake City, Utah, 1982) 400-403.

[9] Stanley P. Hirshon, *The Lion Of The Lord, A Biography of Brigham Young*, (Alfred A. Knopf, New York, 1969) 158-159.

[10] Joseph Smith, *History of the Church of Jesus Christ of Latter-day Saints* (Salt Lake City: Deseret News, 1971), 6: 319-320.

[11] Josiah F. Gibbs, *Mountain Meadows Massacre*, (Salt Lake Tribune Publishing Company, 1910) online book

at: http://www.utlm.org/onlinebooks/meadowscontents. htm.

[12] Heber C. Kimball, in Watt, ed., *Journal of Discourses*, 4:248.

[13] Heber C. Kimball, in Hawkins, ed., *Journal of Discourses*, 6:32-33.

[14] *Nauvoo Expositor*, June 7, 1844, 4. (Reprinted from *Quincy Whig*)

[15] Wilford Woodruff's Journal, Sept. 29, 1857, as cited in *A Comprehensive History of the Church of Jesus Christ of Latter-day Saints*, (Published by the Church, Deseret News Press, Salt Lake City, Utah, 1930) Vol. 4, 160-161.

[16] *A Comprehensive History of the Church of Jesus Christ of Latter-day Saints*, Vol. 4, 166.

[17] Joseph Fielding Smith, *Essentials in Church History*, (Published by The Deseret Book Company for The Church of Jesus Christ of Latter-day Saints, 1979), 422.

[18] Bigler, *Forgotten Kingdom*, 178.

[19] Mountain Meadows Massacre, Special Report by Brevet Major James Henry Carleton, 1859, 57th Congress, House of Representatives, 1st Session, Document No. 605, http://1857massacre.com/MMM/carlton_report. htm.

[20] Ibid.

[21] The Doctrine and Covenants Of The Church Of Jesus Christ Of Latter-day Saints, Containing Revelations Given To Joseph Smith, The Prophet With Some Additions By His Successors In The Presidency Of The Church, Published by The Church of Jesus Christ of Latter-day Saints (Salt Lake City, Utah 1989) 132:26.

[22] Bruce R. McConkie, *Mormon Doctrine*, Bookcraft (Salt Lake City, Utah, 1966) 381.

[23] Ibid., 853.

[24] Wilford Woodruff's Journal, Sept. 29, 1857, as cited in *A Comprehensive History of the Church of Jesus Christ of Latter-day Saints*, (Published by the Church, Deseret News Press, Salt Lake City, Utah, 1930) Vol. 4, 160-161.

[25] Bagley, *Blood of the Prophets*, 186-187.

[26] Brigham Young, in Watt, ed., *Journal of Discourses*, 10:109-110.

[27] Smith, *Essentials in Church History*, 422.

[28] Juanita Brooks, *The Mountain Meadows Massacre*, (University of Oklahoma Press, Norman, 1979) 208-209.

[29] Bruce R. McConkie, *Mormon Doctrine*, Bookcraft (Salt Lake City, Utah, 1958) 314.

[30] Bagley, *Blood of the Prophets*, 361.

[31] Ibid., 158.

[32] Ibid., 145.

[33] *Ogden Standard Examiner*, June 19, 2007, Mountain Meadows stewardship debated, by Jennifer Dobner.

[34] Ibid.

Chapter Ten

THE MARK HOFMANN MURDERS

This chapter, like Chapter Nine, is presented as a demonstration of how the application of Mormon Doctrine has affected people in recent history. This chapter is written in an effort to diffuse the attempts by Mormon apologists to rationalize away the unique Mormon doctrines documented in the previous chapters. The Mountain Meadows Massacre and the Mark Hofmann Murders are presented to give examples of the application of how Mormon Doctrine is linked from past history to relatively recent events. These factual events take on new light when a complete look at Mormon unique doctrines is applied to each incident.

I relied heavily on the information for this chapter from the book: *The Mormon Murders, A True Story of Greed, Forgery, Deceit and Death,* by Steven Naifeh & Gregory White Smith. This chapter will be but a brief synopsis of an extremely complicated case of murder and forgery that involved the highest levels of the Mormon Church and took 458 pages in the above book to describe. However, it clearly demonstrates the power that the Mormon Church wields over its members, even today. I highly recommend getting a copy of the book, *The Mormon Murders*, for a thorough review of this case. To help you with the storyline, the following characters are provided:

<u>Jim Bell</u> – Detective.

<u>David Biggs</u> – Deputy County Attorney, Mormon, Assistant to Prosecuting Attorney Stott.

<u>Steve Christensen</u> – Officer in the investment company, Coordinated Financial Services. Mormon. Returned Missionary. Bombing victim.

<u>Ken Farnsworth</u> – Detective.

<u>Mike George</u> – Chief Investigator with the County Attorney's Office.

<u>Gordon B. Hinckley</u> – 2nd Counselor to Mormon Prophet Spencer W. Kimball, during the Mark Hofmann incident. Currently serving as the 15th Mormon Prophet.

<u>Mark Hofmann</u> – Returned Mormon Missionary, Master Forger, Murderer.

<u>Wilford Kirton</u> – Attorney for the Mormon Church – assisted Mormon Prophet Gordon B. Hinckley.

<u>Dallin Oaks</u> – Mormon Apostle.

<u>Hugh Pinnock</u> – General Authority, First Quorum of Seventy.

<u>Kathy Sheets</u> – Wife of Gary Sheets, business partner of Steve Christensen. Mormon. Bombing victim.

<u>Bob Stott</u> – Deputy County Attorney, Mormon, and the Prosecuting Attorney.

<u>Dawn Tracy</u> – Salt Lake Tribune Reporter.

<u>Brent Ward</u> – U.S. Attorney that refused to file charges against Mark Hofmann. Mormon.

<u>Ron Yengich</u> – Mark Hofmann's Defense Attorney.

THE MORMON MURDERS

It's been over 20 years now since Mark Hofmann, the returned Mormon Missionary, blew up two innnocent people with pipe bombs, and was plea bargained out instead of going to trial (1985-87). Why would't a deranged bomber with 26 felony counts against him and the blood of two innocent people on his hands go to trial? It's really quite simple if you've ever lived in Utah and you understand the power of the Mormon Church over that state. Placing Mark Hofmann on trial would have meant calling Mormon Prophets and Apostles, "The Brethren," to the witness stand. These Mormon General Authorities had been utterly fooled by him into purchasing hundreds of thousands, if not millions, of dollars worth of forged documents about early Mormon history and to have that information publicly disseminated from the witness stand was simply unthinkable.

Mark Hofmann was born and raised as a Mormon and completed his two year mission to southwest England in 1976. Mark was married in 1979 and outwardly appeared to be a good, young Mormon man. Mark had a sinister side though, and he found an easy target in the Mormon Church. Since its beginning, the early foundations of Mormon Church history have been shrouded in claims of fraud, deceit, folklore magic, and mysticism. Also, from its beginning, the Mormon Church has been involved in trying to distance itself from those claims and provide a legimate explanation of its establishment.

Into this fertile ground of proctecting the history of the Mormon Church at all costs, came Mark Hofmann with a plan to make money and make the Mormon Church look foolish – he was successful on both counts!!

THE ANTHON TRANSCRIPT

Mark's first big score was the "Anthon Transcript." Martin Harris, the financier of the first printing of the Book of Mormon in 1830, was skeptical of putting up the money without some proof of the Golden Bible. Joseph Smith would only let him heft the box that supposedly contained the "Golden Plates" from which the Book of Mormon was to be translated. This wasn't enough to satisfy the wealthy farmer; he wanted more. So, Joseph supposedly copied characters from the gold plates and Harris took them to New York City to have the scholars of the day validate the characters. The characters were not of any known language Smith explained to Harris, they were of an unknown language called "Reformed Egyptian."

Harris eventually found his way to Charles Anthon, a professor of Greek and Latin at Columbia College. No one knows for sure what took place at this meeting, except Harris came back declaring Professor Anthon had identified the characters as Egyptian, Chaldean, Assyrian, and Arabic. When Professor Anthon later heard that the Mormons were saying he had validated the characters he wrote a blistering denial.

The "Anthon Transcript" which Martin Harris had taken on his journey was believed lost. Mark Hofmann announced he had found the "Anthon Transcript," much to the joy of the Mormon Church. This incredible find (a forgery) put Mark Hofmann on the inside track with the front office of the Mormon Church. Mark totally fooled every senior Mormon Church leader and walked away with a quick $20,000 dollars for his deceptive efforts; a handsome sum in 1980. Not only did Hofmann fool the Mormon Church leaders of 1980, but the current Mormon Prophet, Gordon B. Hinckley, and the current President of the Quorum of the Twelve Apostles, Boyd K. Packer, were also part of those fooled!

THE SALAMANDER LETTER

Mark's next big scam was the "Salamander Letter." The whole "translation" of the Book of Mormon is steeped in mysticism and fraud. Knowing this, Mark Hofmann dreamed up a letter supposed to have been written by Martin Harris, the financier of the Book of Mormon, that played perfectly off of those claims. His letter "...sounded more like a Grimms' fairy tale than a Sunday-school lesson: kettles of money guarded by spirits, seer stones, enchanted spells, magic "specticles," ghostly visitations. And instead of a benevolent angel, a cantankerous and tricky "old spirit" who transforms himself into a *white salamander!*"[1]

In order to avoid directly involving the Mormon Church in the procurement of this document (too much publicity), Hofmann worked a deal with a "faithful member," a wealthy businessman named Steve Christensen. Steve would purchase the document to prevent it from getting into the "wrong hands." The idea was to allow time to cool off the interest in the documet and then Steve could donate it to the Church and thus ensure a prominent place for himself and his family in the Celestial Kingdom in the next life!

Trying to increase the documents worth, Hofmann selectively leaked portions of the document. Leading Mormon scholars were confident of its authenticity as were "The Brethren." The one voice that rang out in skepticism was Jerald Tanner. Despised by Mormons as an "anti" (anti-Mormon), Jerald and his wife Sandra, the Great-Great Grandaughter of Brigham Young, were known as the leading dissident researchers into the origins of Mormonism. It was Jerald who first voiced the possibility of forgery. The Tanner's detailed research into the foundations of Mormonism is so thorough, that a review of the "Salamander Letter" caused Jerald to remark "This just isn't the Martin Harris I know."[2] It's ironic that the anti-Mormon researchers questioned the document while those who were sustained as "prophets, seers, and revelators," were fooled, "hook, line, and sinker."

THE MCLELLIN COLLECTION

This is the scam that brought Mark Hofmann down. "William E. McLellin was an early Apostle and close associate of Joseph Smith's who had left the Church in 1836 to become one of its bitterest critics. It had long been rumored that McLellin, who kept the minutes at early meetings of the Twelve, had taken with him a pirate's chest full of papers, letters, and journals, all of it incriminating, with which to destroy the Church. But neither the Collection itself, nor any part of it, had ever surfaced. Until now."[3]

This scam was so blatant that Mark Hofmann never even forged the documents. He set a price tag of $185,000 and was working several different people, and the Mormon Church, in the scam. The Mormon Church was so afraid of what might be in this "Collection," all they cared about was that it didn't fall into "enemy" hands. Mark was simply going to take the money and never reveal who supposedly had the "Collection." The perfect scam—take the money and never even produce the goods.

Hofmann was living the high life at this time. He was flying "First Class" back and forth to New York City and other places, supposedly searching for antique documents, and spending money like there was no end to its source. He was attempting to purchase a very expensive house in one of the most affluent neighborhoods in Salt Lake City and he was beginning to run tight on cash.

He went to the Mormon Church Headquarters and told them he needed the $185,000 to acquire the McLellin Collection. Hugh Pinnock, a senior member of the Quorum of Seventy, made a phone call to First Interstate Bank and arranged the loan; Mark simply had to go pick up the check.

Hofmann had also borrowed money from several other Mormons with promises of providing the McLellin Collection. Playing both ends against the middle, time was running out. Mark was under a great deal of pressure to meet all of these various obligations. Steve Christensen (the purchaser of the Salamander Letter) had entered the picture again as Mark was delinquent on his $185,000 loan arranged by the Church. "The Brethren" had asked Steve to help complete the McLellin transaction through a wealthy Mormon Mission President in Nova Scotia, Canada. In his sordid mind, Hofmann believed he could release the pressure cooker he had placed himself in by blowing up Steve and then blowing up one of his business associates; therefore, diverting the investigation away from document dealing and focusing it on a possible bad business deal motive for the bombings.

THE BOMBINGS

On Tuesday October 15, 1985, two bombs took the lives of Steve Christensen and Kathy Sheets. Both bombs were pipe bombs by construction. The one set for Steve Christensen was especially brutal, since it was filled with nails that would absolutely shred its victim. Gary Sheets was the intended target for bomb number two. However, his wife, Kathy, found the bomb outside their home and she became the victim of its deadly power.

No one is sure who was the intended victim of bomb number three. Mark Hofmann was in downtown Salt Lake City in the process of delivering the bomb, when it went off prematurely, and he became its victim. Severly injured, but not killed, Mark was initially thought to be an innocent victim. The investigation, however, clearly showed that Mark was the bomber.

LYING FOR THE LORD

The Mormon Church has a history of "lying for the Lord":

"From the time of the translation of the Book of Mormon through the Nauvoo period and into the time of the Reed Smoot senate hearings, the leadership of the church engaged in a practice that became known as "lying for the Lord." Our leaders used this tactic because they were fearful that if the truth were known about actual church practice or doctrines their adversaries would destroy the Lord's work. (This fear seems somewhat mystifying in light of the promise that "no unhallowed hand shall disrupt my work.") However, we have been assured that the leaders who sought to protect the work by lying will be blessed for their valor. Clearly lying is not always lying, and justice will not always claim those who bear false witness. Under the rule of law, what constitutes lying must ultimately be determined by some interpretation beyond mortality."[4]

Hugh Pinnock, previously noted to be a Mormon General Authority, arranged a $185,000 loan at First Interstate Bank for Mark Hofmann to initially purchase the McLellin Collection. The day after the third bomb explosion that injured Mark Hofmann, Elder Pinnock was interviewed about the crimes:

"...Police Detective Don Bell interviewed him at 1:12 in the afternoon on October 17, the day after the bomb exploded in Hofmann's car.

"Elder Pinnock, this is the deal," Bell began, notebook in hand. "This is a homicide investigation. Do you know Mr. Hofmann?"

Pinnock paused and reflected a moment. 'No, I don't believe I do.'"[5]

This statement by this Mormon General Authority was not truthful. There is no question that he intimately knew and had met with Mark Hofmann on numerous occassions. Detective Bell had questioned Mark Hofmann and Elder Pinnock about the McLellin Collection and the $185,000 loan from First Interstate Bank. His interviews led him to believe both were lying:

> "There was no doubt in Bell's mind: Hofmann was lying, but so was Hugh Pinnock."[6]
> "Pinnock hadn't just lied, he had lied in easily disproved ways; he hadn't just obfuscated, he had obfuscated clumsily; he had contradicted himself and raised more questions than he answered. But worst of all, he violated the prime directive. In his panic, he seemed more interested in protecting himself than in protecting the Church."[7]

When KSL-TV accurately reported that the Mormon Church was involved in arranging document deals and illegal loans, the Mormon Church went ballistic.

> "The Church is upset because we said they helped arrange a loan. Well they *did*! They say it was an individual, not the Church, but that's baloney. It may have been an individual who placed the call, but he was a Church official, sitting in his Church office, on Church time, using a Church phone, and he did it for the benefit of the Church. Nobody else wanted that McLellin Collection except the Church. And the Nova Scotia mission president doesn't *collect* documents. He was just a big-bucks guy who said 'If you need help, I'll help you out.' If the Church says

they weren't helping arrange any buyers for anything, how do you explain the fact that the Church volunteered to get an armored car to go down to Texas and pick the Collection up?"[8]

When current Mormon Prophet, Gordon B. Hinckley, was interviewed by County Prosecuting Attorneys Bob Stott and David Biggs, and Investigator Mike George about his multiple dealings with Mark Hofmann, he was clearly deceptive in his answers:

> "Stott and Biggs shifted uneasily in their chairs. Mike George, the investigator from the county attorney's office who had accompanied Ken Farnsworth on the last interview with Hinckley almost four months before, marveled at how, with time in between to recollect those meetings he *still* couldn't remember a thing.
> "Was he ever in your office?" Stott asked.
> "Probably," said Hinckley.
> *Probably!* thought Biggs. Now he was even forgetting what he had admitted in the press conference."[9]

The above quote was made after the bombings and after the Mormon Church had called a Press Conference to begin damage control operations with respect to their involvement with Mark Hofmann. At that press conference (noted in the quote below) Gordon B. Hinckley had admitted to meeting with Mark Hofmann which clearly shows in the quote above he was being deceptive in his answer.

> "In the back of the auditorium, Detective Don Bell stood against the wall and listened to the Church leaders. He felt momentarily vindicated when Hinckley admitted that he had met with Hofmann. "I knew it," he said softly to himself."[10]

When comparing the notes of the investigators of this crime, it appears that Gordon B. Hinckley, now the current Mormon Prophet had a lapse of memory, or he was hiding the truth from them.

AUTHORS NOTE – SEE APPENDIX THREE FOR MORE INFORMATION ON LYING FOR THE LORD.

IN MORMONISM – YOUR SWORN OATH TO UPHOLD THE LAW IS SUBSERVIENT TO YOUR ALLEGIANCE TO THE CHURCH!

The Prosecuting Attorney on the Hofmann Case was a County Attorney name Robert (Bob) Stott. Why? Mark Hofmann had murdered two innocent victims by blowing them up with pipe bombs. This was a Federal Case for sure — why then was a County Attorney prosecuting this case? The answer: The U.S. Attorney was Brent Ward, a Mormon, and he refused to press charges.

"... Brent Ward was the yuppie lawyer. With his red suspenders, bow tie, and horn-rimmed glasses, he could have been the rising star for some big corporate law firm on the fast track to the top. Which is exactly what he *was* before December 1981, when Orrin Hatch, Utah Senator and a Mormon elder, picked him, at the age of thirty-six, for the U.S. attorney's job.

They may have come from different centuries, but Sheriff Hayward and Brent Ward had one thing in common: political instincts. At the very least, Ward was in line for a federal judgeship if he chose that direction. At his age, that would put him in the running, if Senator Hatch's conservative star continued to rise, for an appeals court, or even, some day, the Supreme Court. **It was no secret that one of the Church's most fervent wishes**

was to seat a Mormon justice on the nation's highest court.

That was the other bottom-line feature of Brent Ward: the Church. More than just a devout Mormon, Ward was an ambitious one. **Of course, in Utah, political ambition and religious ambition were always closely allied. It was difficult to rise to prominent public office without the Church's backing. It was virtually impossible to do so against the Church's opposition.** That was a fact of life in Utah that any good politician understood, and Brent Ward was a very good politician.

In his four years as U.S. attorney, Ward had concentrated his activities on popular causes like pornography and child abuse—causes, not coincidentally, that the Church cared about. When the Hofmann story began to break, more than a few people wondered how the ambitious young U.S. attorney would handle himself in a case that the Church wanted to avoid at all costs.

Like Farnsworth, they soon found out.

Ward's first action was to help arrange to have a key piece of evidence shipped out of state. By the time the police department knew enough to ask the Church for the so-called Salamander Letter, it was already gone— off to the FBI's laboratories in Washington, D.C., for a long and very confidential analysis. **When the county attorney's office requested other Hofmann documents, the Church refused to hand them over. Why would they push one sensitive document into the FBI's hands almost immediately after the bombing and fight to keep other documents out of police hands for weeks?** Church spokesman said they didn't trust local law enforcement.

But they *could* trust the heavily Mormon FBI, which worked hand-in-glove with Brent Ward.

It was Ward's FBI agents who had swooped down on all the major figures in the case in the first few days and taken statements. **By the third day, however, as soon as it became clear that the Church was involved somehow, the FBI stopped sharing its information.** Its agents wouldn't give local police the names of the people they had interviewed. Bell's detectives would arrive only to be told by a beleaguered witness, "What are you doing here? The FBI was here yesterday, asking the same questions. Don't you people talk to each other? Aren't you all law enforcement?" By the end of the first week, some detectives themselves were beginning to wonder.

The police asked if they could go along on FBI interviews. The FBI refused. The police asked to see the FBI interviews, a courtesy routinely extended to local law enforcement agencies on a confidential basis. The FBI refused.

At one point, Farnsworth, Bell, and others from the police department and the county attorney's office were invited to Ward's office. The purpose of the meeting, according to Ward, was to "share information." At last, thought Farnsworth, they're going to let us see what they've got. But it turned out that by "sharing information," Ward meant that the local agents should share *their* information with the federal agents, not the other way around.

The police weren't the only ones who began to wonder whom exactly Brent Ward was collecting this information for. <u>Confidential FBI files were known to have wound up on certain desks in the Church Office Building. Was Ward running a damage-control operation for the Church</u>, sending FBI men out ahead of local police to find out just what the Church's exposure was?

281

That might explain his bizarre insistence on getting a statement from Hofmann. At a meeting on the afternoon of October 24, Ward's assistant Bruce Lubeck, demanded a "statement from Hofmann for the files." Bell and Farnsworth and Gerry D'Elia couldn't believe it. They were in the middle of a furious legal battle to compel nurse Loden to reveal what she had heard in Hofmann's hospital room, and Ward thought that Yengich was going to let Hofmann talk to the cops directly? After the meeting, Bell turned to Farnsworth in disgust. "That's typical. If you don't go down and talk to the suspect so he can tell you to get screwed, they don't feel you've done a complete investigation." Obviously, Ward was reaching — stretching — for excuses not to act.

One thing was obvious from the moment the Church got involved in the case: Brent Ward had no intention of prosecuting *anybody* for *anything* related to the bombings. Hofmann was indicted along with Shannon Flynn for possession of the altered Uzi, but a judge quickly set aside the charge pending the outcome of the state's case. Only a few days after the bombings, ATF agents presented their evidence to Ward. They felt confident they had a federal case against Hofmann, at least for possession of a destructive device, a felony that carried a sentence of ten years in prison. They had the physical evidence, they had the letter jacket, they had the witnesses at the Judge Building. Hell, they had more than they had in most possession cases.

But Brent Ward wouldn't touch it.

And the ATF men thought they knew why. "There was too much at stake," one of them said later. "His political career was at stake. Whether he wanted to secure his political base in Utah or to further strengthen his bond with Mormon Senator Hatch — either way, it would not be helpful to put himself

in a position where he had to subpoena Gordon B. Hinckley and the other Church officials, or to expose the Church's transactions with Mark Hofmann to the full light of day."

If the Church didn't want the truth out, then neither, it appeared, did Brent Ward. If the Church didn't want this case in the headlines, didn't want to get itself involved in the legal process, who was Brent Ward to put it there? **As for his sworn duty to uphold the law, well, there were laws and there were laws. As one investigator on the case saw it: "Brent Ward's got motives above and beyond the law. Do you think a good Mormon in the U.S. Attorney's Office is going to hesitate for one minute deciding to do what's correct for the law or what's best for the Church? This guy was on his way to being a *god*. Next to that, U.S. attorney looks pretty insignificant.**"[11] (*italics* in the original, emphasis added.)

There is no doubt that this U.S. Attorney, who swore an oath to uphold the laws of the United States, saw those laws and his oath to the American people as second place to his allegiance to the Mormon Priesthood and "The Brethren."

IN UTAH – YOU DON'T PUT A MORMON GENERAL AUTHORITY ON THE WITNESS STAND!!

I am going to quote for you Chapter 86, in its entirety, from *The Mormon Murders*. I'll inject commentary in brackets[ ]. I believe this chapter will help you see the overall big picture that has been pieced together in the previous chapters of this book and in Appendix One. It is important to see how this murder case brings to light several of the key points of this book: (1) The revered position of the "Prophets, Seers, and

Revelators"; (2) The power the Mormon Church wields; (3) The belief that the Mormon Church and its leadership are above the law.

"86 Now it was the prosecutors' turn to approach Gordon Hinckley.

Bob Stott must have prayed this day would never come, but by late March, he could no longer avoid it. Church functionaries like Don Schmidt could testify at the preliminary hearing about most of the documents Hofmann had sold the Church, and Hugh Pinnock could take the heat for Dallin Oaks on the McLellin Collection, **but only two people knew about the Joseph Stowell letter, Mark Hofmann and Gordon Hinckley.**

Ironically, Stott had assigned himself the documents side of the Hofmann case, allowing him to control—some said contain—the Church's involvement. **Now, as the prosecutor in charge of the documents scam, he was leading his team into the sanctum sanctorum of Church power, Hinckley's paneled offices.**

Before they even sat down, Hinckley asked the first and most important question: **"<u>Are you members of the church</u>?"**

[This question was asked each time anyone came to interview Mormon Church authorities on the Church's involvement with Mark Hofmann. Why? The answer is simple, those being interviewed wanted to know what level of control could be brought to bear on the person asking the questions. If the interviewer was Mormon, the Church authorities were the ones in control of the interview.]

David Biggs answered, "Yes. But I'm not a particularly good one." He wasn't sure if Hinckley heard him, he seemed so preoccupied with picking up "vibrations." He was, after all, first and foremost a spiritual man with the Lord's business on his mind—and a lawyer, Wilford Kirton, at his side.

Stott explained that they needed to know more about Hinckley's meetings with Mark Hofmann. In particular, they needed to know what kind of pressure Hofmann might have been under to produce the McLellin Collection. Was it the kind of pressure that might lead to murder?

Hinckley looked at them with a *Mona Lisa* smile. Far from putting pressure on Hofmann, he said, he only vaguely *remembered* Mark Hofmann.

[There is no question by the evidence provided in the investigation that Mormon Prophet Gordon B. Hinckley knew Mark Hofmann first hand; he had even called him to wish him a "Happy Birthday." You must hold a significant position of clout in the Mormon Church to have the Prophet call and wish you a "Happy Birthday!"]

Stott and Biggs shifted uneasily in their chairs. Mike George, the investigator from the county attorney's office who had accompanied Ken Farnsworth on the last interview of Hinckley almost four months before, marveled at how, with all the time in between to recollect those meetings, **he *still* couldn't remember a thing.**

"Was he ever in your office?" Stott asked.

"Probably," said Hinckley.

Probably! thought Biggs. Now he was even forgetting what he had admitted in the press conference.

[Hinckley had admitted in the Press Conference that Mark Hofmann had come and talked to him about the possibility of purchasing the Kinderhook Plates. This meeting was confirmed by Church Security as happening at 7:00 a.m., less than two weeks before the bombings.]

"Have you ever bought anything from him yourself?"

"Not directly. A couple of documents may have come through me, but only as a vehicle by which the Church made the purchases."

They tried, ever so gently, to refresh his recollection.

Surely he remembered the morning, only days before the bombings, when Hofmann came to tell him the Kinderhook plates "might be available for the right price"? He did remember the Kinderhook plates?

"I don't know a lot about them," Hinckley said dryly.

George thought, This is *Hinckley*. He's telling us he doesn't know a whole lot about the Kinderhook plates. My God, even I have learned a little bit about them in this investigation. He *has* to know what they're about. They're a big thing in Mormon history.

In a show of cooperativeness, Hinckley walked to his bookshelf, pulled out a book and began to read a passage about the Kinderhook plates as if they were all news to him, like a person who had just heard an interesting word for the first time and wants to look it up—just out of curiosity.

Stott and Biggs pressed. Surely he knew that Steve Christensen had been called by Church officials at all hours of the night to go out and find Hofmann and get him to repay the First Interstate loan?

Hinckley shrugged his shoulders.

Surely, he knew that phone calls have flown back and forth from the Church Office Building and that Christensen was pounding on doors all over Salt Lake City? Surely this indicated that the Church was bringing pressure to bear?

Hinckley could recall nothing.

No matter how evocatively they painted the picture of those last desperate days, Hinckley could recall nothing.

Biggs decided it was time to push a little harder. One thing that had always amazed him, he began innocently, was why no one had investigated the documents the Church bought from Hofmann, not *really* investigated them, not check their provenances, for example. True, Hofmann, like many documents dealers, kept his sources confidential, but the Church had never even *tried* to verify its purchases. And yet it was spending tens of thousands of dollars on these documents.

Biggs wanted to ask: Were these the actions of parties who barely knew each other? Is it credible that you would put that much trust in someone whom you knew only "vaguely"? But he decided instead to ask only half the question, "How is it that you felt comfortable relying on Mr. Hofmann as a sole basis for purchasing these documents?"

Hinckley looked him in the eye. "We relied on Mark Hofmann's integrity," he said gravely. "If we were deceived, then it's to *his* eternal detriment."

[So much for these men being the "oracles" of God. How could God allow his "oracles to be duped in such a colossal way? Mark Hofmann was a celebrity and had direct access to the Prophet and Apostles. He was not a "vague" person.]

Wow, thought Biggs. Heady stuff. But hardly responsive.

They tried another approach. As per Joseph Smith's instructions, every good Mormon is supposed to keep a detailed daily diary of his or her activities. Over the years, the Church's leaders had been extraordinarily conscientious in obeying that injunction. So they asked to see Hinckley's diary entries for his meetings with Mark

Hofmann. "I don't keep a diary," Hinckley responded quickly, as if he were prepared for the question.

After another hour of evasions, memory lapses, and sermonette's, Biggs lost his patience. "President Hinckley. This has been in the news — people have *died* — isn't there any way we can get some information about your meetings with Hofmann?"

[When investigators tried to obtain the log book entry for the day that Mark Hofmann visited President Hinckley on October 4th, from the Church Headquarters Building, Mormon Security refused to provide it.]

Hinckley couldn't contain his indignation. "This is the *least* of my concerns," he huffed. "I am an extremely busy man. I have worldwide concerns. Mr. Hofmann is a postscript..." he reached for the rest of the phrase, "... in the walk of life."

You wish, thought David Biggs.

When Bob Stott finally worked up the courage to talk about Hinckley's testimony at the upcoming preliminary hearing, Wilford Kirton jumped in.

"President Hinckley doesn't wish to testify at the hearing. We think it would be in everyone's best interest to not have him testify."

Someone suggested that he would have to testify at trial.

You don't understand, said Kirton imperiously. President Hinckley does not wish to testify at the hearing, at the trial, at anything.

[Who cares what Gordon B. Hinckley wanted — this was a brutal double murder. That's the point — Mormonism has always placed itself at odds with the law. Brigham Young once said: "I live above the law, and so do this people."[12] Nothing has changed.]

Even Stott had to be outraged. This was putting him, as a devout member of the Church, under wholly unacceptable pressure.

[This is true with any Mormon, they can instantly be put under the most severe pressure imaginable by the Mormon Church. If the Mormon Church wants something done, and a Mormon balks at that pressure, it could cost them their eternity—as noted in Chapter Five.]

Hinckley had obviously wanted to stay out of this discussion, but it was clear from the prosecutors' reaction that nothing less than his personal intervention would calm the furor that Kirton's comments had unleashed. So he decided to give another sermonette, this one on the subject of "priorities." He sat down with Stott as a father would sit down with a wayward son.

"This isn't that significant, as it relates to Church matters," he said softly. "It's the Church that matters. You have to consider the Church first. I don't wish to testify."

[No, you have to consider the law first. No one is exempt from the law—except in Mormonism; it's the Church, the Church, the Church!]

This time Stott said nothing.

But that wasn't all Hinckley wanted. "I think it would be in the best interests of the Church," he added in the same mellow voice, "if you simply dismissed the charge."

Dismiss the charge? Biggs and George were aghast. It took them a moment to realize that he meant only that Stott should dismiss the charge on the Stowell letter, which would let Hinckley off the hook as far as testifying at the preliminary hearing.

Despite the months of investigation, Stott, Biggs, and George still had only the vaguest idea of how much

Hinckley had to lose if Mark Hofmann told all in open court, or even if the complete details of his relationship with Hinckley came into the open. They knew nothing of the forces at work within the ranks of the General Authorities to oust Hinckley from power for his failure of vision, his failure to see the trap that Hofmann had laid for him. If Church conservatives were to read the full details of his misadventures in newspaper accounts of a trial, the consequences for *him*—apart from the consequences for the Church—could be catastrophic. He could disappear from the upper reaches of power or, even worse, of the Celestial Kingdom.

More fervently than the prosecutors could have imagined, Gordon Hinckley must have wanted to say "dismiss the charges," on *all* of Hofmann's crimes. Close the public record, lock him away or buy his silence, put the matter to rest. Make him, as quickly as possible, "just a postscript in the walk of life."

But Bob Stott wasn't ready to do that. **"We are not going to drop the charge,"** he said after he regained his composure. But he did have a compromise question. "If we can get the defense to stipulate as to your testimony, we won't have to call you. But if they won't stipulate, and if we think it's important for you to testify, you will have to testify."

As they left the room, Biggs slapped Stott on the back. He knew that couldn't have been easy."[13] (bracketed information and emphasis added.)

Just a few weeks later in the Preliminary Hearing, Bob Stott began presenting evidence on the charges related to the forged documents. Prosecuting Attorney Stott's last words in the above quote was that he would not drop the charges on the Stowell Letter and without a stipulation from the

Defense Attorney, he would call Gordon B. Hinckley to the stand. President Hinckley was never called. Why?

"There was one element of suspense still hanging over the hearings: Would Gordon Hinckley testify? As late as April 19, the defense had been telling reporters that they expected to see Hinckley on the stand the following week. **Bob Stott's brave determination to subpoena Hinckley seemed to have dissolved in the three weeks since the meeting in Hinckley's office, although no one knew exactly why.** After that meeting, David Biggs and everyone else in the county attorney's office had been cut off from any further contact with Church officials. **Stott insisted that he, and he alone, would deal with the Church.**

Farnsworth, for one, was not reassured. He had seen the way Stott dealt with other, lesser Church officials. Like Hugh Pinnock. In briefing Stott, in preparation for Pinnock's testimony at the hearings, Farnsworth had told him about Pinnock's statement to the effect that he considered the piece of papyrus that Hofmann showed him to be genuine—that is, one of the papyri from which Joseph Smith translated the Book of Abraham. **Stott refused to believe it. "I won't ask Pinnock that on the stand,"** he snapped, **"because I think he's lying."**

"But Bob, this is an important piece of evidence," Farnswoth insisted. **"You've got to ask the questions."** **Stott refused to do it. He refused to be a party to exposing a General Authority to ridicule: either for lying, or for being unable to distinguish between commonplace hieroglyphics and a genuine Joseph Smith papyrus. At the preliminary hearing, Stott stuck to his pledge and skipped over the subject entirely.**

If Stott was that deferential to Pinnock, his colleagues wondered, how could he stand up to Hinckley? **The fact that he was known to have had several one-on-one meetings with Hinckley in the interim only fueled speculation that a deal, explicit or implicit, had already been cut.**

But Hinckley still had a problem. If he wanted to be certain to avoid the witness chair, somebody else needed to sign off on any deal: Ron Yengich. And with the day approaching when Stott was scheduled to put the Stowell letter into evidence, Yengich was still making noises about calling Hinckley to the stand.

That's when Bob Stott paid an unusual visit to the counsel for the defense. For the record, he took David Biggs with him to Yengich's office on 4th South.

"President Hinckley doesn't want to testify," Stott told Yengich. "And we don't want to call him any more than we want to call any other recalcitrant witness. How would it be if we set up an appointment for you to talk to him? And then you come to us, after you talk to him, and see if you can enter into a stipulation as to what his testimony will be." Stott made it sound like his idea, but everyone assumed he could never have offered a meeting if Hinckley hadn't cleared it first.

[There is no way this County Attorney could make such an offer, requiring President Hinckley to meet with the Defense Attorney unless this had been approved by President Hinckley prior to the offer! There is no question that Bob Stott had been put under absolute allegiance to follow "The Brethren"; in this case President Hinckley's direction to work a deal to prevent him from having to testify.]

Yengich accepted the offer.

It was a brief, tense, businesslike meeting. Different as they were, both men had something the other wanted. Hinckley wanted a stipulation that only Yengich could give him. But what did Yengich want? What he *got* was an agreement by Hinckley that Church officials would argue against the death penalty at Hofmann's sentencing.

Hinckley undoubtedly wanted more (a guarantee that Yengich wouldn't call him to testify at trial, for instance), and so did Yengich (an agreement that the Church would push for a plea bargain, perhaps), but those deals would have to wait.

For now, it was a sure sign of how Yengich thought the hearings were going that he was already hedging his bets against the death penalty."[14] (bracketed information and emphasis added.)

How is it possible that the Mormon Church can cut deals in sentencing and guarantee plea bargains instead of trials? If you wield the power over those in public office, then you have the power to make such deals. The Mormon Church was way out of bounds in this terrible murder case. However, rather than allowing justice to take its course they manipulated the outcome to protect their image.

IN UTAH – YOU DON'T EMBARASS THE MORMON CHURCH!!!

The case against Mark Hofmann was overwhelming with two Murder One Counts and 26 Felony Charges. There was no question he would be convicted of 1st Degree Murder and receive the death penalty for his despicable crimes. Yet, he only received a mere slap on the wrist for murdering two innocent people by blowing them up with pipe bombs and, not only defrauding the Mormon Church out of hundreds of thousands, if not millions of dollars, but other people as well.

"It was clear to everyone by now that Bob Stott was determined to avoid a trial no matter what. Said one policeman when the news of the bargain began to spread through the department like the smell of a gas leak, **"Even if we had a *confession*, Stott would have given Yengich anything he wanted."**[15] (*italics* in the original, emphasis added.)

Later, when a *Los Angeles Times* reporter flew to Salt Lake City to cover the breaking plea-bargain story, he told Dawn Tracy [Salt Lake Tribune Reporter] that the most surprising aspect of the entire case was the attitude of the prosecution. "The typical prosecutor," the reporter said, "goes out and gets the bad guys. He goes out and stirs things up. Here, they're so nice and cooperative. What a *nice* plea bargain. **In any other state, you'd see this thing go on trial, because that's how prosecutors' reputations are made.** Going to trial and getting bad guys, big splashes, lot of exposure. Here you have a nice plea bargain.

"Hey," said Tracy, "**You don't rise in this state embarrassing the Mormon Church or making them look bad.**"[16] (bracketed information and emphasis added.)

Who cares about truth? Who cares about justice – in Mormonism you must protect the "Myth" at all costs!!

The Mormon Prosecutor, Bob Stott, would not execute the responsibilities of his office, because in Mormonism, the attitude toward truth is "faith before facts!"[17]

WHAT'S THE POINT?

Utah is supposed to be a state—not some third world country. How is it possible that such a horrendous murder/bombing/forgery case could be plea bargained at the level of "armed robbery?"[18] An objective analysis of this case leaves no question that the Mormon Church manipulated the Justice System to their own advantage and the tools of the manipulation were the Mormons that filled the Government positions at the Federal, State, County and City levels. The Mormon Church has the ability to wield the power of the allegiance factor, through the oaths and covenants sworn at Baptism, each week when they take the sacrament, ordination into each Priesthood Office and most especially when they swear the secret oaths in the Temple Ceremonies.

The one and only reason that these various men, investigators, FBI agents and prosecuters, would not fulfill their <u>sworn obligations</u> to the people of the State of Utah, and this Nation, was because their <u>sworn allegiance was to the Mormon Church, first and foremost</u>!!

[1] Steven Naifeh & Gregory White Smith, *The Mormon Murders, A Story of Greed, Forgery, Deceit, and Death*, (Weidenfeld & Nicolson, New York, 1988) 127.

[2] Ibid., 145.

[3] Ibid., 164.

[4] Doug Ward, The Law that Brings Life, *Dialogue: A Journal of Mormon Thought*, Vol. 28, No. 1 Spring 1995 (Dialogue Foundation, Salt Lake City, Utah, 1995) 61. As found on *"New Mormon Studies CD-ROM*, (Smith Research Associates, Signature Books, Inc. Salt Lake City, Utah, 1998)

[5] *The Mormon Murders*, 246-247.

[6] Ibid., 249.

[7] Ibid., 254.

[8] Ibid., 389.
[9] Ibid., 355-356.
[10] Ibid., 264.
[11] Ibid., 295-297.
[12] Brigham Young in Watt, ed., *Journal of Discourses*, 1:361. (26 volumes)
[13] *The Mormon Murders*, 355-358.
[14] Ibid., 387-388.
[15] Ibid., 420-421.
[16] Ibid., 421.
[17] Ibid., 439.
[18] Ibid., 440.

CONCLUSION

This book has very concretely shown that Mormonism is not just Protestantism with a few problems. It is a unique religious system when compared with the various religions of the world. One thing that sets Mormonism apart from other world religions is its specific oaths and covenants required for varying levels of membership. Another aspect of Mormonism that is quite troubling is its absolute requirement for allegiance to its Priesthood, beginning with its Prophet and Apostles and working itself to the local level of Priesthood organization.

The "Priesthood" is the all consuming entity that powers Mormonism through its living Prophet. Without the "Priesthood," there is no Mormon Church. Likewise, without its living Prophet, there is no Mormon Church either. The "Priesthood" controls every facet of Mormonism. No meeting can be held, no event can take place, no doctrine can be taught, and no person can serve in any capacity, without the knowledge and approval of the Mormon Priesthood. Local level Priesthood Officers have and hold their authority to serve through an organizational chain of authority that culminates in the living Mormon Prophet. He holds all the

Priesthood "Keys" (the power to direct the labors of the various responsibilities and functions of the Priesthood) on earth. Mormonism believes that the Priesthood is the power by which men may speak and act for God on earth and their living Prophet is, in fact, God's real time "oracle."

Part of the responsibility of holding the Priesthood are the covenants that come with it at ordination. Profoundly significant is the covenant to "receive my servants." Every male Priesthood holder must accept this covenant when he is ordained into any Priesthood office. This covenant states that he will obey the Priesthood authorities over him or he will have no forgiveness in this world nor the world to come. That obligation puts every Mormon male into a "doctrinal vice" with respect to obeying Mormon Church leaders.

This "doctrinal vice" not only controls males, but females as well. All Mormons are under direct Priesthood leadership, no matter their position in the Church. The Mormon Church holds itself as "the only true and living church on the face of the whole earth,"[1] and eternal salvation can only be obtained through the "Church." Mormon Apostle Mark E. Petersen made this point very plain: **<u>"salvation is in the Church, and of the Church, and is obtained only through the Church.</u>"[2]**

The domination of Mormonism begins with the covenants agreed upon in being baptized into the Church. These covenants include standing as a witness for God at all times and in all places. Since the Mormon Church believes it alone is the only true church on earth, that means a Mormon covenants to stand up for it at all times. Mormons also covenant to keep all of God's commandments—in Mormonism, part of the commandments of God is to obey His earthly leaders, the Mormon Priesthood. Each Sunday these covenants are renewed with the partaking of the sacrament (communion).

The absolute control in Mormonism is exercised in the Church's belief that it is led by a living Prophet who is the literal mouthpiece of God on earth. The Mormon Prophet, his two Counselors, and the Twelve Apostles of the Church ("The Brethren") are held in reverence as "prophets, seers, and revelators." Following their direction and counsel leads to eternal life: **"Let us hearken to those we sustain as prophets and seers, as well as the other brethren, as if our eternal life depended on it, because it does!"**[3]

Mormonism's belief is that it is the only true church on earth, is led by a living Prophet who speaks for God in all things, and maintains control through its Priesthood authority that it alone possesses. These beliefs together advance the requirement for absolute allegiance to the Church and its Leadership. Since salvation can only be gained through the Church, and eternal life only by hearkening to those sustained as "prophets, seers, and revelators," utter dependency is placed in the Church and its leaders, and with that comes subjugation.

Mormonism is dependent upon its Golden Rule: "Follow the Prophet!" The conditioned belief in Mormonism is that its living Prophet is God's literal mouthpiece on earth, speaks for Him in all things, can never lead the Church astray, and to follow him is to directly obey God: ergo, blind obedience.

The Mormon Prophet, as well as "The Brethren," by virtue of their esteemed position in Mormon doctrine, command absolute obedience from the Mormon people. Couple this doctrinal position of power and authority with the belief that the Mormon Church is God's literal "Kingdom" on earth, both temporally and spiritually, and you have the potential for abuse of power. Mormonism's migratory history was a result of this abuse of power wherever the Church was physically located. The conflicts with the local populace were driven by this abuse of power and were the reason the Mormons were "driven" from state to state until they finally settled in a previously uninhabited area. The belief that the Mormons were driven out simply because of religious persecution is incorrect and a Mormon self-promoting myth when compared with the objective evidence of history.

The belief that the Mormon Church is God's "Kingdom" on earth, in and of itself wields a declaration of power: **"The Church is a kingdom. The Lord Jesus Christ is the Eternal King, and the President of the Church, the mouthpiece of God on earth, is the earthly king. All things come to the Church from the King of the kingdom in heaven, through the king of the kingdom on earth."**[4] Holding to the position that the Mormon Prophet is the "king of the kingdom on earth" through whom God controls, and communicates all things, places all Mormons in a position of servitude to the king.

The Mormon Church believes it will be the governing entity of the world when Jesus returns to the earth: **"The Church of Jesus Christ of Latter-day Saints as it is now constituted is the *kingdom of God on earth*. Nothing more needs to be done to establish the kingdom. (D. & C. 35:27; 38:9, 15; 50:35; 62:9; 65; 136:41.) The kingdom is here, and it is the same kingdom which Daniel said would be set up in the last days."**[5]

Historically, and by definition of the 13th Prophet of the Mormon Church, Ezra Taft Benson, as cited in Chapter Five, the Mormon Prophet **"can receive revelation on any matter—temporal or spiritual and the prophet may be involved in civic matters."**[6] The mating together of Church and State cannot be divorced from Mormonism because they are one in the Kingdom of God—which is the Mormon Church! This opens "Pandora's Box" for the abuse of power, which has demonstrated itself repeatedly in Mormon history.

As noted by Ezra Taft Benson in his *Fourteen Fundamentals in Following the Prophet*, number 14 states: **"The prophet and the presidency—the living prophet and the First Presidency—follow them and be blessed;**

reject them and suffer."[7] This absolute allegiance factor in Mormonism is reinforced and supported through its system of oaths, covenants and Temple Endowments, as discussed in Chapter Six.

Mormonism's culminating event on earth is its Temple Ceremony where a Mormon receives their endowment. As noted in Chapter Six, four different "Laws" are presented in the Temple Ceremony where secret oaths are sworn that unconditionally bind a Mormon to those laws by covenant. The first is the "Law of Obedience." The Mormon Temple participants swear by oath to obey God's commandments which include following the Mormon Priesthood. The second is the "Law of Sacrifice." The Mormon Temple participants swear that they **"should covenant to sacrifice all that we possess, even our own lives if necessary, in sustaining and defending the Kingdom of God."**[8] Here the Mormon swears to sacrifice everything they possess, even their own life if called upon, to sustain and defend Mormonism. The third law is the "Law of the Gospel." Mormons agree here to avoid impure and unholy actions and are specifically instructed to avoid **"evil speaking of the Lord's anointed."**[9] This command is to avoid speaking out in disagreement of those placed in a Priesthood Leadership position over the Mormon. The fourth law is the "Law of Consecration." In this oath and covenant a Mormon swears to **"consecrate yourselves, your time, talents, and everything with which the Lord has blessed you, or with which he may bless you, to the Church of Jesus Christ of Latter-day Saints, for the building up of the Kingdom of God on the earth and for the establishment of Zion."**[10] This oath and obligation is all encompassing to the Mormon. It obligates them to covenant all that they have now and all that they have in the future — time, talents, and everything with which the Lord has blessed them — to the Mormon Church.

These four secret oaths of the Mormon Temple place any Mormon who has been through the Temple and received their "Endowment" in an unconditional position of subjection to the Mormon Church and its controlling power: The Priesthood. This power obviously peaks in the office of its Prophet, but extends to the local level of Priesthood leadership as well.

As thoroughly documented in this book, a Mormon, by oath and covenant, is subjugated to the Mormon Church. Mormonism believes it is in fact God's Kingdom on earth, controlled by His Priesthood and its leaders are God's direct oracles. Not only does Mormonism exercise earthly control over its membership, but its authority reaches beyond the grave. Mormonism's belief that its Prophets and Apostles will stand side-by-side with Jesus Christ on "Resurrection Morning" having a direct impact on the eternal destiny of an individual, places a yoke of bondage on a Mormon that is insurmountable.

This leverage, this ecclesiastical weight, cannot be underestimated. As detailed in the analysis of the Mountain Meadows Massacre and the Hofmann Murders, this undue influence played a governing role in these events. There is no question that Mormons acted contrary to reason and normal behavioral patterns because of the direct pressure placed upon them by the power of Mormonism. Because of the extraordinary power that Mormonism exercises over its membership, a Mormon truly is not an independent person. Within the bonds of Mormonism, a person is not their own.

Elder Brigham H. Roberts, one of the Seven Presidents of the Seventy brings this all together in a speech given at General Conference:

"It is sometimes urged that the permanent realization of such a desire is impossible, since the Latter-day Saints hold as a principle of their faith that God now reveals

Himself to man, as in ancient times; that the priesthood of the Church constitute a body of men who have, each for himself, in the sphere in which he moves, special right to such revelation; that the President of the Church is recognized as the only person through whom divine communication will come as law and doctrine to the religious body; <u>that such revelation may come at any time, upon any subject, spiritual or temporal, as God wills; and finally that, in the mind of every faithful Latter-day Saint, such revelation, in whatsoever it counsels, advises or commands, is paramount.</u> Furthermore it is sometimes pointed out that the members of the Church are looking for the actual coming of a Kingdom of God on earth, that shall gather all the kingdoms of the world into one visible, divine empire, over which the risen Messiah shall reign. **<u>All this, it is held, renders it impossible for a 'Mormon' to give true allegiance to his country, or to any earthly government.</u>**"[11] (emphasis added.)

This statement, by a Mormon General Authority is very cogent. Without provocation he sums up the principle of this book: There is a conflict between Mormonism and the public trust.

<u>WHAT'S THE POINT?</u>

"<u>When Salt Lake City Calls</u>," what will a member of the Mormon Church do? The religion of Mormonism places a Mormon in servitude to its human leadership. This bondage is real, it is expressed in its doctrinal passages, is reinforced twice yearly by the sustaining vote for the leadership, and obedience to it is required for a member to be considered in "good standing," and to have any expectation to go on to exaltation (Godhood) in the next life.

The Mormon Church is in effect "The Ultimate Lobbyist." With eternal consequences at stake, the Mormon Church can influence its membership in a role that reaches beyond the grave. Furthermore, this influence cannot be legislated away. This is America, and as long as Mormons abide by the law, they are free to exercise their religious freedoms as per the dictates of their own conscience. I would never deny them that; however, the American voter has a right to know what undue influence may be brought to bear upon their public servants. Lobbying laws to control the ability of outside entities to unduly influence government officials are right and proper. Our Republic form of Government was originally drawn up by the Founding Fathers to place representatives in Congress that would be independent and unencumbered. A Mormon, by definition of their own doctrine, having been placed in a multiple covenanted relationship with their Church, is not independent or unencumbered. Mormonism not only functions by oath, it is conditioned by rote and ritual and all Mormons are bound by obligation to its Priesthood authorities. There are no "Sunshine Laws" in Mormonism. Under the guise of "sacredness," Mormons will not tell what oaths and covenants they have obligated themselves to in their secret rituals.

President John F. Kennedy, in his statement to the Southern Baptist Leaders in 1960, speaking with respect to his Presidential Candidacy, makes a point that is applicable to all levels of public service across the board of American Democracy:

"I want a chief executive whose public acts are responsible to all and obligated to none — who can attend any ceremony, service or dinner his office may appropriately require him to fulfill — and whose fulfillment of his Presidential office is not limited or conditioned by any religious oath, ritual or obligation."[12]

The mandatory requirements of President Kennedy's statement cannot be met within the context of Mormonism. "**When Salt Lake City Calls**," what will a member of the Mormon Church do? The doctrinal position as fully documented in this book, says the answer to that question is: "WAKE UP, YE ELDERS OF ISRAEL, AND LIVE TO GOD and none else; and learn to do as you are told....But if you are told by your leader to do a thing, do it. **NONE OF YOUR BUSINESS WHETHER IT IS RIGHT OR WRONG**."[13] (emphasis added.)

[1] *Doctrine and Covenants* 1:30.

[2] *Ensign*, July 1973, p. 108.

[3] 12th Mormon Prophet, Spencer W. Kimball, *Search These Commandments, Melchizedek Priesthood Personal Study Guide*, (Published by The Church of Jesus Christ of Latter-day Saints, Salt Lake City, Utah, 1984) 276.

[4] Bruce R. McConkie, *Mormon Doctrine* (Bookcraft: Salt Lake City, Utah, 1966) 416.

[5] Ibid., 415.

[6] *Fourteen Fundamentals in Following the Prophet* by Ezra Taft Benson, http://www.lds-mormon.com/fourteen.shtml

[7] Ibid.

[8] Chuck Sackett, *What's Going On In There?*, (Sword of the Shepherd Ministries, Inc., Thousand Oaks, California, 1982) 31.

[9] Ibid., 39.

[10] Ibid., 44.

[11] Elder Brigham H. Roberts, *Conference Report*, April 1907, Afternoon Session., 46.

[12] John F. Kennedy, Address to the Southern Baptist Leaders, http://usinfo.state.gov/usa/infousa/facts/democrac/66.htm

[13] Heber C. Kimball, in Hawkins, ed., *Journal of Discourses*, 6:32.

APPENDIX ONE

NILES' NATIONAL REGISTER- AUGT. 31, 1844— THE MORMONS.

Below is a transcript of the *Niles' National Register* of August 31, 1844, printed in Baltimore, Maryland. It contained a reprint of an article from the front page of the *Quincy (Illinois,) Whig*, dated July 24, 1844, just 27 days after Joseph Smith's murder. The City of Quincy was a voice of reason and stability in the area surrounding Nauvoo that was awash with anti-Mormon sentiment. Quincy was the "City of Refuge" for the Mormons upon their expulsion from the State of Missouri in 1838-1839, prior to their settling in Nauvoo. This article provides sound insight for the reason tension and unrest existed between the citizens in the surrounding areas and the Mormons. Mormon historians would have us believe that the Mormons were persecuted purely because of their religious beliefs and were the victims of bigotry and unreasoned hatred. No mention is ever provided in the annals of Mormon history of the usurpation of the laws of the nation and state by their leaders as cause for the tensions and poor relations between the Mormons and the citizenry surrounding them in the various areas they lived in throughout their migratory history.

The author of this article makes some very strong points that wherever the Mormons settled conflicts erupted where none had existed before. Again, Mormon historians would have us believe that the Mormons were simply an innocent people seeking to practice their religious freedoms. No mention is ever made that in each instance the leadership of Mormonism placed itself above the law and operated outside of the laws of the nation, state, and local governments. When defiance of the law reached a point where the local citizenry rose up in opposition and demanded compliance therewith, Mormon leaders cried "religious persecution" and moved to a new location where they again came into conflict with the laws of the land. This pattern repeated itself until the United States forced compliance under the Edmund-Tucker Act of 1887. The choice was given: comply with the laws of the United States or the Mormon Church would be unincorporated and broken apart. Relocated to a remote area where conflict with an existing citizenry was removed (Utah), and forced into compliance with national law by the United States Government, the Mormon Church has now become an accepted part of the American landscape. Mormon historians have been quite successful at rewriting history to place Mormons as the innocent victims and that all problems occurring around them was due to "religious persecution" by evil people.

A review of the *Niles National Register* reprinted article provides an insightful observation. When I first read this piece I was struck with the reasoned analysis of the original situation by the writer and how applicable their observations are even to this day.

NILES' NATIONAL REGISTER

FIFTH SERIES.—No. 27. –Vol. XVI.] BALTIMORE, AUGUST 31, 1844 [Vol. LXVI.—WHOLE No. 1,718

THE PAST—THE PRESENT—FOR THE FUTURE
PRINTED AND PUBLISHED, EVERY SATURDAY, BY
JEREMIAH HUGHES, EDITOR AND PROPRIETOR,
AT FIVE DOLLARS PER ANNUM, PAYABLE IN
ADVANCE.

THE MORMONS.

From the Quincy (Illinois,) Whig.

"The recent death of Joseph Smith and his brother, by lawless violence, while confined in jail, has been justly reprobated by the public voice, as well in the county of Hancock, where it happened, as in the state of Illinois generally, and in other parts of the Union. No man, so far as my knowledge extends, has been found to justify that rash and guilty act, however much he might believe that the crimes of the prisoners had deserved punishment at the hands of the law.

But it seems to me that *public sentiment,* as is often the case, is in danger of re-acting with so much force to overbear what, for want of a better term, I shall call *public reason.* In other words, our feelings have been so much revolted by this instance of *anti-Mormon* violence, that we sympathize with the *Mormons* alone; we are strongly set against their opponents: we forget the past conduct of the prophet and his followers; we lose sight of the causes which led to the catastrophe, and the Mormons are becoming in our eyes a peaceful, law-abiding people, while their dead leaders assume the semblance of innocence and martyred victims. This is by no means an unusual revulsion in public feeling. But it is necessary to a just understanding of a question, which may at no distant day be of the highest importance to ourselves, that we arrest this current of sympathy, and calmly examine the actual position of things, before we are hurried away from the ground we have heretofore occupied.

I need not review the history of the Mormons in this and other states. From the many and conflicting statements published, enough may be gathered to satisfy us of these facts: that they have every where been troublesome neighbors; and wherever they have established themselves they have bred difficulties, where none before existed; and that, taken as a body of people, especially if collected in strong settlements, they have always manifested a disposition to resist or evade the general laws of the state when applied to restrain their action. Such is the testimony against them in other states, and such is our own experience of them in Illinois.

The causes of this insubordination and turbulence on their part are neither obscure nor uncertain; they are to be found in their peculiar tenets of faith and principles of government. Other religious sects are as enthusiastic as the Mormons, as devoted to the worship of the creed of their choice; but they form no distinct, civil, or political community; they are all (however variant from one another in religious opinion) citizens of a common government, and all recognise the supreme obligations of the constitutions, state and federal, and the laws made in pursuance there of. Each man looks to those laws as the measure of his duties and his rights, and is prepared to sustain their authority against all who oppose it.

But the Mormons have heretofore proceeded upon a different system. The aim and object of him who called himself their prophet was to collect about him a people devoted to his will and obedient to all his commands. To this end he pretended to be inspired by God himself, to be favored with frequent revelations, and to announce to his followers, from time to time, the commands of the great Jehovah. To make his influence over them more direct and powerful, they were gathered, as much as possible, into communities, separate and distinct from other citizens; and, if people of a different persuasion have settled among them, they have been too few and weak to make head against the authority of the prophet. The Mormons, thus associated and thus taught, have been the blind, fanatical, unreasoning followers of an arch impostor. They have fed his luxury with the contributions of money and property. They have pampered his pride and lust of power by their obedience and adulation. And, more than all, they have set up his will as paramount to the laws of the land, and have shown themselves on more than one occasion ready to support him by force in his opposition thereto. What else indeed, could be expected? The word of God, say they, is of far greater obligation than the word of man. God speaks by the mouth of Joseph—man speaks by human laws. Shall we not, therefore, rather obey God than man?

Time will not permit me to exhibit the many illustrations of what I have stated above, which will readily occur to all who are familiar with the conduct of these people in Hancock county for the last three or four years. It is true that the grant of powers in the charter of the city of Nauvoo has furnished them with a pretext for some of the usurpations and encroachments of which they have been guilty. But it was but a pretext, and a flimsy one; it could not and did not deceive the designing men, who used it as a cloak for deliberate tyranny; it could not have served the purpose of deceiving any community not enslaved by the debasing influence of superstition; nor was that city charter necessary for the accomplishment of these purposes. Had that pretext been wanting, others would have been found. The ground work existed in the hearts of the deluded people; it was easy for the hand of their ruler to raise upon it his edifice of fraud, vice, and tyranny.

Who does not know the fact that one short year since Joseph Smith, when arrested by the authority of the governor of this state, upon a demand made by the governor of Missouri, discharged himself from custody by a mock trial upon *habeas corpus* before his creatures, the city council of Nauvoo, he himself being president of that same city council, as mayor of the city!

Who does not know that this successful defiance of the laws of this state, and of process emanating from its highest executive authority, is but one instance out of many. Let me enumerate a few of them. The authorities of Nauvoo have assumed and exercised the power—

To establish a recorder's office for the record of deeds, independent of that provided for by the state laws in every county.

To grant marriage licenses, independently of the state laws requiring them to issue from the clerk of the county commissioners' court.

To try cases of slander and causes the jurisdiction whereof is vested exclusively in the circuit courts of the state.

To punish by fine and imprisonment persons guilty of speaking words disrespectful of Joseph Smith, and other alleged offences, which, if cognizable any where, belonged exclusively to the circuit courts.

To arrest and annoy peaceable visiters to the city, by vexatious confinement and examination, under pretence of regulating its police.

To discharge persons from arrest upon civil or criminal process from any court of the state, by writs of *habeas corpus* emanating from the city council.

And they passed an ordinance prohibiting any civil officer to serve process from the state courts in Nauvoo, unless it was countersigned by their mayor, under penalty of fine and imprisonment, which the governor of the state is forbidden to remit by his pardon!

But, not to fatigue your readers with further enumerations, I will proceed briefly to relate the facts which led to the late occurrences in Hancock county, and from one example, they may learn all the rest.

Certain seceding Mormons, for reasons satisfactory to themselves, disavowed the authority of their late master a few weeks ago, and set up a newspaper in Nauvoo, which was designed to expose his hypocrisy and vices. The prophet, in his capacity as mayor, called together the city council, and took into consideration this enterprise of the seceders, and the first number of the paper which had then been published. It was resolved by the city council and the mayor *that the paper was a public nuisance, and ought to be abated,* and forthwith a warrant was issued to the city marshall to take a sufficient force with him and to destroy the press and type. That officer obeyed his instructions, and on the same day, by force, broke into the office, broke up the press, and scattered the types into the street.

One of the proprietors of the press went immediately to Carthage, the county seat, and complained on oath against the mayor, the city council, the marshal, and others concerned, for a riot in the destruction of his press. Upon his affidavit, a warrant was issued to a constable, who went to serve it, attended by only one individual. He served it first upon the two Smiths, and afterwards upon the others. The prophet at first tried threats and intimidation against the constable, swore great oaths that he would lose the last drop of his blood rather than go to Carthage, and finally resorted to the never-failing *habeas corpus.* He issued writs for the other defendants, some of them (being the city council) issued a writ for him: they tried each other and discharged each other; and the constable was dismissed by the city marshal (himself a defendant) with the assurance that, whether they were discharged or not, he should never take them out of that city.

The constable reported to his fellow citizens in other parts of the county the resistance which he had met with, and called upon them for a force sufficient to enable him to execute the writ. It was known long before that Nauvoo boasted a large force under military organization, which was reported to be well supplied with arms. It was therefore necessary to make serious preparations for the collision. The volunteer companies of the county were called out; new companies raised and organized; aid was solicited from other counties; arms, ammunition, and provisions were collected, and messengers were despatched to the governor, to inform him of the state of things and ask his interference. The Mormons, on their part, were not idle. Their friends were collected from the settlements into Nauvoo; the troops were daily paraded and drilled; guards were stationed about the city, who permitted no one to pass in or out without leave of the city authorities; means and munitions of war were procured as fast as possible, and the whole city was put under strict military regulations, and, as many say, *martial law* was proclaimed. Nay, even after the governor arrived in the county, the United States mail was stopped and sent back some distance, and detained a considerable time, until leave to proceed was given by the Mormon authorities.

Such was the state of affairs when the governor arrived in the county. He recognised the propriety of the action of the citizens, and, after a short correspondence, demanded of the prophet and his codefendants an unconditional surrender of themselves to the constable who had served the writ. After some shuffling for two or three days, the accused finally came in and gave themselves up on a promise of protection from violence, which the governor gave them, and which he received an assurance of from the troops. After their surrender upon this charge, which they acknowledged, and for which they gave bail, the two Smiths were detained upon the further charge of treason; and, the trial being postponed in order to procure witnesses, they were committed to jail for safe-keeping.

There is no doubt but that some evil disposed persons were during all this time engaged in stirring up the wrath of the people against the two Smiths, and endeavoring to incite them to violence. But there is reason to believe, from the course of events, that such a result might not have taken place but for one or two unlucky circumstances. The governor had ordered the troops at Warsaw and Carthage to rendezvous on Thursday, the 27th June, at Golden's Point, and to march upon Nauvoo. His object I do not know, but I presume it was to make a display of force to the Mormons, and to convince them of their incapacity to resist the arms of the state. On the morning of that day, however, apprehending disturbances if he marched so large a force into the city, he ordered all the troops to be disbanded, with the exception of some 200 men, part of whom were in Nauvoo and a part in Carthage. With one company of these he set out himself for Nauvoo.

Upon the same day an attempt was detected to convey into the jail a bundle containing clothes, which were evidently intended to disguise the prisoners: and the report became general that a rescue and escape was contemplated. Doubtless the disbanding of the troops was also urged as a proof of the governor's connivance at it. These were topics well calculated to inflame the minds of men, already strongly excited by the annoyance and tyranny of the Mormon rulers, and the recent expectation of actual hostilities. They produced a most unfortunate effect. A body of armed men marched hastily upon the jail, overpowered the guard, and put to death the two Smiths, and in that act inflicted a deep wound upon the honor of the state, and wrought a lasting injury to all who were opposed to the Mormon dynasty."[1]

[1] *NILES' NATIONAL REGISTER.*, Fifth Series.—No. 27.— Vol. XVI], Baltimore, August 31, 1844., [Vol. LXVI.— Whole No. 1,718, page 433. (copy in possession of the author).

APPENDIX TWO

EXTRA MATERIAL SUPPORTING THE MORMON DOCTRINAL POSITION DENYING THE TRADITIONAL CHRISTIAN BELIEF OF THE VIRGIN BIRTH

This appendix provides additional Mormon source material from numerous Prophets and Apostles on the Mormon doctrine of the "Virgin Birth," which denies the traditional Biblical account. Rather than overload the Eighth Essential Fundamental of Christianity, The Virgin Birth, in Chapter Two, I've provided some additional quotes here. The 6th Mormon Prophet, Joseph F. Smith, is quoted in the January 2006 issue of the Church magazine *Ensign*, under the "The Fulness of the Gospel" section, as follows:

> President Joseph F. Smith (1838-1918) taught: "God the Eternal Father...is the literal Parent of our Lord and Savior Jesus Christ, and of the spirits of the human race....We are God's children."[1]

The above quote ties the paternity of Jesus to the paternity of the spirits of the human race. There is no question in Mormon doctrine that God the Father was the physical progenitor (sire) of the spirits of all mankind in the "Pre-existence." For this Mormon Prophet to align these two events, Jesus' conception and the fatherhood of the spirits of mankind, together in one sentence is definitive. The pro-creative action of both subjects is one and the same. Placing the literal parenting of the pre-mortal spirits and Jesus by "God the Father" in one sentence, with the unquestioned Mormon doctrinal position of a physical relationship to create "the spirits of the human race," leaves no other option for that of Jesus Christ.

The 13th Mormon Prophet, Ezra Taft Benson, is quoted in several different sources as stating the conception of Jesus was that of being "sired." I have listed a little more context in the quote below so you can absolutely see that this former Mormon Prophet is specifically teaching the physical pater-nity of Jesus by God the Father, the exalted man who has a body of flesh and bones.

Jesus Is Divine Because of His Divine Birth

The most fundamental doctrine of true Christianity is the divine birth of the child Jesus. This doctrine is not generally comprehended by the world. **The paternity of Jesus Christ is one of the "mysteries of godliness" comprehended only by the spiritually-minded.**

The apostle Matthew recorded: "Now the birth of Jesus Christ was on this wise: When as his mother Mary was espoused to Joseph, before they came together, she was found with child of the Holy Ghost." (Matthew 1:18.)

Luke rendered a plainer meaning to the divine concep-tion. He quoted the angel Gabriel's words to Mary: "The Holy Ghost shall come upon thee, and *the power of the Highest shall overshadow thee*: therefore also that holy [being] which shall be born of thee shall be called the Son of God." (Luke 1:35; italics added.)

[Prophet Benson sets the above words in *italics* because he is highlighting the person: *the Highest*. This rendering in Mormonism is God the Father.]

Some six hundred years before Jesus was born, an ancient prophet had a vision. He saw Mary and described her as "a virgin, most beautiful and fair above all other virgins." **He then saw her "carried away in the Spirit . . . for the space of a time." When she returned, she was "bearing a child in her arms . . . even the Son of the Eternal Father." (Book of Mormon, 1 Nephi 11:15, 19-21.)**

Thus the testimonies of appointed witnesses leave no question as to the paternity of Jesus Christ. **God was the Father of Jesus' mortal tabernacle, and Mary, a mortal woman, was His mother. He is therefore the only person born who rightfully deserves the title "the Only Begotten Son of God."**

From the time of Christ's heaven-heralded birth, **heresies have crept into Christianity intended to dilute or undermine the pure doctrines of the gospel**. **These heresies, by and large, are sponsored by the philosophies of men and, in many instances, advocated by so-called Christian scholars. Their intent is to make Christianity more palatable, more reasonable, and so they attempt to humanize Jesus and give natural explanations to those things which are divine.**

An example is Jesus' birth. The so-called scholars seek to convince us that the divine birth of Christ as proclaimed in the New Testament was not divine at all and that Mary was not a virgin at the time of Jesus' conception. They would have us believe that Joseph, the foster-father of Jesus, was His physical father, and that therefore Jesus was human in all attributes and characteristics. They appear generous in their praise of Him when they say that He was a great moral philosopher,

319

perhaps even the greatest. But the import of their effort is to repudiate the divine Sonship of Jesus, for on that doctrine rest all other claims of Christianity.

The Church of Jesus Christ of Latter-day Saints proclaims that Jesus Christ is the Son of God in the most literal sense. The body in which He performed His mission in the flesh was sired by that same Holy Being we worship as God, our Eternal Father. Jesus was not the son of Joseph, nor was He begotten by the Holy Ghost. He is the Son of the Eternal Father![2] (bracketed information and emphasis added.)

Mormon Apostle James E. Talmage, wrote about the paternity of Jesus in his foundational Mormon book, the *Articles of Faith*:

"...His [Christ's] unique status in the flesh as the offspring of a mortal mother [Mary] and of an immortal, or resurrected and glorified, Father [Elohim];..."[3] (bracketed information added.)

In the quote below, Brigham Young very specifically aligns the "Father" who sired Jesus' spirit in the Pre-existence and the spirits of mankind. The bolded line makes a direct reference to Mormon doctrine that God is just an exalted man. There would be no reason to make a statement, "of letting any other man do it" except that "God Himself was once as we are now and is an exalted man."[4] There is no other explanation possible for this quote from Brigham Young except that God the exalted man came to earth and committed the physical act necessary to produce Jesus rather than allow any other man to do it. These are not my words, they are Brigham Young's words!

"When the time came that His first-born, the Saviour, should come into the world and take a tabernacle [body], **the Father came Himself and favoured that spirit with a tabernacle instead of letting any other man do it.** The Saviour was begotten by the Father of His spirit, by the same Being who is the Father of our spirits, and that is all the organic difference between Jesus Christ and you and me."[5] (bracketed information and emphasis added.)

This next series of quotes are from Mormon Apostle Bruce R. McConkie who served as a General Authority for 38 years, 15 of those years as an Apostle until he passed away in 1985. He was probably the most prolific writer for Mormonism in the 20th Century. He wrote a series of books, called *"The Messiah Series,"* published during the 1978-1982 timeframe while he was an Apostle.

This quote is a little lengthy, however you can't miss the point by this Mormon Apostle who was sustained as a "prophet, seer, and revelator," at least 25 times by the Mormon Church in a physical vote at their semi-annual General Conference. I will add commentary in [] brackets:

How Messiah Became Mortal

Messiah is the firstborn Spirit Son of Elohim. How came he into mortality that he then might be raised in immortality and become like his Father in the full and eternal sense? What was the process by which he traveled from his primeval spirit home to that of resurrected glory which he now possesses, and in which he has received "all power...in heaven and in earth"? (Matt. 28:18.)

In most respects his coming was comparable to that of all mortals; in one respect—and oh, how vital this is!—his coming was singled out and set apart and different from that of any other person who ever has or ever will dwell on earth. That the true account of his coming might be had among the faithful, Matthew begins his recitation of how the Messiah became mortal; how he took upon himself flesh and blood; how he made clay his tabernacle; how our Elder Brother [Mormonism de-Deifies Jesus by making Him merely our "Elder Brother"] in the spirit took upon himself that mortality which we all undergo—that all this might be known, Matthew commences his account by saying: "Now the birth of Jesus Christ was on this wise," and then follows a recitation of what took place.

Thus, the Messiah was born! On the one hand, his birth was like that of all men; on the other it was unique, unlike that of any of the infinite hosts of our Father's children. And so Matthew says: "When as his mother Mary was espoused to Joseph, before they came together, she was found with child of the Holy Ghost." The marriage discipline of the day called, in effect, for two ceremonies. The participating parties were considered to be husband and wife after the first ceremony, comparable to a formal engagement in our culture, but they did not commence their association as husband and wife until the final marriage ceremony, which often was performed an appreciable period later. It was during this period that Mary "was found with child," a situation that would cause great embarrassment and sorrow among those who believed in and followed the divine laws of chastity and virtue.

Thus the record says: "Then Joseph her husband, being a just man, and not willing to make her a publick example, was minded to put her away privily"—a reaction that dramatizes the compassion and spiritual stature of the one destined to be the foster father of our Lord—"But while he thought on these things, behold, the angel of the Lord appeared unto him in a dream, saying, Joseph, thou son of David, fear not to take unto thee Mary thy wife: for that which is conceived in her is of the Holy Ghost. And she shall bring forth a son, and thou shalt call his name JESUS: for he shall save his people from their sins.... Then Joseph being raised from sleep did as the angel of the Lord had bidden him, and took unto him his wife: And knew her not till she had brought forth her firstborn son: and he called his name JESUS." (Matt. 1:18-25.)

Jesus was thus conceived in the womb of Mary. He took upon himself the nature of man in the same way that all men do. **And yet the account is particular to say Mary "was found with child of the Holy Ghost," and "that which is conceived in her is of the Holy Ghost." If this is interpreted to mean that the Holy Ghost is the Father of our Lord, we can only say the record has come down to us in a corrupted form, for the Holy Spirit and the Father are two separate personages.** [Mormonism denies the Trinity and teaches that God the Father has a body of flesh and bones, and the Holy Ghost (Spirit) is a male "Personage" of spirit; He occupies time and space. If the Holy Ghost was standing in front of you he would be visible.] But providentially there are parallel passages that clarify and expand upon the paternity of Him whom Mary bare.

The Messianic language of Abinadi, [Book of Mormon Prophet] speaking of things to come as though they had already happened, says: "He was conceived by the power of God." (Mosiah 15:3.)

Gabriel's great proclamation to Mary was: "Behold, thou shalt conceive in thy womb, and bring forth a son, and shalt call his name JESUS. He shall be great, and shall be called the Son of the Highest: and the Lord God shall give unto him the throne of his father David: And he shall reign over the house of Jacob for ever; and of his kingdom there shall be no end." Mary asked how this could be, "seeing I know not a man?" Gabriel replied: "The Holy Ghost shall come upon thee, and the power of the Highest shall overshadow thee: therefore also that holy thing which shall be born of thee shall be called the Son of God." (Luke 1:31-35.)

All ambiguity and uncertainty of meaning, if there is any, is removed by Alma, [Book of Mormon Prophet] whose Messianic utterance announced: "The Son of God cometh upon the face of the earth. And behold, he shall be born of Mary,...she being a virgin, a precious and chosen vessel, who shall be overshadowed and conceive by the power of the Holy Ghost, and bring forth a son, yea, even the Son of God." (Alma 7:9-10.) **Jesus, thus, is the Son of God, not of the Holy Ghost, and properly speaking Mary was with child "by the power of the Holy Ghost," rather than "of the Holy Ghost,"** and she was, of course, "overshadowed" by the Holy Spirit, in a way incomprehensible to us, when the miraculous conception took place.

"A Virgin Shall Conceive"

An easy heresy to grow into would be that since **the Messiah is a God;** since he is the Eternal One, the Lord Jehovah, who created all things; since he has all power, all might, and all dominion—and yet must be born among men—surely he must have more than a mortal woman as a mother. High prelates and persons of note and influence in the Catholic fold have argued that Mary should be proclaimed co-redemptrix with Christ, making her bear equally with him the sins of the world. But lest there be any misconceptions in the minds of men, the Messianic messages are pointed and clear as to the person and status of the one chosen to be the mother of God's Son.

In extolling his maternal source, a certain woman said to Jesus, "Blessed is the womb that bare thee, and the paps which thou hast sucked." Our Lord's response admitted the blessed status of her to whom Gabriel had truly said, "Blessed art thou among women" (Luke 1:28), but adroitly turned the thinking of the conversationalist away from undue adoration and toward that which all men must do to be saved. He said: "Yea rather, blessed are they that hear the word of God, and keep it." (Luke 11:27-28.)

Mary's name and appointment to be the chief mother in Israel were known and discussed by them of old. Ammon [Book of Mormon Prophet] testified: "I have seen my Redeemer; and he shall come forth, and be born of a woman, and he shall redeem all mankind who believe on his name." (Alma 19:13.) Jeremiah proclaimed: "The Lord hath created a new thing in the earth, A woman shall compass a man." (Jer. 31:22.) The angelic preacher who taught the doctrine of the atonement to King Benjamin said: "He shall be called Jesus Christ, the Son of God,...and his mother shall be called Mary." (Mosiah 3:8.) As we have already seen, Alma called her Mary and spoke of her as "a virgin, a precious and chosen vessel" (Alma 7:10); she herself told Gabriel she had never known a man (Luke 1:34), and Matthew left us the witness that she was with child before she and Joseph had associated together as man and wife (Matt. 1:18-25). The great Biblical pronouncement as to the virgin birth comes, of course, from Isaiah, who foretold: "A virgin shall conceive, and bear a son, and shall call his name Immanuel." (Isa. 7:14.) Matthew tells us this prophecy was fulfilled in the birth of Jesus. (Matt. 1:22-23.) And Nephi [Book of Mormon Prophet] bears a like

testimony, as we shall now see in discussing the condescension of God. (1 Ne. 11:13-19.) **For our present
purposes, suffice it to say that our Lord was born of
a virgin, which is fitting and proper, and also natural,
since the Father of the Child was an Immortal Being.**
[Notice the teaching point this Mormon Apostle just
made in this bolded sentence. There is no need for
this sentence unless there is some conflict between the
Orthodox Christian belief in the "Virgin Birth" and the
Mormon doctrine that an "Immortal Being," who is an
exalted man was in fact the Father, physically, of Jesus.]

"Knowest Thou the Condescension of God?"

Nearly six hundred years before Mary was with
child of God, by the power of the Holy Ghost, Nephi
saw in vision what would transpire in time's meridian.
"I beheld the city of Nazareth," he says, "and in the city
of Nazareth I beheld a virgin, and she was exceedingly
fair and white." Clearly the vision was intended to show
the high and holy place of Mary. She was foreordained.
There is only one Mary, even as there is only one Christ.
We may suppose that she was more highly endowed spiritually than any of her mortal sisters, but with it all, **she
was a mortal, not a God.** Her mission was to bring the
Son of God into the world, not to redeem mankind, not to
intercede for them. She was destined to be a mother, not
a mediator; hers was the blessed privilege, being mortal,
to bring into the world Him by whom immortality should
come. And blessed is she forever!

Asked by an angel what he saw, Nephi said: "A virgin,
most beautiful and fair above all other virgins." Then,
from the lips of the heavenly being came this question
of eternal import: **"Knowest thou the condescension of
God?"** And since even the greatest of prophets do not

know all things—their knowledge, as with the rest of us, coming line upon line and precept upon precept—Nephi responded: "I know that he loveth his children; nevertheless, I do not know the meaning of all things." Thereupon the angel answered his own question by saying: "Behold, the virgin whom thou seest is the mother of the Son of God, after the manner of the flesh."

The angelic answer is perfect. **The great God, the Eternal Elohim, the Father of us all, the Supreme Being, the Maker and Upholder and Preserver of all things, the Creator of the sidereal heavens, the One whose might and omnipotence we can scarcely glimpse and cannot begin to comprehend, this Holy Being to whom we, by comparison, are as the dust of the earth, this Almighty Personage, in his love, mercy, and grace, <u>condescended to step down from his Almighty throne, to step down to a lesser and benighted state</u>, as it were, and become the Father of a Son "<u>after the manner of the flesh</u>.""** [There can be no question what is being conveyed here, God condescends to step down from His throne, to a lesser benighted (ignorant) state to Father the child "after the manner of the flesh." Why would these statements be made if it was a "miraculous" event—because it wasn't a "miraculous" event, it was a "physical" event, according to Mormonism.]

"And it came to pass that I beheld," Nephi writes, "that she was carried away in the Spirit; and after she had been carried away in the Spirit for the space of a time the angel spake unto me, saying: Look! And I looked and beheld the virgin again, bearing a child in her arms. And the angel said unto me: Behold the Lamb of God, yea, even the Son of the Eternal Father!" **<u>This then is the condescension of God—that a God should beget a man; that an Immortal Parent should father a mortal Son; that the Creator of all things from the begin-</u>**

**ning should step down from his high state of exalta-
tion and be, for a moment, like one of the creatures
of his creating.** [No need for this bolded sentence if
the conception was "miraculous." This sentence is only
needed if God the "exalted man" becomes the physical
parent of Jesus.]

Later the angelic ministrant bade Nephi to look and
behold the condescension of God, meaning this time that
of the Son, and Nephi did so, seeing the persecutions
and trials of the Redeemer of the world as he, in condescension, ministered among his fellow mortals. (1 Ne.
11:13-36.)

Messiah Is the Only Begotten

**We have spoken plainly of our Lord's conception
in the womb of Mary; in reality the plain assertions
are found in the revealed word, and we have but certi-
fied that the words mean what they say and cannot be
spiritualized away. And as it is with reference to our
Lord's mother, so it is as pertaining to his Father. The
scriptures say that Jesus Christ is the Only Begotten
Son. The problem is that the intellectually led ministry
and laity of the day assume, as Satan leads them to do,
that a name-title of this sort is simply figurative and
does not have the same literal meaning as when the
words are spoken in ordinary conversation. Perhaps
again the best service we can render, on the issue here
involved, is somehow to get the message across that
words mean what they say, and that if Christ is the
Only Begotten of the Father, it means just that.** [This
Mormon Apostle is very clearly saying there is nothing
figurative in the language—it is literal: Jesus is the Son
of an Immortal Father.]

Some words scarcely need definition. They are on every tongue and are spoken by every voice. The very existence of intelligent beings presupposes and requires their constant use. Two such words are *father* and *son.* Their meaning is known to all, and to define them is but to repeat them. Thus: A son is a son is a son, and a father is a father is a father. I am the son of my father and the father of my sons. They are my sons because they were begotten by me, were conceived by their mother, and came forth from her womb to breathe the breath of mortal life, to dwell for a time and a season among other mortal men.

And so it is with the Eternal Father and the mortal birth of the Eternal Son. The Father is a Father is a Father; he is not a spirit essence or nothingness to which the name Father is figuratively applied. And the Son is a Son is a Son; he is not some transient emanation from a divine essence, but a literal, living offspring of an actual Father. God is the Father; Christ is the Son. The one begat the other. Mary provided the womb from which the Spirit Jehovah came forth, tabernacled in clay, as all men are, to dwell among his fellow spirits whose births were brought to pass in like manner. There is no need to spiritualize away the plain meaning of the scriptures. **There is nothing figurative or hidden or beyond comprehension in our Lord's coming into mortality. He is the Son of God in the same sense and way that we are the sons of mortal fathers. It is just that simple. Christ was born of Mary. He is the Son of God—the Only Begotten of the Father.**[6] (bracketed information and emphasis added.)

The statements here are quite clear: Jesus was conceived "in the same sense and way that we are the sons of mortal fathers." Biology 101!

Continuing in the same book, Apostle McConkie makes the distinction that Jesus inherited physical traits from His parents just as all children do—that would have to happen from a physical chromosome provided from a physical, exalted God-man:

"Who Shall Declare His Generation?"

"But perhaps Isaiah's query "Who shall declare his generation?" has a greater Messianic meaning than is found in a mere attempt to trace genealogical ancestry. It is a true principle that "no man can say [or, rather, know] that Jesus is the Lord, but by the Holy Ghost." (1 Cor. 12:3.) The testimony of Jesus, which is also the spirit of prophecy, is to know by personal revelation that Jesus Christ is the Son of the living God. In the full and complete sense of the word no one ever knows that Jesus is Lord of all except by personal revelation; and all persons to whom that testimony or revelation comes are then able to declare His generation, to assert from a standpoint of personal knowledge that they know that Mary is his mother and God is his Father. And so, in the final analysis it is the faithful saints, those who have testimonies of the truth and divinity of this great latter-day work, who declare our Lord's generation to the world. **Their testimony is that Mary's son is God's Son; that he was conceived and begotten in the normal way; that he took upon himself mortality by the natural birth processes; that he inherited the power of mortality from his mother and the power of immortality from his Father—in consequence of all of which he was able to work out the infinite and eternal atonement.** This is their testimony as to his generation and mission."[7] (emphasis added.)

This next quote is from Apostle McConkie's book *"The Mortal Messiah."* I could shorten it up a bit, but I don't want to be accused of taking this explicit statement about Jesus' conception out of context:

"Knowest Thou the Condescension of God?"
(1 Nephi 11:16)

John is now conceived in Elisabeth's womb; the son of Zacharias will soon be born; our Lord's forerunner, destined to be six months his senior, shall soon breathe the breath of life. **The words of Gabriel are coming to pass, and soon the Son of God must be sired, conceived, born, and laid in a manager.** [Notice that "sired" and "conception" are distinguished as two separate acts.]

But how can a God be born into mortality? How can the Eternal One take upon himself flesh and blood, and let himself be fashioned as a Man? **A child—any child, including the Child—must have progenitors; he must have parents, both a father and a mother. Gabriel will soon tell the Virgin of Galilee that she shall be the mother. As to the father—he is Elohim. The Son of God shall have God as his Father; it is just that simple, and it could not be otherwise. The doctrine of the divine Sonship lies at the foundation of true religion; without it, Christ becomes just another man, a great moral teacher, or what have you, without power to ransom, to redeem, and to save.**

Having seen in vision—more than six hundred years before the events themselves transpired—the city of Nazareth and a gracious and beautiful virgin therein, Nephi was asked by an angel: "Knowest thou the condescension of God?" He responded by saying he knew of the Lord's love for his children, but not the full answer to the profound query framed by angelic lips. Then the angel answered his own question by saying: "Behold, the virgin whom thou seest is the mother of the Son of God, after the manner of the flesh." **That is to say, the condescension of God lies in the fact that he, an exalted Being, steps down from his eternal throne to become the Father of a mortal Son, a Son born "after the manner of the flesh."**

Immediately after hearing these words, Nephi saw that the virgin "was carried away in the Spirit; and after she had been carried away in the Spirit for the space of a time," Nephi saw "the virgin again, bearing a child in her arms." Thereupon the angel said: "Behold the Lamb of God, yea, even the Son of the Eternal Father!" **To be "carried away in the Spirit" means to be transported bodily from one location to another, as witness the fact that Nephi, at the very time he beheld these visions, had been "caught away in the Spirit of the Lord" and taken bodily "into an exceeding high mountain," which he never "had before seen," and upon which he "never had before" set his "foot." (1 Ne. 11:1, 13-21.)**

Without overstepping the bounds of propriety by saying more than is appropriate, let us say this: God the Almighty; the maker and Preserver and Upholder of all things; the Omnipotent One; he by whom the sidereal heavens came into being, who made the universe and all that therein is; he by whose word we are, who is the Author of that life which has been going on in this system for nigh unto 2,555,000,000 years; God the Almighty, who once dwelt on an earth of his own and has now ascended the throne of eternal power to reign in everlasting glory; who has a glorified and exalted body, a body of flesh and bones as tangible as man's; who reigns in equity and justice over the endless billions of his spirit children

who inhabit the worlds without number that roll into being at his word—God the Almighty, who is infinite and eternal, elects, in his fathomless wisdom, to beget a Son, an Only Son, the Only Begotten in the flesh.

God, who is infinite and immortal, condescends to step down from his throne, to join with one who is finite and mortal in bringing forth, "after the manner of the flesh," the Mortal Messiah.[8] (emphasis added.)

The word "join" used here in this statement is conclusive. Webster's Dictionary defines **join: "1 to bring or come together (with); connect; unite 2 to become a part or member of (a club, etc.) 3 to participate (in a conversation, etc.)."** The word "join" is a verb—it is an action word. In order for an infinite, immortal God to "join," "with one who is finite and mortal in bringing forth, 'after the manner of the flesh,'" He had to come together, connect, unite. This Apostle very specifically stated above that words mean things and are to be taken "literally": join means what it says—to bring or come together (with); connect; unite!!

How does this physical act happen? Mormon Apostle McConkie sheds light on the logistics of this event:

Gabriel Comes to Mary
(Luke 1:26-38; JST, Luke 1:28-29, 34-35)

Mary asked, "How shall this be, seeing I know not a man?" Obviously she could, at the proper time, know Joseph, and he could be the father of all her children, not just those who would come after the Firstborn. She knew that. But already the concept was framed in her mind that the promised Son was not to originate from any power on earth. This offspring was to be himself almighty—God's Almighty Son. How and by what means and through whose instrumentality does such a conception come?

> Gabriel explains: "The Holy Ghost shall come upon thee, and the power of the Highest shall overshadow thee: therefore also that holy thing [better, that holy child] which shall be born of thee shall be called the Son of God."
>
> Again the answer is perfect. There is a power beyond man's. When God is involved, he uses his minister, the Holy Ghost, to overshadow the future mother and **to carry her away in the Spirit. She shall conceive by the power of the Holy Ghost, and God himself shall be the sire.** It is his Son of whom Gabriel is speaking. **A son is begotten by a father: whether on earth or in heaven it is the same.**[9] (emphasis added.)

Apostle McConkie says children are begotten "whether on earth or in heaven it is the same." And, as we saw in note [8] above, "To be "carried away in the Spirit" means to be transported bodily from one location to another, as witness the fact that Nephi, at the very time he beheld these visions, had been "caught away in the Spirit of the Lord" and taken bodily "into an exceeding high mountain," which he never "had before seen," and upon which he "never had before" set his "foot." Apostle McConkie is saying that Mary was physically carried away from earth to heaven to be brought into the presence of God the Father to be physically impregnated (see note [63] in Chapter Two to compare with Mormon Apostle Melvin J. Ballards explanation of this event).

Apostle McConkie is right—words do mean things. In Chapter Two as well as here, I have provided numerous quotes from Mormon Prophets and Apostles that clearly state that the Mormon doctrine of the birth of Jesus denies the Virgin Birth as defined by the Bible and as understood in Orthodox Christianity.

[1] *Ensign*, January 2006, p. 51.

[2] Ezra Taft Benson, *Come unto Christ*, (Deseret Book Company, Salt Lake City, Utah, 1983) 3-4. (Also cited in "*Teachings of Ezra Taft Benson*," pg 7.)

[3] James E. Talmage, *A Study of the Articles of Faith*, (University Press, Cambridge, Mass., 1949) 472.

[4] Joseph Smith, *Teachings of the Prophet Joseph Smith*, Deseret Book Company, Salt Lake City, Utah, 1974) 345.

[5] Brigham Young in Richards, ed., *Journal of Discourses*, 4:218.

[6] Bruce R. McConkie, *The Promised Messiah, The First Coming of Christ*, Deseret Book Company, Salt Lake City, Utah, 1978) 462-469.

[7] Ibid., 472-473.

[8] Bruce R. McConkie, *The Mortal Messiah, From Bethlehem to Calvary, Book 1*, Deseret Book Company, Salt Lake City, Utah, 1979) 313-315.

[9] Ibid., 318-319.

APPENDIX THREE

LYING FOR THE LORD

This appendix is meant to show that there has been a fundamental problem identified with Mormon leaders telling the truth when the subject deals with the Mormon Church. Note [4] of Chapter Ten of this book is very telling and is provided for review:

> "From the time of the translation of the Book of Mormon through the Nauvoo period and into the time of the Reed Smoot senate hearings, **the leadership of the church engaged in a practice that became known as "lying for the Lord."** Our leaders used this tactic because they were fearful that if the truth were known about actual church practice or doctrines their adversaries would destroy the Lord's work. (This fear seems somewhat mystifying in light of the promise that "no unhallowed hand shall disrupt my work.") **However, we have been assured that the leaders who sought to protect the work by lying will be blessed for their valor. Clearly lying is not always lying, and justice will not always claim those who bear false witness. Under the rule of law, what constitutes lying must ultimately be deter-**

mined by some interpretation beyond mortality."[1]
(emphasis added.)

In an essay printed in "*History of the Church*" Joseph Smith provides a foundation for deception based upon a principle of man's limited understanding:

"Happiness is the object and design of our existence; and will be the end thereof, if we pursue the path that leads to it; and this path is virtue, uprightness, faithfulness, holiness, and keeping all the commandments of God. But we cannot keep all the Commandments without first knowing them, and we cannot expect to know all, or more than we now know unless we comply with or keep those we have already received. **That which is wrong under one circumstance, may be, and often is, right under another.**

God said, "thou shalt not kill;" at another time He said "Thou shalt utterly destroy." This is the principle on which the government of heaven is conducted— by revelation adapted to the circumstances in which the children of the kingdom are placed. **Whatever God requires is right, no matter what it is, although we may not see the reason thereof till long after the events transpire.**...

... **But in obedience there is joy and peace unspotted,** unalloyed; and as God has designed our happiness—and the happiness of all His creatures, he never has— **He never will institute an ordinance or give a commandment to His people that is not calculated in its nature to promote that happiness** which He has designed, and which will not end in the greatest amount of good and glory to those who become the recipients of his law and ordinances."[2] (emphasis added.)

Joseph Smith, here lays out a premise for acceptable deceit: **"That which is wrong under one circumstance, may be, and often is, right under another."** Adding to this wall of rationalization is the concept that we as humans simply don't have the "big picture," and may not see all that is going on: **"Whatever God requires is right, no matter what it is, although we may not see the reason thereof till long after the events transpire."** Attach to those building blocks the ideas that **in obedience "is joy and peace unspotted,"** and that **God will never give a commandment that is not calculated to promote our happiness** and you have the all the ingredients necessary to "Lie for the Lord." If you believe that whatever you are lying about is from God then you can rationalize away the deception.

Daniel H. Wells, 2nd Counselor to Brigham Young was found to be lying under oath about polygamy:

> "One significant aspect of the case was the testimony of Daniel H. Wells, the high-ranking LDS authority, who had wedded Miles to Owens. Wells had no problem recalling that particular ceremony, but when asked about Miles having another wife (or wives), the Mormon leader suddenly could "not remember." He refused to answer other questions because they involved "secret" Mormon ceremonies. Wells also denied the bloody oaths and threats of death contained in the temple rituals. He was fined $100 and jailed for two days on contempt of court charges.
>
> **The Miles case showed U.S. authorities that prosecuting polygamy would be virtually impossible given Mormon leadership's willingness to lie under oath.**"[3]

(emphasis added.)

Two Mormon Prophets (4th Wilford Woodruff and 6th Joseph F. Smith) and one 1st Counselor in the First Presidency (George Q. Cannon) were all found to by lying under oath:

> "Wilford Woodruff, Joseph F. Smith, and George Q. Cannon unflinchingly swore in court to the Federal Master-in-Chancery, Charles Loofbourow, that the Manifesto: 1) prohibited plural marriages; and 2) required polygamous men to live with only one of their wives, thus ending illegal cohabitation in Utah. These LDS authorities gave assurances that all Mormons were obeying the new policy. Woodruff remarked: "As shepherds of a patient, suffering people we ask amnesty for them and pledge our faith and honor for their future." **His testimony remains a stunning example of perjury under oath by a high-profile witness.**
> **Lying, either to bring about a "greater good" or to protect the church, has always been an acceptable practice within Mormonism, and continues to be an unspoken tenet of the faith.**"[4] (emphasis added.)

Authors Richard and Joan Ostling discovered this aspect of Mormonism in their research as well:

> "Post-Manifesto Mormons were in a situation analogous to that in Nauvoo. Polygamy was again secret, denied in public, and causing division inside the church itself. The high authorities, as well as the rank and file, included members who were uncomfortable with contorted evasions of truth. But what Hardy calls "pretzeled language" became common public discourse on the subject of plural marriage. Matthias Cowley [Mormon Apostle] could say in one breath, **"I am not dishonest and not a liar and have always been true to the work and to the brethren,"** and in the next breath, **"We**

have always been taught that when the brethren were in a tight place that it would not be amiss to lie to help them out."[5] (bracketed information and emphasis added.)

In an address given to the faculty, students, and alumni of BYU on September 12, 1993, Mormon Apostle Dallin H. Oaks continues the theme of "theocratic" or "situational ethics" with respect to telling the truth:

"In the matter of lying, the essential question is not whether we have a duty to tell the truth and nothing but the truth. We clearly have that duty. We must not lie. I know of no category of justified lies.

The difficult question is whether we are morally responsible to tell the whole truth. When we have a duty to disclose, we are morally responsible to do so. Where there is no duty to disclose, we have two alternatives. **We may be free to disclose if we choose to do so, but there will be circumstances where commandments, covenants, or professional obligations require us to remain silent.**

In short, my brothers and sisters, the subject of lying is clear-cut in a majority of instances. **But there are a lot of situations where people are sometimes charged with lying where the charge is not well founded. You will read that kind of charge in the literature and in current commentary, as if a person were under a duty to tell everything he or she knew, irrespective of any other duties or obligations.**

I urge you who are lawyers and lawyers-in-preparation to be sophisticated as you think about these subjects. Be unqualified in your commitment to the truth. Be unqualified in your determination to tell the truth and nothing but the truth. But also be prepared for circumstances that may be painful and contrary to your personal interest and comfort where you must keep confidences, even if someone calls you a liar. **It requires sophisticated analysis of the circumstances and a finely tuned conscience to distinguish between the situation where you are obliged by duty to speak and the situation where you are obliged by duty, commandment, or covenant to remain silent.**"[6] (emphasis added.)

This counsel by Apostle Oaks appears to have been well taken by the current Mormon Prophet, Gordon B. Hinckley:

"Since taking the lead of Mormonism in 1995, ninety-one-year-old Gordon B. Hinckley has effectively distanced the Mormon church from anything that might make it appear non-Christian. Journalist Richard Ostling observes:

> Hinckley has held an unprecedented number of open press conferences from New York to Albuquerque to Seoul to Tokyo, and has granted interviews to newspapers, magazines, and TV's Mike Wallace and Larry King. In these appearances, ever the professional publicist, he conveys an upbeat philosophy and smooths over the most controversial LDS teachings.

During some interviews, Hinckley has gone so far as to answer pointed doctrinal questions in a manner not altogether straightforward; one might even say, deceptively vague. For example, during a March 1997 interview with religion writer Don Lattin, Hinckley was asked about the LDS doctrine concerning God being a mortal man with a body (a belief highly offensive to Christians). **To the question, "Don't Mormons believe that God was once a man?," the LDS presi-**

dent responded: "I wouldn't say that... That gets into some pretty deep theology that we don't know very much about." In actuality, this doctrine is one of Mormonism's key tenets about which a great deal is known, according to countless quotes from LDS leaders on the subject.

Later in 1997, during the PBS *NewsHour with Jim Lehrer*, Hinckley made an equally deceptive comment about the classic LDS doctrine affirming potential godhood for the Saints. Hinckley refused to say that Mormons hope to become a god, but instead, said: "[Latter-day Saints] can achieve to a godly status, yes, of course they can." He went on to side-step the godhood issue to say: "We believe in the eternity and the infinity of the human soul, and its great possibilities."

Then, in August 1997, Hinckley again was evasive during an interview with *Time*. The magazine asked: "God the father was once a man as we were. This is something that Christian writers are always addressing. Is this the teaching of the church today, that God the Father was once a man like we are?" Hinckley not only professed to have little knowledge of this cherished belief, but added that he did not even know if the LDS Church taught such a thing! In response to the query about God once being a man, Hinckley answered:

I don't know that we teach it. I don't know that we emphasize it. I haven't heard it discussed for a long time in public discourse. I don't know. I don't know all the circumstances under which that statement was made. I understand the philosophical background behind it. But I don't know a lot about it and I don't know that others know a lot about it.

Making Hinckley's response all the more disingenuous is his self-professed role in the LDS Church as a spiritual leader whose job it is to declare doctrine. Interestingly, Hinckley sang a rather different tune shortly afterward when speaking to an all Mormon audience at the LDS church's General Conference. In an apparent reference to the prior interviews during which he feigned ignorance of key Mormon beliefs, Hinckley wryly commented: "None of you need worry because you read something that was incompletely reported. You need not worry that I do not understand some matters of doctrine. I think I understand them thoroughly." At this comment his audience laughed with a sense of pride that they were indeed being led by a clever, as well as politically savvy, prophet."[7]

The documentation is without question that Joseph Smith, the founding Prophet of Mormonism, was found to be lying on many occasions. The early Church initiated many unorthodox doctrines that were very strange and offensive to Christianity. In order to prevent exposure of these offensive doctrines, an element of secretiveness and clannishness developed which is very much a part of the Mormon religion today. The history of Mormonism is wrought with Prophets and Apostles which have been caught in lying and deceitful practices. This is often rationalized away with the apologetic position of the Church that these are mere men who sometimes exhibit human frailties. This statement is very dangerous when coupled with the absolute allegiance that is given to these men and the belief that they are God's direct oracles on earth.

In his above quotes, the current Prophet, Gordon B. Hinckley, has perpetuated the practice of giving evasive, disingenuous answers which expands the distrust against Mormonism that has developed over the years.

[1] Doug Ward, The Law that Brings Life, *Dialogue: A Journal of Mormon Thought*, Vol. 28, No. 1 Spring 1995 (Dialogue Foundation, Salt Lake City, Utah, 1995) 61. As found on *"New Mormon Studies CD-ROM*, (Smith Research Associates, Signature Books, Inc. Salt Lake City, Utah, 1998)

[2] Joseph Smith, *History of the Church of Jesus Christ of Latter-day Saints, Period 1, History of Joseph Smith, the Prophet, by Himself*, (The Deseret Book Company, Salt Lake City, Utah, 1970) Vol. V, 134-135.

[3] Richard Abanes, *One Nation Under Gods: A History of the Mormon Church* (New York: Four Walls Eight Windows, 2002) 312-313.

[4] Ibid., 326.

[5] Richard N. Ostling and Joan K. Ostling, *Mormon America: The Power and the Promise*, (HarperCollins Publishers Inc., San Francisco, 1999) 89.

[6] Dallin H. Oaks, "Gospel Teachings About Lying", http://www.lds-mormon.com/oakslying.shtml

[7] *One Nation Under Gods: A History of the Mormon Church*, 386-389.

APPENDIX FOUR

"OATH OF VENGEANCE"

Many Mormons will argue that the "Oath of Vengeance" is a myth, a "vicious rumor," which never existed. Their argument is based on ignorance rather than on any objective evaluation of the evidence for its existence.

It was removed from the Mormon Temple Ceremony on February 15, 1927, so who cares whether it existed or not? Two very important points are related to its existence: (1) It reinforces the facts that have consistently shown that the Mormon Church, since its inception, has defied the laws of the United States, and has often placed itself above those laws. (2) The oath states that the participants are to teach this oath "to your children and to your children's children unto the third and fourth generation."

By reviewing the words given in the "Oath of Vengeance," it is very much still in effect today. Born as a 6th generation Mormon, both sets of my grandparents participated in the Mormon Temple Ceremony prior to February 15, 1927; therefore, I am only the 2nd generation removed from this oath. In accordance with the oath, in Mormonism, there are still two generations behind me that are under the obligations of this oath. This oath shows some very unsettling characteristics of the foundations upon which the Mormon Church of today is built.

Has the Mormon Church ever "officially" denounced this "Oath of Vengeance?" The answer is: No. Below I have provided an extract from the United States Senate Hearings on Senator Reed Smoot from Utah. The Senate Committee that investigated the matter of whether or not the Senator from Utah could serve in the Senate because he had taken this "Oath of Vengeance," ruled as follows: "*Resolved*, That Reed Smoot is not entitled to a seat as a Senator of the United States from the State of Utah."

OATH OF VENGEANCE

In the protest signed and verified by the oath of Mr. Leilich it is claimed that Mr. Smoot has taken an oath as an apostle of the Mormon Church which is of such a nature as to render him incompetent to hold the office of Senator. From the testimony taken it appears that Mr. Smoot has taken an obligation which is prescribed by the Mormon Church and administered to those who go through a ceremony known as "taking the endowments." It was testified by a number of witnesses who were examined during the investigation that one part of this obligation is expressed in substantially these words:

You and each of you do covenant and promise that you will pray and never cease to pray Almighty God to avenge the blood of the prophets upon this nation, and that you will teach the same to your children and to your children's children unto the third and fourth generation.

An effort was made to destroy the effect of the testimony of three of these witnesses by impeachment of their reputation or veracity. This impeaching testimony was not strengthened by **the fact that the witnesses by**

348

whom it was given were members of the Mormon Church, and would naturally disparage the truthfulness of one who would give testimony unfavorable to that church. The testimony of the witnesses for the protestants, before referred to, was corroborated by the testimony of Mr. Dougall, a witness sworn in behalf of Mr. Smoot, and no attempt was made to impeach the character of this witness. It is true that a number of witnesses testified that no such obligation is contained in the endowment ceremony; **but it is a very suspicious circumstance that every one of the witnesses who made this denial refused to state the obligation imposed on those who take part in the ceremony.**

The evidence showing that such an obligation is taken is further supported by proof that during the endowments ceremonies a prayer is offered asking God to avenge the blood of Joseph Smith upon this nation, and certain verses from the Bible are read which are claimed to justify the obligation and the prayer. The fact that such a prayer is offered and that such passages from the Bible are read was not disputed by any witness who was sworn on the investigation. Nor was it questioned that by the term "the prophets" as used in the endowment ceremony, reference is made to Joseph and Hyrum Smith.

That an obligation of vengeance is part of the endowment ceremony is further attested by the fact that shortly after testimony had been given on that subject before the committee, Bishop Daniel Connelly of the Mormon Church denounced the witnesses who had given this testimony as traitors who had broken their oaths to the church.

The fact that an oath of vengeance is part of the endowment ceremonies and the nature and character of such oath was judicially determined in the third judicial court of Utah in the year 1889 in the matter of

the application of John Moore and others to become citizens of the United States. In an opinion denying the application, the court say:

> In these applications the usual evidence on behalf of the applicants as to residence, moral character, etc., was introduced at a former hearing and was deemed sufficient. Objection was made, however, to the admission of John Moore and William J. Edgar upon the ground that they were members of the Mormon Church, and also because they had gone through the endowment house of that church and there had taken an oath or obligation incompatible with the oath of citizenship they would be required to take if admitted. * * *
>
> Those objecting to the right of these applicants to be admitted to citizenship introduced eleven witnesses who had been members of the Church of Jesus Christ of Latter Day Saints, commonly called the "Mormon Church." Several of these witnesses had held the position of bishop in the church, and all had gone through the endowment house and participated in its ceremonies. The testimony of these witnesses is to the effect that every member of the church is expected to go through the endowment house, and that nearly all do so; that marriages are usually solemnized there, and that those who are married elsewhere go through the endowment ceremonies at as early date thereafter as practicable in order that the marital relations shall continue throughout eternity.
>
> **On behalf of the applicants fourteen witnesses testified concerning the endowment ceremonies, but all of them declined to state what oaths are taken, or what obligations or covenants are there entered into, or what penalties are attached to**

their violation; and these witnesses, when asked for their reason for declining to answer, stated that they did so "on a point of honor," while several stated they had forgotten what was said about avenging the blood of the prophets. * * *

The witnesses for the applicants, while refusing to disclose the oaths, promises, and covenants of the endowment ceremonies and the penalties attached thereto, testified generally that there was nothing in the ceremonies inconsistent with loyalty to the Government of the United States, and that the Government was not mentioned. One of the objects of this investigation is to ascertain whether the oaths and obligations of the endowment house are incompatible with good citizenship, and it is not for the applicants' witnesses to determine this question. **The refusal of applicants' witnesses to state specifically what oath, obligations, or covenants are taken or entered into in the ceremonies renders their testimony of but little value, and tends to confirm rather than contradict the evidence on this point offered by the objectors. The evidence established beyond any reasonable doubt that the endowment ceremonies are inconsistent with the oath an applicant for citizenship is required to take, and that the oaths, obligations, or covenants there made or entered into are incompatible with the obligations and duties of citizens of the United States.** (Vol. 4, pp. 340-343)

The obligation hereinbefore set forth **is an oath of disloyalty to the Government which the rules of the Mormon Church require,** or at least encourage, every member of that organization to take.

It is in harmony with the views and conduct of the leaders of the Mormon people in former days, when they openly defied the Government of the United States, and is also in harmony with the conduct of those who give the law to the Mormon Church to-day in their defiant disregard of the laws against polygamy, and polygamous cohabitation. **It may be that many of those who take this obligation do so without realizing its treasonable import; but the fact that the first presidency and twelve apostles retain an obligation of that nature in the ceremonies of the church shows that at heart they are hostile to this nation and disloyal to its government.**

And the same spirit of disloyalty is manifested also in a number of the hymns contained in the collection of hymns put forth by the rulers of the Mormon Church to be sung by Mormon congregations.

There can be no question in regard to the taking of the oath of vengeance by Mr. Smoot. He testified that he went through the ceremony of taking the endowments in the year 1880 and the head of the Mormon Church stated in his testimony that the ceremony is now the same that it has always been.

An obligation of the nature of the one before mentioned would seem to be wholly incompatible with the duty which Mr. Smoot as a member of the United States Senate would owe to the nation. It is difficult to conceive how one could discharge the obligation which rests upon every Senator to so perform his official duties as to promote the welfare of the people of the United States and at the same time be calling down the vengeance of heaven on this nation because of the killing of the founders of the Mormon Church sixty years ago.

MR. SMOOT NOT ENTITLED TO A SEAT
IN THE SENATE

The more deliberately and carefully the testimony taken on the investigation is considered, the more irresistibly it leads to the conclusion that the facts stated in the protest are true; that Mr. Smoot is one of a self-perpetuating body of men, known as the first presidency and twelve apostles of the Church of Jesus Christ of Latter-Day Saints, commonly known as the Mormon Church; that these men claim divine authority to control the members of said church in all things, temporal as well as a spiritual; that this authority is, and has been for several years past, so exercised by the said first presidency and twelve apostles as to encourage the practice of polygamy in polygamous cohabitation in the State of Utah and elsewhere, contrary to the constitution and laws of the State of Utah and the law of the land; that the said first presidency and twelve apostles do now control, and for a long time past have controlled, the political affairs of the State of Utah, and have thus brought about in said State a union of church and state, contrary to the constitution of said State of Utah and contrary to the Constitution of the United States, and that said Reed Smoot comes here, not as the accredited representative of the State of Utah in the Senate of the United States, but as the choice of the hierarchy which controls the church and has usurped the functions of the State in said State of Utah.

It follows, as a necessary conclusion from these facts, that Mr. Smoot is not entitled to a seat in the Senate as a Senator from the State of Utah, and your committee report the following resolution:

<u>*Resolved,* That Reed Smoot is not entitled to a seat as a Senator of the United States from the State of Utah</u>.

J.C. BURROWS,
Chairman.[1]
(emphasis added).

The following is a transcription of the photocopy of a letter dated February 15, 1927, from Mormon Apostle George F. Richards to the President of the St. George Temple, discontinuing the "Oath of Vengeance" from the Temple Endowment Ceremony:

Salt Lake Temple
Salt Lake City, Utah
<u>FEBRUARY 15. 1927</u>

<u>Pres. St George Temple</u>
<u>St. George, Utah</u>

Dear Brother;

We have the Temple ordinances written into the books for the Presidents of Temples and are At request of President Grant we have already adopted some of the changes decided upon, and it will be in order for you to do the same. In sealing for the dead, whether one or both is dead, omit the kissing. **<u>Omit from the prayer in the circles all references to avenging the blood of the Prophets</u>. <u>Omit from the ordinance and lecture all reference to retribution</u>.** This last change can be made with a day's notice to those taking the parts that contain such reference.

This letter is written with the approval of the Presidency.

Sincerely your brother,
George F. Richards
(Signature)[2] (emphasis added.)

AUTHOR'S NOTE: In the first bolded sentence above in the letter to the President of the St. George Temple, note the reference to "Omit from the prayer in the circles all references to avenging the blood of the Prophets." In note [31] of Chapter Nine, author Will Bagley discusses the events that took place on the killing field of Mountain Meadows immediately following the killings. Notice how the men where assembled in a "prayer circle" and that **"they had been privileged to keep a part of their covenant to avenge the blood of the prophets."**[3] This is not a coincidence. The prayer circle was part of the Mormon Temple Ceremony and the "Oath of Vengeance" was part of that "prayer circle" portion of the ceremony.

[1] 59th Congress, *1st Session*. SENATE. DOCUMENT No. 486, Proceedings Before The Committee On Privileges And Elections Of The United States Senate In The Matter Of The Protests Against The Right Of Hon. Reed Smoot, A Senator From The State Of Utah, To Hold His Seat., (VOLUME IV, WASHINGTON: GOVERNMENT PRINTING OFFICE. 1906.) 495-498.

[2] Chuck Sackett, *What's Going On In There?*, (Sword of the Shepherd Ministries, Inc., Thousand Oaks, California, 1982) 62.

[3] Will Bagley, *Blood of the Prophets, Brigham Young and the Massacre at Mountain Meadows*, (University of Oklahoma Press, Norman, 2002) 158.

APPENDIX FIVE

MORMON RACISM

The theme of this book is to point out the obligations that Mormons are under that leverage them to their Church in every aspect of their lives and that they are not autonomous with respect to their being able to act independently to serve the people freely when they serve in any public office; whether that office is local, state or federal.

Another factor I feel obligated to bring to the attention of the voting public is the fact that the doctrinal position of the Mormon Church, with respect to race, is prejudicial to the extreme. The Mormon Church Public Relations Department has done a great job of smoothing the issue of racism over. However, the prejudicial doctrines remain and cannot help but bias those of the Mormon faith when dealing with the races which populate our great country. One cannot be indoctrinated with prejudicial teachings and have no bias as a result of that indoctrination; it's just not possible.

Do we as Americans wish to have people in public service whose professed "Faith" is prejudicial to people of color? Can we trust a public servant whose core beliefs state that anyone who is not white was cursed by God and that their skin color is a punishment for their performance in a

"Pre-earth Life?" Will these people be non-prejudicial or unbiased in their attitudes toward anyone of color when their belief system indoctrinates them otherwise? These are some very serious questions that every American voter should be concerned about.

This Appendix is sure to infuriate Mormons. However, I'm just the reporter of the facts. This isn't my belief. I didn't make these quotes up. I am simply accurately reporting the doctrinal position of the Mormon Church with respect to its teachings on how the races of the world came to be, and that teaching begins in its doctrine on the "Pre-existence." The Mormon Church doctrine on "Pre-existence" is unquestionably prejudicial to anyone who is not white.

I am going to say right up front that there are parts of this information that are quite inflammatory, and downright derogatory towards anyone who is not white. I will use the term "negro," often in this text. I'm not using it to offend anyone, it is simply the term used in the majority of the quotes, as it was the vernacular of the day, and I will be responding to the quotes of Mormon leaders using this term.

Please don't get mad at the messenger. I will simply accurately and truthfully document all that I present. This information will undoubtedly offend both Mormons and non-Mormons alike; however, the truth needs to be told. I could have left this appendix out of this book, but I'm not willing to avoid the hard issues. I've researched them and I'm providing the information to you, because you have a right to know what Mormonism really stands for. Why was this book written? Because the Mormon Church will never show you the information that is presented here. Modern Mormonism is all about hiding or rewriting the past and being disingenuous about its current doctrines and teachings, to hide the embarrassing truth!

I have spent hundreds of hours of research on this topic, and all the while one thing has rung through loud and clear: Of all the subjects on Mormonism I have studied to date, and I have studied many, no single Mormon Doctrine more clearly shows that Mormon leaders are mere men, with no "higher calling" placed upon them, as Mormonism claims, than this "Anti-Black/Anti-African Doctrine."

PENALTY AGAINST AFRICANS REMOVED
OFFICIAL DECLARATION—2

To Whom It May Concern:

On September 30, 1978, at the 148ᵗʰ Semiannual General Conference of The Church of Jesus Christ of Latter-day Saints, the following was presented by President N. Eldon Tanner, First Counselor in the First Presidency of the Church:

In early June of this year, the First Presidency announced that a revelation had been received by President Spencer W. Kimball extending priesthood and temple blessings to all worthy male members of the Church. President Kimball has asked that I advise the conference that after he had received this revelation, which came to him after extended meditation and prayer in the sacred rooms of the holy temple, he presented it to his counselors, who accepted it and approved it. It was then presented to the Quorum of the Twelve Apostles, who unanimously approved it, and was subsequently presented to all other General Authorities, who likewise approved it unanimously.

President Kimball has asked that I now read this letter:

June 8, 1978

To all general and local priesthood officers of The Church of Jesus Christ of Latter-day Saints throughout the world:

Dear Brethren:

As we have witnessed the expansion of the work of the Lord over the earth, we have been grateful that people of many nations have responded to the message of the restored gospel, and have joined the Church in ever-increasing numbers. This, in turn, has inspired us with a desire to extend to every worthy member of the Church all of the privileges and blessings which the gospel affords.

Aware of the promises made by the prophets and presidents of the Church who have preceded us that at some time, in God's eternal plan, all of our brethren who are worthy may receive the priesthood, and witnessing the faithfulness of **those from whom the priesthood has been withheld,** we have pleaded long and earnestly in behalf of these, our faithful brethren, spending many hours in the Upper Room of the Temple supplicating the Lord for divine guidance.

He has heard our prayers, and by revelation has confirmed that the **long-promised day has come** when every faithful, worthy man in the Church may receive the holy priesthood, with power to exercise its divine authority, and enjoy with his loved ones every blessing that flows therefrom, including the blessings of the temple. **Accordingly, all worthy male members of the Church may be ordained to the priesthood without regard for race or color.** Priesthood leaders are instructed to follow the policy of carefully interviewing all candidates for ordination to either the Aaronic or the Melchizedek Priesthood to insure that they meet the established standards for worthiness.

We declare with soberness that the Lord has now made known his will for the blessing of all his children throughout the earth who will hearken to the voice of his authorized servants, and prepare themselves to receive every blessing of the gospel.

Sincerely yours,

SPENCER W. KIMBALL
N. ELDON TANNER
MARION G. ROMNEY

The First Presidency

Recognizing Spencer W. Kimball as the prophet, seer, and revelator, and president of The Church of Jesus Christ of Latter-day Saints, it is proposed that we as a constituent assembly accept this revelation as the word of and will of the Lord. All in favor please signify by raising your right hand. Any opposed by the same sign.

The vote to sustain the foregoing motion was unanimous in the affirmative.

Salt Lake City, Utah, September 30, 1978[1]
(emphasis added.)

NEGROES NOT ENTITLED TO FULL BLESSINGS OF THE GOSPEL

Why was there a need for a "Revelation" to allow all **worthy** brethren to receive the Mormon Priesthood? Let's hear from the highest level of the Mormon Church: Letter of LDS First Presidency to Dr. Lowery Nelson, July 17, 1947:

"From the days of the Prophet Joseph even until now, it has been the doctrine of the Church, never questioned by any of the Church leaders, that the **Negroes are not entitled to the full blessings of the Gospel.**"[2] (emphasis added.)

MORMON LEADERS, ORACLES OF GOD ON EARTH

As you can see, the Mormon Church believed that blacks were not entitled to "the full blessings of the gospel" (remember in the Mormon vocabulary, "gospel" means Mormonism). Twice I've quoted the First Presidency of the Mormon Church, 31 years apart, contradicting each other. As defined in Chapter Five, the "First Presidency" (Mormon Prophet and his two counselors) and the Mormon Twelve Apostles are believed to be God's living oracles on earth and are sustained as "Prophets, Seers, and Revelators," to the Mormon Church.

It is important to understand the Mormon belief about these fifteen men (the Prophet, his two counselors and the Twelve Apostles). They are believed to be God's living oracles on earth and "They have the **right,** the **power,** and **authority to declare the mind and will of God** to his people..."[3] (emphasis added.) I'm going to be quoting men who held these offices. It is also important to note that each of the men currently serving in one of these fifteen positions, and all who have ever served in one of them, have/had been sustained twice a year by the complete Church, as a prophet, seer, and revelator, as long as they held the office. We have already seen in the two quotes from the First Presidency, the historical Mormon stance that blacks were not entitled to the "full blessings of the gospel".

MORMONISM DENIES NEGROES THE PRIESTHOOD, AND DOES NOT PREACH TO THEM

Mormon Apostle Bruce R. McConkie, in his foundational work, Mormon Doctrine, said:

"Negroes in this life are denied the priesthood; under no circumstances can they hold this delegation of authority from the Almighty. (Abra. 1:20-27.) **The gospel message of salvation is not carried affirmatively to them** (Moses 7:8, 12, 22) although sometimes negroes search out the truth, join the Church, and become by righteous living heirs of the celestial kingdom of heaven. President Brigham Young and others have taught that **in the future eternity** worthy and qualified negroes will receive the priesthood and every gospel blessing available to any man. (*Way to Perfection*, pp. 97-111.) ... **The negroes are not equal with other races where the receipt of certain spiritual blessings are concerned, particularly the priesthood and the temple blessings** that flow therefrom, **but this inequality is not of man's origin. It is the Lord's doing, is based on his eternal laws and grows out of the lack of spiritual valiance of those concerned in their first estate.**"[4] (emphasis added).

What we clearly see here from this Mormon Apostle, who has "special authority," and is an oracle of God on earth (and of note he is quoting two former Mormon Prophets) are four primary Mormon doctrinal points:

    (1) Negroes are denied the priesthood in this life, and under no circumstances can they hold it;

    (2) That the gospel message (Mormonism) is not carried affirmatively to them;

    (3) That they are not equal with other races where the receipt of certain spiritual blessings are concerned;

(4) <u>These prejudices are based on Eternal Law and grow out of the lack of spiritual valiance of those concerned in their "first estate"</u> ("first estate" in the Mormon vocabulary refers to the unique Mormon Doctrine of "Pre-existence" – that man pre-existed in a Spirit World, "first estate," prior to coming to earth, his "second estate").

MORMONISM'S DOCTRINE OF THE RACES

So, in a nutshell, what did we just cover? Blacks are denied the Mormon Priesthood; Mormonism was not to be preached to them; they were not equal to other races as far as Mormon blessings were concerned; and, this is all due to their lack of spiritual valiance in their pre-earth life (Pre-Existence - "first estate").

Mormonism teaches that the races of people here on earth began in a pre-existent, pre-earth life. Christianity does not teach or believe this, because it is not taught in the Bible. The premise for this belief comes entirely from Mormon unique scriptures.

BLACKS CURSED WITH A DARK SKIN

Mormonism teaches that blacks, because of their lack of valiancy in the "pre-existence" were cursed with a dark skin, and in order to come to this earth had to come through the lineage of Cain, who Mormonism teaches was cursed with a black skin for killing his brother Abel. In the "History of the Church" under the date of January 25, 1842, in Nauvoo, Illinois, Joseph Smith taught that negroes were the "sons of Cain":

"In the evening debated with John C. Bennett and others to show that the Indians have greater cause to complain of the treatment of the whites, than the **negroes, or sons of Cain.**"[5] (emphasis added.)

"Those who were less valiant in pre-existence and who thereby had certain spiritual restrictions imposed upon them during mortality are known to us as the *negroes*. Such spirits are sent to earth through the lineage of Cain, **the mark put upon him for his rebellion against God and his murder of Abel being a black skin.**"[6] (emphasis added.)

BLACKS AN INFERIOR RACE

The 10TH Mormon Prophet, Joseph Fielding Smith, in his book "The Way to Perfection," taught that not only were blacks the sons of Cain, but that they were an inferior race:

"Not only was Cain called upon to suffer, but because of his wickedness **he became the father of an inferior race.** A curse was placed upon him and that curse has been continued through his lineage and must do so while time endures. **Millions of souls have come into this world cursed with a black skin** and have been denied the privilege of Priesthood and the fulness of the blessings of the Gospel. These are the descendants of Cain. Moreover, **they have been made to feel their inferiority and have been separated from the rest of mankind from the beginning.** Enoch saw the people of Canaan, descendants of Cain, and he says, '**and there was a blackness came upon all the children of Canaan, that they were despised among all people.**'"[7] (emphasis added.)

NEGRO LINEAGE THROUGH THE FLOOD

Mormon Apostle Bruce R. McConkie taught that Noah's son Ham carried the negro lineage through the flood:

"Noah's son Ham married Egyptus, a descendant of Cain, thus preserving the negro lineage through the flood. (Abra. 1:20-27)"[8]

A SINGLE DROP OF BLOOD

According to Mormonism, what qualified a person to be considered a negro? A **"single drop"** of negro blood. Mormon Apostle Mark E. Petersen gave an address at the Convention of Teachers of Religion on the College Level at Brigham Young University, Provo, Utah, on August 27, 1954. He said, quoting the former 4th Mormon Prophet, Wilford Woodruff:

President Wilford Woodruff added, "The Lord said, 'I will not kill Cain, but I will put a mark upon him, and that mark will be seen upon every face of every Negro upon the face of the earth. And it is the decree of God that mark shall remain upon the seed of Cain, until the seed of Abel shall be redeemed, and Cain shall not receive the priesthood until the time of that redemption. **Any man having one drop of the blood of Cain in him cannot receive the priesthood.** But the day will come when all that race will be redeemed and possess all the blessings which we now have.'"[9] (emphasis added.)

CURSE REMAINS UNTIL ABEL'S SEED IS REDEEMED IN THE NEXT LIFE

According to Mormon doctrine blacks were given the mark of Cain, a black skin, and that mark will remain until the seed of Abel shall be redeemed. When will that day come? When will the negro receive all the blessings? As the above quote states, that can only happen after the "seed of Abel shall be redeemed." But Cain killed Abel; so, Abel didn't have any seed (children). How will the seed of Abel be redeemed? Mormonism teaches this redemption will happen in the next life.

As previously quoted (Official Declaration—2), in 1978 the First Presidency removed the curse of Cain. What is the Mormon teaching of when the curse will be removed? On December 3, 1854, Brigham Young said:

> "**When all the other children of Adam have had the privilege of receiving the Priesthood,** and of coming into the kingdom of God, and of being redeemed from the four quarters of the earth, **and have received their resurrection** from the dead, **then it will be time enough to remove the curse from Cain and his posterity.** He deprived his brother of the privilege of pursuing his journey through life, and of extending his kingdom by multiplying upon the earth; and because he did this, he is the last to share the joys of the kingdom of God."[10] (emphasis added.)

On August 19, 1866, Brigham Young continued:

> "Why are so many of the inhabitants of the earth cursed with a **sin (sic) [skin] of blackness?** It comes in consequence of their fathers rejecting the power of the Holy Priesthood, and the law of God. They **will go down to death.** And when all the rest of the children have received their blessings in the Holy Priesthood, then that curse will be removed from the seed of Cain, and they will then come up and possess the priesthood, and receive all the blessings which we now are entitled to. The volition of the creature is free; this is a law of their existence, and **the Lord cannot violate his own law;** were he to do that, **he would cease to he God.**"[11] (bracketed information and emphasis added.)

Brigham Young says the negroes "will go down to death" and when all the rest of human kind have received their blessings in the holy priesthood, then the curse will be removed, and not until. He states that it is the Law of the Lord and He cannot violate His law or He would cease to be God.

This doctrine that blacks are inferior has its roots in the Mormon unique doctrine of man's pre-existence. Let's look at that Mormon unique belief. The second Mormon "Prophet," Brigham Young, said on December 28, 1862:

> "**There never was a time when man did not exist,** and there never will be a time when he will cease to exist. Eternity is without confines, and all things animate and inanimate have their existence in it. **The Priesthood of God,** that was given to the ancients and is given to men in the latter-days, as **co-equal in duration with eternity**—is without beginning of days or end of life. It is unchangeable in its system of government and its Gospel of salvation. **It gives to Gods and angels their supremacy and power,** and offers wealth, influence, posterity, exaltations, power, glory, kingdoms and thrones, ceaseless in their duration, to all who will accept them on the terms upon which they are offered."[12] (emphasis added.)

As you can see from this quote, Brigham Young brought forward some strange teachings that are totally foreign to the Bible and are "Anti-Christian":

1) That man existed eternally.
2) The "priesthood" of God given to man in the latter-days, is what makes man co-equal with God.
3) The "priesthood" of Mormonism gives to Gods and angels their supremacy and power.

4) For those who accept this Mormon Priesthood, it offers them <u>wealth</u>, <u>influence</u>, <u>posterity</u>, <u>exaltations</u>, <u>power</u>, <u>glory</u>, <u>kingdoms</u> and <u>thrones</u>.

The belief and indoctrination that a Mormon male who holds the Mormon priesthood will be given <u>wealth</u>, <u>influence</u>, <u>posterity</u>, <u>exaltations</u>, <u>power</u>, <u>glory</u>, <u>kingdoms</u> and <u>thrones</u>, and holds the same power that gives the "Gods and angels their supremacy and power," really puffs up the flesh of a man.

Mormon Apostle Orson Pratt taught extensively on the Mormon unique doctrine of a pre-earth life:

> "I have already told you that the spirits of men and women, all had a previous existence, thousands of years ago, in the heavens, in the presence of God; and I have already told you that among them are many spirits that are more noble, more intelligent than others, that were called the great and mighty ones, reserved until the dispensation of the fulness of times, to come forth upon the face of the earth, through a noble parentage that shall train their young and tender minds in the truths of eternity..."[13]

PRE-EXISTENCE

In a nutshell, let me briefly describe the Mormon doctrine of pre-existence:

Mormonism teaches that anyone who ever has, or ever will, live on this earth existed in a pre-existent life prior to coming to earth. This doctrine states that we all existed eternally as **"pure intelligence."** Then through a celestial marital relationship between our polygamous God father and one of his many wives, our "pure intelligence" was converted into a "spiritual" pregnancy in our God mother. Nine months later we, all humans born on this earth, were born as spirit babies into the "pre-existence."

We grew up to adult spirithood in the "pre-existence" and progressed as far as we could as spirits; then something had to be done, as we could progress no further as spirits. We needed a mortal body to continue our progression to "Godhood." So, Mormon doctrine says, a "Council of the Gods" was convened and all the "great ones" were there: Abraham, Isaac, Jacob, Joseph Smith, Brigham Young, Jesus and even Lucifer – yes in Mormonism Lucifer was a God.

The "Council of the Gods" convened to decide what to do with all of God's spirit children. Lucifer stood up and addressed the council and proposed a plan where an earth would be created for the spirit children to go and receive their mortal bodies. He, Lucifer, would go to earth and usher all of God's children through life and not allow them to sin. For his efforts, he believed he should receive all the glory for doing this. When he had finished addressing the council, he sat down.

Then Elohim, the Mormon name for the head God of this earth, called on Lucifer's brother to address the council. His name is Jesus. Yes, in Mormonism, Lucifer and Jesus are brothers. Jesus proposed a plan to build an earth for God's spirit children to come to and receive their mortal bodies. However, he proposed that man should be given "free-agency" to live life as they saw fit. Man could follow God or live a life of sin. Jesus proposed that he would come to earth and die for the sin of man, for those who would repent, so they could come and live with their "Father God" again.

Elohim, accepted Jesus' plan, which made Lucifer so furious that he rebelled against God and started a war in heaven. When the war was over, one third of all the "spirit children," including Lucifer, were cast out of heaven and destined to become the devil and his demons here on earth.

Your performance in the "pre-existence" and how valiant you were in the war in heaven, determined your status of birth in this life. The more valiant in heaven, the whiter your skin color. The most valiant were reserved to be born white and born into a Mormon home on this earth. The more color in your skin the less valiant you were in heaven. Mormon teaching is that Blacks sided with Lucifer but didn't actually fight with him. Therefore, they were not kicked out of heaven, but were instead cursed with a black skin and were denied the future privilege on earth of receiving the Mormon Priesthood.

"***There is a reason why one man is born black*** and with other disadvantages, while ***another is born white*** with great advantages. The reason is that we once had an estate before we came here, and we were obedient; more or less, to the laws that were given us there. *Those who were faithful in all things there received greater blessings here, and those who were not faithful received less.*"[14] (*italics* in the original, emphasis added.)

"**According to the doctrine of the Church, the negro, because of some condition of unfaithfulness in the spirit—or preexistence, was not valiant and hence was not denied the mortal probation, but was denied the blessings of the priesthood.**"[15] (emphasis added.)

These last two quotes are from the 10th Mormon Prophet, Joseph Fielding Smith, who served as Prophet from January 1970 until his death in July 1972. The next quote from him is quite specific that those of African descent have a black skin because they "merit" it:

"NO NEUTRALS IN HEAVEN. There were no neutrals in the war in heaven. *All took sides either with Christ or with Satan.* Every man had his agency there, and men receive rewards here based upon their actions there, just as they will receive rewards hereafter for deeds done in the body. The Negro, evidently, is receiving the reward he merits."[16] (*italics* in the original.)

Mormon Apostle Alvin R. Dyer very specifically spells out, with respect to the "Pre-existence," why "a Negro is a Negro"—they rejected the Priesthood of God in the pre-existence:

"I suppose, and you may have often heard missionaries say it or have asked the question: **Why is a Negro a Negro?** And, you have heard this answer. 'Well, they must have been neutral in the pre-existence or they must have straddled the fence.' That is the most common saying—they were neither hot nor cold, so the Lord made them Negroes. This, of course, is not true. **The reason that spirits are born into Negro bodies is because those spirits rejected the Priesthood of God in the pre-existence. This is the reason why you have Negroes upon the earth.**"[17] (emphasis added.)

BLATANT PREJUDICE

Let's look at a statement by Mormon Apostle Melvin J. Ballard. Remember, as an Apostle in Mormonism, he has the **"right, the power and authority to declare the mind and will of God"**[18]:

"Now, my brothers and sisters, I would like you to understand that long before we were born into this earth we were tested and tried in our pre-existence. Of the thousands of children born today, a certain proportion of them went to the **Hottentots** of South Africa; thousands went to **Chinese** mothers; thousands went to **Negro**

372

mothers; thousands to **beautiful white Latter-day Saint mothers**. Now you cannot tell me that all these spirits were just arbitrarily designated, marked, to go where they did, that they were **men and women of equal opportunities**. There are no infant spirits born. They had a being ages before they came into this life. They appear in infant bodies, but they were **tested, proven souls**. Therefore, I say to you that long before we came into this life all groups and races of men existed as they exist today. Like attracts to like.

Why is it in this Church **we do not grant the priest-hood to the Negroes**? It is alleged that the **Prophet Joseph said**—and I have no reason to dispute it—that it is because of some act committed by them before they came into this life. I am convinced it is because of some **things they did before they came into this life** that they have been denied the privilege. **The races of today are very largely reaping the consequences of a previous life**."[19] (emphasis added.)

This doctrine of pre-existence has no basis in Biblical teachings. It was the product of Joseph Smith's teachings and his supposed translation of the Book of Abraham from Egyptian papyri (which has now been shown to be a fraud). This teaching is so prejudicial it defies description. Notice in the above quote that the other races of the world (African, Chinese) were people of "unequal opportunities." Only those who were "tested, proven souls" and who earned their placement based on a "previous life," come to earth through **"beautiful white Latter-day Saint mothers."**

This concept is amplified by Mormon Apostle Mark E. Petersen on page 6 of a speech he gave at the Convention of Teachers of Religion on the College Level at Brigham Young University on August 27, 1954:

"Let us consider the great mercy of God for a moment. **A Chinese, born in China with a dark skin, and with all the handicaps of that race seems to have little opportunity.** But think of the mercy of God to Chinese people who are willing to accept the gospel. **In spite of whatever they might have done in the pre-existence to justify being born over there as Chinamen,** if they now, in this life, accept the gospel and live it the rest of their lives they can have the Priesthood, go to the temple and receive endowments and sealings, and that means they can have exaltation. Isn't the mercy of God, marvelous?"[20] (emphasis added.)

THUS SAITH THE LORD – NOT!

The Mormon Church Canon contains four books of scripture. One of those is named "The Doctrine and Covenants." This book purportedly contains the revelations given to Joseph Smith, the founding Prophet of Mormonism, and is revered by Mormons as scripture. In these "revelations" from God given to Joseph Smith, God spoke directly to Joseph as evidenced by the statements penned by Joseph stating "Thus saith the Lord." The quotes from "The Doctrine and Covenants" leave no room for questioning these revelations as being from God.

When Joseph Smith and his successor, Brigham Young, died, God must have changed his way of communicating with His modern day prophets, because the last two "Revelations" received, on polygamy and prejudice, have glaringly been missing the "Thus saith the Lord" delivery. Why is it that the last two revelations, given because of direct pressure on the Mormon Church to change its doctrinal positions, don't have God speaking? Maybe it is because these last two revelations were human realization, vice Holy Revelation. (Now, don't get me wrong here, I do not believe the "Revelations" received by Joseph Smith were from God, anything but. I'm using this line of reasoning to make a point.)

The letter from the Mormon Presidency which reverses the Mormon Church's Anti-Black Doctrine is attempting to rewrite Mormon History as to when the blacks will be allowed to hold the Mormon Priesthood. Let's look at what the Mormon "First Presidency" wrote:

"Aware of the **promises made by the prophets and presidents** of the Church who have preceded us **that at some time, in God's eternal plan, all of our brethren who are worthy may receive the priesthood,** and witnessing the faithfulness of those from whom the priesthood has been withheld, we have pleaded long and earnestly in behalf of these, our faithful brethren, spending many hours in the Upper Room of the Temple supplicating the Lord for divine guidance.

He has heard our prayers, and <u>by revelation has confirmed that the long-promised day has come</u> when every faithful, worthy man in the Church may receive the holy priesthood, with power to exercise its divine authority, and enjoy with his loved ones every blessing that flows therefrom, including the blessings of the temple."[21] (emphasis added.)

This letter leads the uninformed to believe that previous "Prophets and Presidents" promised that at some time in the future, the time would come that blacks could receive all of the blessings everyone was entitled to.

TWO BIG, MAJOR STIPULATIONS

What is the whole story here? Whenever you deal with Mormonism, you have take the Paul Harvey approach, you have get "The Rest of the Story." When did these previous

"Prophets and Presidents" say "all of our brethren who are worthy may receive the priesthood," was going to happen? In the book "The Church and the Negro" published in 1967, 11 years before "The Revelation" changing the anti-black doctrine, Mormon writer John L. Lund discusses the two stipulations before the priesthood can be given:

> "The prophets have declared that there are at least two major stipulations that have to be met before the Negroes will be allowed to possess the Priesthood. The first requirement relates to time. The Negroes will not be allowed to hold the Priesthood during mortality, in fact, not until after the resurrection of all of Adam's children. The other stipulation requires that Abel's seed receive the first opportunity of having the Priesthood."[22] (emphasis added.)

NEGROES CANNOT HOLD THE PRIESTHOOD IN MORTALITY

Let's look at what these previous prophets had to say. Brigham Young, on December 3, 1854, said that the negroes will not have the privilege of receiving the priesthood until:

> "...all the other children of Adam have had the privilege of receiving the Priesthood, and of coming into the kingdom of God, and of being redeemed from the four quarters of the earth, and have received their resurrection from the dead, then it will be time enough to remove the curse from Cain and his posterity."[23]

Twelve years later, on August 19, 1866, Brigham Young, speaking on the negro and the priesthood, said:

"**They will go down to death**. And **when all the rest of the children have received their blessings** in the Holy Priesthood, **then that curse will be removed from the seed of Cain,** and they will then come up and possess the priesthood, and receive all the blessings which we now are entitled to. The volition of the creature is free; **this is a law of their existence, and the Lord cannot violate his own law;** were he to do that, he would cease to be God."[24] (emphasis added.)

These quotes from the second Mormon Prophet, clearly show that the negroes must pass through mortality, they must die, before they can hold the Mormon Priesthood. Brigham Young stated that this law was from the Lord and that He cannot violate His law or He ceases to be God.

ABEL'S SEED MUST FIRST BE RESURRECTED

Another quote from the book "The Church and the Negro": "The second major stipulation that needs to be met before the Negroes can be allowed to possess the priesthood is the requirement that Abel's seed receive the opportunity of holding the priesthood first."

"The Prophet Joseph taught that Negroes could not hold the Priesthood or act in any of its offices until the seed of Abel received that Priesthood."[25]

The book *"The Church and the Negro"* answers the obvious question for us: "When will Abel's seed receive the priesthood?"

"It will first of all be necessary that **Abel marry, and then be resurrected,** and ultimately exalted in the highest degree of the Celestial Kingdom so that he can have a continuation of his seed. **It will then be necessary for Abel to create an earth for his spirit children to come to and experience mortality.** These children will have to be "redeemed" or resurrected. **After the resurrection or redemption of Abel's seed, Cain's descendants, the Negroes, will then be allowed to possess the Priesthood.** Joseph Fielding Smith has said that "the Lord decreed that the children of Cain should not have the privilege of bearing the priesthood until **Abel had posterity** who could have the priesthood and **that will have to be in the far distant future.** When this is accomplished **on some other world**, then the restrictions will be removed from the children of Cain who have been true to their 'second' estate." This earth life is considered the "second" estate and those Negroes who prove through their individual righteousness their worth will certainly be blessed by God to possess the Priesthood **in that distant future when Abel's seed has been redeemed.**"[26] (emphasis added.)

These quotes of the 1st, 2nd, and 10th Mormon Prophets, without question show that the negroes cannot hold the Mormon Priesthood in this life, it will only happen in a future world. According to Brigham Young, this is God's Law and if He were to change it "He would cease to be God." Then along comes Mormon Prophet number 12, Spencer W. Kimball, who up and changes God's Law. So, according to Brigham Young, GOD CEASED TO BE GOD, or ALL THE MORMON PROPHETS FROM NUMBER 1, JOSEPH SMITH, TO NUMBER 11, HAROLD B. LEE, WERE WRONG – WHICH MAKES THEM FALSE PROPHETS! The Mormon Church can't have it both ways. **ACCORDING TO THEIR OWN PROPHETS, EITHER GOD CEASED TO BE GOD AND ALL PROPHETS BEFORE KIMBALL WERE FALSE, OR**

<u>**HE (KIMBALL) WAS A FALSE PROPHET.**</u> The facts simply do not bear out any other conclusion.

<u>PROMOTING A NEW IMAGE</u>

The "Church News" is an official publication of the Mormon Church. It is published weekly by the Deseret Newspaper Company which is owned by the Mormon Church. On the front cover of the May 31, 2003 issue are two black men sporting white shirts and black name tags, which identify them as Mormon Missionaries. The cover says:

25 years since priesthood revelation

'The long-promised day has come when every faithful, worthy man in the Church may receive the holy priesthood.' Official Declaration – 2, Doctrine and Covenants

Denial and deceit appears to be the way the Mormon Church intends to avoid facing the reality that their anti-black doctrine proves that Mormonism is a false religion.

The front cover of the Church News was laid out such that, under the picture of the two black missionaries, was the above statement that **"The long-promised day has come..."** That statement perpetuates the lie the Mormon Church is putting forward to hide the truth of their anti-black doctrine. The statement simply ignores history, and insinuates that the previous Mormon Prophets all prophesied that a "Day would come." That is true, they did all prophecy that "a day would come" when the blacks could hold the priesthood. But, that day, they all said, or agreed with the position of the previous prophets, was to be in the next life - after the resurrection, in another world.

<u>ON SOME OTHER WORLD</u>

The 10th Mormon Prophet, Joseph Fielding Smith, wrote a series of books called "Answers to Gospel Questions." In

Volume 2 of that series he answers a question concerning when Negroes will be allowed to receive the Mormon Priesthood:

> "Since Cain slew his brother Abel in order to obtain all the rights of priesthood to descend through his lineage, the Lord decreed that **the children of Cain should not have the privilege of bearing the priesthood until Abel had posterity who could have the priesthood** and that will have to be in the <u>**far distant future**</u>. When this is accomplished <u>**on some other world,**</u> then the restrictions will be removed from the children of Cain who have been true to their 'second' estate."[27] (emphasis added.)

WAIT A MINUTE!! Oracle number 10 and all previous Oracles, back to number 1, say the blacks will not be allowed to hold the priesthood until after the resurrection in another world. Oracle number 12 comes along and reverses the doctrine. HOW CAN THAT BE? <u>**One of the Oracles has to be wrong!**</u> As outlined in Chapter Five, the 13th Prophet of the Mormon Church, Ezra Taft Benson, gave a speech at BYU on February 26, 1980, while President of the Quorum of the Twelve Apostles. This speech was after the reversal of the anti-black doctrine. The speech by Apostle Benson was called "FOURTEEN FUNDAMENTALS IN FOLLOWING THE PROPHETS." Let me quote from the speech concerning the Fourth Fundamental:

FOURTH: <u>The Prophet Will Never Lead The Church Astray</u>.

President Wilford Woodruff stated:

> **"I say to Israel, the Lord will never permit me or any other man who stands as president of the**

Church to lead you astray. It is not in the program. It is not in the mind of God." (The Discourses of Wilford Woodruff, pp 212-213)

President Marion G. Romney tells of this incident which happened to him:

"I remember years ago when I was a Bishop I had President (Heber J.) Grant talk to our ward. After the meeting I drove him home ... Standing by me, he put his arm over my shoulder and said: '**My boy, you always keep your eye on the President of the Church, and if he ever tells you to do anything, and it is wrong, and you do it, the Lord will bless you for it.**' Then with a twinkle in his eye, he said, 'But you don't need to worry. **The Lord will never let his mouthpiece lead the people astray.**'"[28]

"HOUSTON, WE HAVE A PROBLEM!"

To quote a famous line from the movie "Apollo 13" – "Houston we have a problem." We see that the Mormon Church teaches that Prophets and Apostles are God's Oracles on Earth. They have the "**Right, the Power, and the Authority to declare the mind and the will of God**," and the Lord will never permit them to lead you astray.

WELL, SOMEONE HERE IS LEADING SOMEONE ASTRAY!! THE MORMON CHURCH CAN'T HAVE IT BOTH WAYS!

The 12th Mormon Prophet can't come along and reverse what 11 other Prophets have all stated directly or indirectly was God's Law. Either they were all wrong and led the Church astray, or number 12 led the Church astray; or God just couldn't make up His mind! Which is it?

JESUS' CHARGE TO HIS APOSTLES (Mark 16:15)

In the Bible in the book of Mark, Chapter 16 verse 15, we read: "And he said unto them, Go ye into **all the world,** and preach the gospel to **every creature.**"

What was the Mormon Church's doctrinal position up until June 8, 1978? In the foundational work, Mormon Doctrine, by Apostle Bruce McConkie we read:

"Negroes in this life are denied the priesthood; under no circumstances can they hold this delegation of authority from the Almighty. (Abra. 1:20-27.) The message of the gospel is not carried affirmatively to them..."[29] (emphasis added.)

Now let's look at the utter hypocrisy that the Mormon Church is putting forth today; a complete denial of "God's Law" as taught by their Prophets and Apostles. An article was printed in the June 1990 "Ensign" magazine, titled "A Hike to Eternity." This article shows the absolute denial of Mormonism about their racist doctrine. The article tells of a mixed race family that lived down the hill from the Oakland, California Temple. A quote from the article:

"We had lived just below the Oakland Temple for more than a year, but we had never gone near it. We were an interracial family and, though we had heard the Mormons now allowed blacks to hold the priesthood, we were certain we wouldn't be welcome there. Besides, we really weren't interested in going anywhere near a church with such a well-known image of discrimination against blacks ... Michael, I don't think we'd better go there," I said. "Mormons don't like blacks, and they especially don't like mixed families."[30]

The story continues with the family taking a hike and ending up at the Temple. They sneak into a tour group and the Mormons leading the group are so nice to them. One thing leads to another and they take the missionary lessons and join the Mormon Church. The article concludes with this:

> "In the intervening decade, our family's 'hike to eternity' has carried us halfway around the world and back again to our present home in Oregon. We've taken some wrong turns and detours along the way, and some of the trail has been rough. But in all our wanderings, we have never found hide nor hair of the racism we had worried about. What we have found is a world filled with Bodines and Nelsons—Church member 'co-hikers' who are always ready to reacquaint us with the map and put us back on the right path to eternity."[31]

This article perpetuates a lie that the Mormon Church has never been racist and fully accepts **"MIXED RACE MARRIAGES."**

MIXED RACE MARRIAGES

What did Brigham Young say about mixed race marriages?

> **"Shall I tell you the law of God in regard to the African race? If the white man who belongs to the chosen seed mixes his blood with the seed of Cain, the penalty, under the law of God, is death on the spot. This will always be so."**[32] (emphasis added.)

Do you see the deception? The Mormon Church is in utter denial of its past. One can say, "Well, men of other Christian Churches made racial statements over the years." That is absolutely right; however, the Mormon Church says its leaders are **God's Oracles** on earth and have the **"Right, the Power, and the Authority to declare the mind and the will of God,"** and the Lord will never permit them to lead the Church astray. No one else says that. Christian denominational leaders and pastors tell their membership to validate what they say against God's Word: The Bible. Mormonism says, its living leaders are the living word and trump the written word. This Appendix clearly shows that the Mormon Prophets and Apostles weren't led by God; rather, they are simply sinful men led by their environment and egos.

PREJUDICIAL STATEMENTS

In an interview with LOOK Magazine on October 22, 1963, the 10th Mormon Prophet, Joseph Fielding Smith, said:

> **"I would not want you to believe that we bear any animosity toward the Negro. 'Darkies' are wonderful people, and they have their place in our church."**[33] (emphasis added.)

The 3rd Mormon Prophet, John Taylor, said blacks were the Devil's representatives on earth:

> "And after the flood we are told that the curse that had been pronounced upon Cain was continued through Ham's wife, as he had married a wife of that seed. And why did it pass through the flood? Because **it was necessary that the Devil should have a representative upon the earth** as well as God;"[34] (emphasis added.)

The 2ⁿᵈ Mormon Prophet, Brigham Young, said:

"**You see some classes of the human family that are black, uncouth, uncomely, disagreeable and low in their habits, wild, and seemingly deprived of nearly all the blessings of the intelligence that is generally bestowed upon mankind.**"[35] (emphasis added.)

The Book of Mormon, touted by the LDS Church as scripture, makes very prejudicial statements. All four of these next quotes are from the current Mormon scripture: The Book of Mormon:

2 Nephi 5:21. And **he had caused the cursing to come upon them**, yea, even a sore cursing, **because of their iniquity.** For behold, they had hardened their hearts against him, that **they had become like unto a flint**; wherefore, as **they were white, and exceedingly fair and delightsome, that they might not be enticing** unto my people the Lord **God did cause a skin of blackness to come upon them.** (emphasis added.)

[As you can plainly see in this Mormon scripture, God cursed these people because of their iniquity with a skin of blackness. They previously were "white, and exceedingly fair and delightsome," but God didn't want them to be "enticing," so he cursed them with a skin of "blackness."]

2 Nephi 30:6. And then shall they rejoice; for they shall know that it is a blessing unto them from the hand of God; and **their scales of darkness shall begin to fall from their eyes**; and **many generations shall not pass away among them**, save they shall be a **pure and a delightsome people.** (emphasis added.)

[The last phrase of this verse "pure and a delight-some people," was changed after the 1978 "revelation" allowing blacks to hold the Mormon Priesthood. The word "pure" was originally "white." The verse actually doesn't make sense with the change to pure, as, why does it take several generations to become "pure?" If it was a physiological change—black skin to white skin—it would take several generations, which makes sense in the original, prejudicial, reading.]

Alma 3:6. **And the skins of the Lamanites were dark, according to the mark**, which was set upon their fathers, **which was a curse upon them because of their transgression and their rebellion** against their brethren, who consisted of Nephi, Jacob, and Joseph, and Sam, who were just and holy men. (emphasis added.)

[The dark skin of the Lamanites was a "mark," which was a curse placed on them because of their transgression and rebellion against just and holy men.]

Mormon 5:15. And also that the seed of this people, may more fully believe his gospel, which shall go forth unto them from the Gentiles; for **this people shall be scattered and shall become a dark, a filthy, and a loathsome people,** beyond the description of that which ever hath been amongst us, yea, even that which hath been among the Lamanites, and this **because of their unbelief and idolatry.** (emphasis added.)

[The association here is very clear: dark-filthy-loathsome. Why do they become dark, filthy and loathsome: because of their unbelief and idolatry.]

Nowhere in Christian scripture, the Bible, do you find such "cursings;" or black, or dark skin, that is identified as being done by God because of sinfulness. In the above Mormon scriptures, dark skin is identified with cursings from God because of the peoples' transgressions, rebellion, hardened hearts, unbelief and idolatry. White skin is identified as "delightsome." This prejudicial, doctrinal teaching is deeply entrenched in Mormonism and has been taught since its foundation—the Book of Mormon being published in 1830, just before the Mormon Church was officially organized.

Mormonism today promotes a story that the Church was opposed to slavery. NOT TRUE. Joseph Smith, the founding Prophet of Mormonism, under the date of May 8, 1838, while answering 20 frequently asked questions, said the Church was opposed to setting the Negro free:

Thirteenth-"Are the Mormons Abolitionists?"

"No, unless delivering the people from priestcraft, and the priests from the power of Satan, should be considered abolition. **But we do not believe in setting the negroes free.**"[36] (emphasis added.)

The Mormon Church today is deceitful about its position on slavery in the past. In an article in the Church's magazine the "Ensign," April 1996, titled "Shepherding in Mississippi's Jackson Stake," under the subheading "No Prejudice Within These Walls," we see the deception:

"**More than a century ago, the United States was ripped apart over the issue of slavery.** But today **the restored gospel continues to be a healing balm** and force for mutual understanding and unity among members of all races and backgrounds. They attend church together, worshipping and learning about love, service, and Heavenly Father's plan for them."[37] (emphasis added.)

The key word here is "**continues.**" The insinuation is that more than a century ago when the United States was ripped apart over the issue of slavery, that the Mormon Church was opposed to it and "continues" to be a healing balm and force for mutual understanding....**However, the**

truth to the matter is that Utah was the only Western State or Territory to practice slavery!!

The Mormon viewpoint with reference to the peculiar institution of the South was admirably set forth in the famous interview between abolitionist Horace Greeley, editor of the <u>New York Tribune</u>, and President Brigham Young, at Salt Lake City, July 13, 1859:

"H.G. – What is the position of your church with respect to slavery?"

"B.Y. – We consider it of <u>DIVINE INSTITUTION</u>, and <u>not to be abolished</u> until the curse pronounced on Ham shall have been removed from his descendants."

"H.G. – Are there <u>SLAVES</u> now held in this territory?"

"B.Y. – <u>THERE ARE</u>."

"H.G. – Do your territorial laws uphold slavery?"

"B.Y. – Those laws are printed – you can read them for yourself. If slaves are brought here by those who owned them in the states, <u>we do not favor their escape from the service of those owners</u>."[38] (emphasis added.)

Slavery in America was anything but a "DIVINE INSTITUTION" as Brigham told Horace Greely. I have a copy of those laws of the Territory of Utah – The Act of Organizing the Territory of Utah, dated 1852. As written on pages 80 through 82, "An Act in Relation to Service," the laws for slavery in Utah are explained.

Utah was the only state or territory in the West that allowed slavery, and it was drawn up by a legislature that was 100% Mormon men. The Mormon Church is trying its best to promote an image of universal acceptance of all men as equals. The Mormon Church may have changed its position in allowing blacks to hold the Mormon Priesthood and enter their temples to perform the ordinances they believe are required to becomes Gods, but the teachings that blacks are an inferior race and have been cursed with a black skin because of their actions in the "Pre-existence" have not changed, and are still part of Mormon doctrine!

No other doctrine of Mormonism more clearly shows the contradictions between present and past Mormon Prophets and Apostles. These men were not, are not, "Called of God."

My attempt in this appendix is to expose the prejudicial Mormon doctrine and teachings on the African race. Today the Mormon Church is promoting a two faced position towards blacks: (1) welcoming them with open arms, while (2) retaining those false prejudicial teachings in their official doctrine. The Mormon Church is not just another "Christian" church. Its doctrines and teachings are unique to its self proclaimed scripture and are prejudicial to the core.

[1] *Doctrine and Covenants*, 1989, Official Declaration—2.

[2] John J. Stewart, *Mormonism and the Negro*, (Bookmark A Division Of Community Press Publishing Company, Provo, Utah, 1960, Twelfth Printing 1973) 42-43.

[3] *Teachings of the Living Prophets*, Student Manual Religion 333, Published by The Church of Jesus Christ of Latter-day Saints (Salt Lake City, Utah, 1982) 9.

[4] Bruce R. McConkie, *Mormon Doctrine* (Bookcraft: Salt Lake City, Utah, 1966) 527-528.

[5] Joseph Smith, statement of January 25, 1842, *History of the Church of Jesus Christ of Latter-day Saints* (Salt Lake City: Deseret Book Company, 1970) vol. 4, 501.

[6] Bruce R. McConkie, *Mormon Doctrine*, Bookcraft (Salt Lake City, Utah, 1966) 527.

[7] Joseph Fielding Smith, *The Way to Perfection*, (Published by the Genealogical Society of Utah, Press of Zion's

Printing and Publishing Co., Independence, Jackson County, Mo., 1943) 101-102.

[8] McConkie, *Mormon Doctrine,* 527.

[9] Mark E. Petersen, as quoted from "Mormons and Negroes," by Jerald and Sandra Tanner, (Utah Lighthouse Ministry, P.O. Box 1884, Salt Lake City, Utah 84110, 1970) 10, from the speech *"Race Problems—As They Affect the Church"* August 27, 1954.

[10] Brigham Young, in Watt, ed., *Journal of Discourses,* 2:142.

[11] Brigham Young, in Watt, ed., *Journal of Discourses,* 11: 272.

[12] Brigham Young, in Watt, ed., *Journal of Discourses,* 10:5.

[13] Orson Pratt, in Watt, ed., *Journal of Discourses,* 1:62-63.

[14] Joseph Fielding Smith, *Doctrines of Salvation: Sermons and Writings of Joseph Fielding Smith.* 3 vols., compiled by Bruce R. McConkie. (Bookcraft, Salt Lake City, 1954-56) 1:61.

[15] Joseph Fielding Smith, as quoted from "Mormons and Negroes," by Jerald and Sandra Tanner, (Utah Lighthouse Ministry, P.O. Box 1884, Salt Lake City, Utah 84110, 1970) 4, letter dated April 10, 1963.

[16] Smith, *Doctrines of Salvation,* 1:65-66.

[17] Alvin R. Dyer, as quoted from "Mormons and Negroes," by Jerald and Sandra Tanner, (Utah Lighthouse Ministry, P.O. Box 1884, Salt Lake City, Utah 84110, 1970) 6.

[18] *Teachings of the Living Prophets,* Student Manual Religion 333, Published by The Church of Jesus Christ of Latter-day Saints (Salt Lake City, Utah, 1982) 9.

[19] John Lewis Lund, *The Church And The Negro, A Discussion of Mormons, Negroes and the Priesthood,* (Copyright 1967, John Lewis Lund) 98.

[20] Mark E. Petersen, as quoted from "Mormons and Negroes," by Jerald and Sandra Tanner, (Utah Lighthouse Ministry, P.O. Box 1884, Salt Lake City, Utah 84110, 1970) from the speech *"Race Problems— As They Affect the Church"* August 27, 1954, page 6.

[21] *Doctrine and Covenants*, 1989, Official Declaration—2.

[22] Lund, *The Church And The Negro*, 47.

[23] Brigham Young, in Watt, ed., *Journal of Discourses*, 2:143.

[24] Brigham Young, in Watt, ed., *Journal of Discourses*, 11:272.

[25] Lund, *The Church And The Negro*, 48.

[26] Ibid., 49.

[27] Joseph Fielding Smith, *Answers To Gospel Questions*, 5 vols., (Deseret Book Company, Salt Lake City, Utah,1968) 2:188.

[28] *Fourteen Fundamentals in Following the Prophet* by Ezra Taft Benson, http://www.lds-mormon.com/fourteen.shtml

[29] McConkie, *Mormon Doctrine*, 527.

[30] *Ensign*, June 1990, "A Hike to Eternity", as found on the CD "LDS Church Magazines 1971-1999" published by The Church of Jesus Christ of Latter-day Saints.

[31] Ibid.

[32] Brigham Young, in Watt, ed., *Journal of Discourses*, 10:110.

[33] Bill McKeever & Eric Johnson, *Mormonism 101*, (Baker Books, Grand Rapids, Michigan, 2000) 233.

[34] John Taylor, in Gibbs, ed., *Journal of Discourses*, 22:304.

[35] Brigham Young, in Watt, ed., *Journal of Discourses*, 7:290.

[36] Joseph Smith, *History of the Church of Jesus Christ of Latter-day Saints* (Salt Lake City: Deseret News, 1970), 3:29.

[37] *Ensign*, April 1996, "Shepherding in Mississippi's Jackson Stake," as found on the CD "LDS Church Magazines 1971-1999" published by The Church of Jesus Christ of Latter-day Saints.

[38] A. L. Neff, *History of Utah*, page 618, as re-printed in Jerald & Sandra Tanner, *Mormonism-Shadow or Reality?*, (Modern Microfilm Company, Salt Lake City, Utah, 1982) 278.

GLOSSARY OF MORMON TERMINOLOGY

(TERMS AND PRIMARY PEOPLE)

<u>AARONIC PRIESTHOOD</u> – Lower level Priesthood organization. Offices consist of: Deacon, Teacher, and Priest.

<u>APOSTATE</u> – Anyone who was a Mormon and, for whatever reason, left. Their lot at the "Judgment" will be to become the "Sons of Perdition."

<u>BAPTISM FOR THE DEAD</u> – This is an ordinance that is performed for those who are dead. Mormonism believes that those who are dead, and not Mormons, are in a spirit world called Spirit Prison. Mormon Missionaries who are also dead, who reside in Paradise, go to the Spirit Prison and preach Mormonism to those who are there. If they decide they want to become Mormons, they cannot until they have been baptized by proxy, by a living person in a Mormon Temple back on earth.

<u>BENSON, EZRA TAFT</u> – The 13th "Prophet" of the Mormon Church. He served as President from November 10, 1985 until his death on May 30, 1994. He served as U.S. Secretary of Agriculture, 1953-61.

<u>BISHOP</u> – The presiding ward officer; the senior ecclesiastical leader in the ward.

BISHOPRIC – A Bishop and his two counselors. They preside over a ward to direct all matters pertaining thereto.

BLOOD ATONEMENT – A Mormon doctrinal position that claims the "Blood of Jesus Christ" does not cover all sins. There are sins that a person can commit that require the shedding of their own blood to "atone" for.

BOOK OF MORMON – A book Mormons consider to be additional scripture to the Bible. Joseph Smith said an angel appeared to him and told him about "Golden Plates" which had inscribed on them the history of the American Continent from the Tower of Babel until the year 421 A.D. No physical proof has ever been found to validate any claims that The Book of Mormon is an actual history of the Americas.

BRANCH – The lowest level of ecclesiastical organization in the Mormon Church. This is a very small congregation – not large enough to become a Ward.

BRANCH PRESIDENT – The ecclesiastical leader of a Branch – equivalent of a Bishop, but on a smaller scale.

BRETHREN (THE BRETHREN) – The President/Prophet of the Mormon Church, his two Counselors, and the Twelve Apostles.

CALLING – An office/position in the Church where a member is "called" to serve.

CELESTIAL KINGDOM – Highest of the three Kingdoms of Glory after death. It is the Kingdom of God. Mormons who achieve this Kingdom have the possibility of becoming a God themselves.

CHURCH (THE) – The Church of Jesus Christ of Latter-day Saints, for the Mormon, is the only "true and living Church on the face of the whole earth" and is simply referred to by them as "The Church."

COUNCIL OF THE TWELVE – The Quorum of the Twelve Apostles.

<u>DAME, WILLIAM</u> – Colonel of the Militia that executed the Mountain Meadows Massacre. He was the Stake President of Parowan.

<u>DANITES</u> – A secret police/underground para-military organization formed in June 1838. Its two stated purposes: (1) intimidation of Mormon dissenters; (2) warfare against anti-Mormon militia units. They were originally organized as the "Daughters of Zion"; also known as "Destroying Angels."

<u>DEACON</u> – Lowest Office in the Aaronic Priesthood. Primarily they pass the Sacrament each Sunday; they also collect Fast Offerings and serve as a junior companion to an Elder for Home Teaching.

<u>DOCTRINE AND COVENANTS</u> – A book considered by Mormons to be additional scripture to the Bible. It is a book of purported revelations given to the Prophet Joseph Smith with some additions by his successors in the Presidency of the Church. More than 95% of the book is made up of the revelations of Joseph Smith. Many false prophecies are contained in the book.

<u>ELDER</u> – Office of the Melchizedek Priesthood. Specifically known as "ministers of Christ"; they are to administer in spiritual things. They can perform any function of any Aaronic Priesthood Office.

<u>ELOHIM</u> – God the Eternal Father's name.

<u>ENSIGN</u> – The "Official" monthly magazine of the Mormon Church.

<u>ENDOWMENT</u> – Special temple ceremony (see Chapter Six). In this ceremony, Mormons are elevated into a doctrinal position called "Eternal Increase," where they believe they will become Gods and will be sexually fertile for eternity, producing children to populate the planet that each Mormon male will organize within each universe he puts together.

ETERNAL INCREASE – The teaching in Mormonism that when a Mormon becomes a God/Godess, they will be sexually fertile and will be able to procreate children forever as they populate their future planets.

ETERNAL PROGRESSION – The Mormon doctrinal position that after the resurrection, a Mormon can continue to progress until they achieve a state of perfection like unto the state that God the Eternal Father exists in now: Godhood. Mormon doctrine teaches that man may become a God; just as God is now.

EXALTATION – What Mormon doctrine calls achieving Godhood.

FAST AND TESTIMONY MEETING – The first Sunday of each month is "Fast and Testimony" meeting and is conducted during Sacrament Meeting. Instead of having someone give a "talk," the pulpit is opened up for Mormons to come and "bear their testimony" about how they "know" that Joseph Smith was a Prophet, that the line of authority continues today in their current Prophet and how they "know" the Church is true.

FAST OFFERING – Each Mormon family is to abstain (fast) from eating two meals the first Sunday of each month and provide the funds for those two meals to the poor through a "Fast Offering."

FILE LEADER – A person in a leadership role over another Mormon.

FIRST PRESIDENCY – The Prophet along with his 1st and 2nd Counselors (part of "The Brethren"). The highest tier of the Mormon Church power pyramid.

GENERAL AUTHORITIES – The First Presidency, Council of the Twelve (12 Apostles), Assistants to the Twelve, First Quorum of the Seventy, Second Quorum of the Seventy, and the Presiding Bishopric.

GENERAL CONFERENCE – A special meeting held twice a year (first week of April and first week of October) in Salt Lake City, Utah, where Mormons believe their General Authorities provide them "real time" revelations. Mormons believe in continuing revelation from God and General Conference is seen as a time when this revelation is given to the Saints. Of significance, at each General Conference all members of the Church are asked to "sustain" the "The Brethren" as "Prophets, seers, and revelators," of the Church. This sustaining vote reinforces the absolute allegiance to these men and the Mormon Church.

GENTILE – Anyone, including a Jew, who is not a Mormon, is identified as a "Gentile."

GOSPEL – Mormonism.

GRANT, HEBER J. – The 7th "Prophet" of the Mormon Church. He served as President from November 23, 1918 until his death on May 14, 1945.

HAIGHT, ISAAC – Cedar City Mayor, Stake President and Lt. Colonel in the Iron County Militia. He was the senior local ecclesiastical and civic leader that ordered the Mountain Meadows Massacre.

HELL – The place in the spirit world where, after death, wicked people will await "Judgment." After "Judgment," the wicked will be dispersed to the "Telestial Kingdom" or to the "Lake of Fire," which is not Hell; thus Hell will have an end.

HIGBEE, JOHN M. – 1st Counselor to Stake President Isaac Haight. Major in the Iron County Militia. Marshall of Cedar City. Major planner and participant in Mountain Meadows Massacre.

HIGH COUNCIL – Each Stake has a High Council made up of 12 High Priests. The main functions are judicial and administrative in nature.

HIGH PRIEST – Office in the Melchizedek Priesthood. Specifically called to minister in spiritual things. Can perform all functions of a Seventy, Elder, or any Aaronic Priesthood Office.

HINCKLEY, GORDON B. – The 15th "Prophet" of the Mormon Church. He was set apart as the 15th Prophet of the Church on March 12, 1995 until present, September 2007.

HOPKINS, CHARLES – Private in Iron County Militia. Participant at Mountain Meadows Massacre.

HUNTER, HOWARD W. – The 14th "Prophet" of the Mormon Church. He served as President from June 5, 1994 until his death on March 3, 1995.

INNOCENT BLOOD – A child under the age of eight years old is in a state of "innocence." In Mormon Doctrine, killing a child under the age of eight is "shedding innocent blood," and there is no forgiveness for this sin in this world or the world to come.

INSPIRED VERSION – Joseph Smith's version of the Bible as he felt through inspiration how it should read.

JESUS – In Mormonism, Jesus was born as the offspring of Elohim and one of his wives into a "Spirit World," before he came to earth. He was the first born son of Elohim; Lucifer (or Satan) was the second born son.

JOSEPH SMITH TRANSLATION (JST) – Not a translation, as no ancient manuscripts were used - Joseph Smith's version of the Bible as he felt through inspiration how it should read.

JOURNAL OF DISCOURSES – A 26 Volume set of "public Sermons, Discourses, Lectures, etc., delivered by the Presidency, the Twelve, and others." It was officially sanctioned by Brigham Young and his two Counselors (The First Presidency of The Church of Jesus Christ of Latter-day Saints).

KEYS (OF THE PRIESTHOOD) – The power to direct the labors of the various responsibilities and functions of the Priesthood. The Prophet of the Church holds all the "keys." Various quorum leaders hold the keys respective to their quorum, but ultimately through the Prophet of the Church.

KIMBALL, HEBER C. – 1st Counselor to Brigham Young.

KIMBALL, SPENCER W. – The 12th "Prophet" of the Mormon Church. He served as President from December 30, 1973 until his death on November 5, 1985.

KLINGENSMITH, PHILIP – Bishop of the Cedar Ward. Private in the Iron County Militia. Participant at Mountain Meadows Massacre.

LATTER-DAY SAINTS – Abbreviated from the official name of the Mormon Church: The Church of Jesus Christ of Latter-day Saints.

LDS – Mormons often refer to themselves as LDS – abbreviated from Latter-day Saints. This abbreviation is used on the "dog-tags" of Mormons who are members of the Armed Forces of America.

LEE, HAROLD B. – The 11th "Prophet" of the Mormon Church. He served as President from July 7, 1972 until his death on December 26, 1973.

LEE, JOHN D. – Bishop of Harmony Ward, Major in the Fort Harmony Militia. He was the Indian Agent, known as the Indian "Farmer." He directed the Indians to commit the initial attack at Mountain Meadows. He rode into the encampment with a white truce flag and tricked the emigrants to lay down their arms and walk out into the Meadows to be massacred. The only person ever put on trial and held accountable for the Massacre.

LORD'S ANOINTED – Those who have been ordained into Priesthood positions of authority in the Church. Very specific doctrines are laid out to "speak not against the Lord's Anointed."

LUCIFER (SATAN) – In Mormonism Lucifer is Jesus' brother. Jesus being the first born son into the "Spirit World"; Lucifer being the second. Jesus and Lucifer, as well as the entire human race, are Elohim's direct physical offspring.

MANIFESTO – The revelation, called "Official Declaration—1," that ended polygamy. Officially dated October 6, 1890. Issued by Wilford Woodruff.

McLELLIN COLLECTION – A supposed collection of papers from William E. McLellin, early Mormon Apostle, associate of Joseph Smith, and bitter critic of the Church.

McKAY, DAVID O. – The 9th "Prophet" of the Mormon Church. He served as President from April 9, 1951 until his death on January 18, 1970.

MELCHIZEDEK PRIESTHOOD – Upper level Priesthood organization. Offices consist of: Elder, Seventy and High Priest.

MORMON – Nickname given to members of The Church of Jesus Christ of Latter-day Saints. It comes from the association of the Church with its primary additional book of scripture: The Book of Mormon.

MORONI – According to Joseph Smith, this was the name of the angel who appeared to him and gave him the "Golden Plates" to be translated into The Book of Mormon.

MOUNTAIN MEADOWS MASSACRE – September 11, 1857, 120 innocent men, women, and children were brutally slaughtered by the Mormon Priesthood at Mountain Meadows in Southern Utah. The Mormon Church disavows complicity.

OLDER BROTHER – In Mormonism Jesus is often referred to as our "Older Brother." This concept originates from the Mormon doctrine of "Pre-existence."

ORACLES OF GOD – Mormonism teaches that the Prophet, his two Counselors, and the Twelve Apostles, are God's Living Oracles on earth. They have the "**right,** the **power,** and **authority to declare the mind and will of God** to his people…"

ORDAINED – Having Mormon Priesthood holders place their hands on a person's head, normally while they are seated, and provide a prayer/blessing to place (ordain) them into an office or position in the Church or Priesthood.

OUTER DARKNESS – A place reserved for the worst sinners of mankind. Those who leave the Mormon Church are called "Sons of Perdition" and will be sent to "outer darkness." This is a place after death and prior to the "Judgment." After the "Judgment," "Sons of Perdition," along with Satan and his demons will be sent into the "Lake of Fire."

PEARL OF GREAT PRICE – A book considered by Mormons to be additional scripture to the Bible. It contains the books of "Moses and Abraham" and "Extracts from the History of Joseph Smith, The Prophet." The Book of Abraham was "translated" by Joseph Smith from a roll of Egyptian papyrus obtained in the year 1835. The original papyrus was believed lost until found in 1967 by the Metropolitan Museum of Art in New York City. It was subsequently turned over to the Mormon Church. It has been translated and conclusively shows that Joseph Smith's claim that it contained the writings of Abraham is fraudulent.

PRE-EXISTENCE – Mormon doctrinal position that all of mankind was born into a pre-earth life, a "Spirit-World" called "Pre-Existence." Mormonism teaches that God was once a man and lived on another planet. He died on that planet, was resurrected and continued progressing until he became a God. He then created this universe, including this earth, and as part of the plan to populate this earth, he had physical relationships with his harem of polygamous wives and we, the human race, as a result of this pro-creation activity, were born as spirits into this "spirit-world." A plan was concocted whereby an earth was organized that we, the spirit children, could come to "earth" and get a mortal body so that we could die, be resurrected from this earth, and continue our progression to become Gods as well; and, then go and create our universes and populate our own earths.

PRESIDENT – The senior ecclesiastical leader of the Mormon Church is referred to as the President of the Church. He is also revered as a living "Prophet."

PRIEST – Highest Office of the Aaronic Priesthood. They have authority to baptize and primarily bless the Sacrament each Sunday; they also serve as junior companions to Elders for Home Teaching.

PRIESTHOOD – The power and authority in Mormonism to act in the name of God, in all things, on earth.

PRIESTHOOD KEYS – The authority to act in a Priesthood function.

PRIMARY – Children's Auxiliary Organization (children ages 3-11 attend).

PROPHET – The leader of the Mormon Church is believed to be, and is extolled as a modern day, living Prophet. He is God's direct mouthpiece on earth – He speaks for God. The Prophet is also referred to as the President of the Church.

QUORUM – A primary Priesthood organizational structure within the Mormon Church. All members of each Priesthood office (Deacon, Teacher, Priest, Elder, Seventy, High Priest) at the Ward or Stake level are organized into "quorums." At the highest levels of the Church, the First Presidency is the Presiding Quorum of the Church. The Twelve Apostles of the Church are commonly referred to as The Quorum of the Twelve.

RELIEF SOCIETY – Women's Auxiliary Organization organized to work for the temporal and spiritual salvation of women in the Church.

RIGHT ARM TO THE SQUARE – Bringing your right arm to be horizontal from the shoulder to the elbow, then bending the arm 90 degrees upward at the elbow so the fingers are pointing straight up (a right hand turn signal if driving a car, except done with the right arm instead of the left).

SACRAMENT – What Christians would call Communion, or the Lord's Supper. It is served as white store bought bread (several slices of Sunbeam bread), broken into small pieces and water is used instead of grape juice or wine.

SACRAMENT MEETING – Christian equivalent of a regular morning service, however, the Bishop does not "preach" sermons as Christians are used to (only General Authorities can teach Church doctrine—or approved Church manuals for Sunday School, Priesthood Meeting, etc.). Different members of the Ward, or sometimes Mormons come from outside the Ward, and speak on various subjects. The "talks" as they are called, are usually light on "doctrine" and long on "feelings."

SAINTS – Abbreviated reference to Mormons. This stems from the term LDS (Latter-day Saints).

SALVATION – In Mormonism, there are two salvations: General and Individual. General "salvation" will be experienced by all* – being resurrected (joining the spirit with the physical body). Individual "salvation" is experienced only by Mormons who achieve glory in the Celestial Kingdom and go on to Godhood.

* The one exception to General "salvation," resurrection, does not apply to Sons of Perdition.

SATAN (LUCIFER) – In Mormonism Satan is Jesus' brother. Jesus being the first born son into the "Spirit World"; Satan (then known as Lucifer) being the second. Jesus and Satan, as well as all of the human race, are Elohim's direct physical offspring.

SEALING – Special Temple Ceremony where husbands and wives are married (sealed) for time and all eternity – similarly, children are sealed to parents eternally as well. These ceremonies can be done for the living or the dead.

SET APART – To be ordained to serve in a particular Church office/position.

SEVENTY – Office in the Melchizedek Priesthood. Specifically called to function as Missionaries. Can perform all the functions of an Elder and all Offices of the Aaronic Priesthood.

SEVENTY (THE, OR THE QUORUM OF THE SEVENTY) – Directly under the Quorum, or Council of the Twelve Apostles in rank of the General Authorities, are members of the Quorum of Seventy. Currently there are five Quorums of the Seventy. Only members of the first two Quorums of the Seventy are recognized as General Authorities. They specifically oversee the Church's Missionary Program.

SMITH, GEORGE A. – Was 2nd Counselor to Brigham Young until Heber C. Kimball's death, when he became 1st Counselor. He was directly involved in delivering counsel to Southern Utah Mormon leaders that set the stage for the Mountain Meadows Massacre.

SMITH, GEORGE ALBERT – The 8th "Prophet" of the Mormon Church (son of George A. Smith, Brigham Young's 1st Counselor, who was Joseph Smith's (1st Mormon Prophet) cousin. He served as President from May 21, 1945 until his death on April 4, 1951.

SMITH, HYRUM – Joseph Smith's (1st Mormon Prophet) older brother. He was killed in a gun battle with a mob while incarcerated in the Carthage Jail, Carthage, Illinois, along with his brother Joseph, on June 27, 1844.

SMITH, JOSEPH Jr. – The founding "Prophet" of the Mormon Church. He was killed in a gun battle with a mob while incarcerated in the Carthage Jail, Carthage, Illinois, June 27, 1844, at the age of 38. He served as President from April 6, 1830 (the day the Mormon Church was organized) until his death on June 27, 1844.

SMITH, JOSEPH F. – The 6th "Prophet" of the Mormon Church (son of Hyrum Smith, and nephew of Joseph Smith, Jr., the founding Prophet). He served as President from October 17, 1901 until his death on November 19, 1918.

SMITH, JOSEPH FIELDING – The 10th "Prophet" of the Mormon Church (son of Joseph F. Smith, 6th Prophet of the Mormon Church). He served as President from January 23, 1970 until his death on July 2, 1972.

SNOW, LORENZO – The 5th "Prophet" of the Mormon Church. He served as President from September 13, 1898 until his death on October 10, 1901.

SON OF PERDITION – Those who knew the truth, Mormonism, and left "the only true and living Church on the face of the whole earth." They will be cast into "Outer Darkness" with Satan and his demons, and eventually into the Lake of Fire. This is the worst fate that can be placed upon any member of the human race.

STAKE – Regional geographic organization usually comprised of 6-8 Wards. Depending on membership density, a stake may cover just a few square miles, or a whole country that has a small Mormon population.

STAKE CONFERENCE - A special meeting held twice a year at the local "Stake" level. Mormons hear from many local, senior ecclesiastical leaders and often from a visiting General Authority who presides over the "Conference." Just like at General Conference held in Salt Lake City, all members of the Church are asked to "sustain" the "The Brethren" as "Prophets, seers, and revelators," of the Church. They also "sustain" their local level Priesthood Leadership (Stake President, High

Council). This sustaining vote reinforces the absolute allegiance to these men and the Mormon Church.

STAKE PRESIDENT – The presiding stake officer; the senior ecclesiastical leader in the stake.

STANDARD WORKS (THE) – Mormons refer to their four volumes of scripture as the *Standard Works*: The Book of Mormon, The Doctrine and Covenants, The Pearl of Great Price, and the Bible (King James Version only).

SUSTAIN – Members of the Mormon Church are selected to various positions, or offices, in the Church by the gift of revelation in that person who it is appointed to select that position, or office. However, before they can begin to serve in that position they must receive a "sustaining vote," a vote of approval, from the people over whom they are to preside.

TALKS – A sermon or speech. However, Mormons don't use either of these terms with respect to presentations given in their church services.

TAYLOR, JOHN – The 3rd "Prophet" of the Mormon Church. He served as President from October 10, 1880 until his death on July 25, 1887.

TEACHER – Middle Office of the Aaronic Priesthood. Their primary jobs are to be a junior companion to an Elder for Home Teaching and to prepare the Sacrament each Sunday.

TELESTIAL KINGDOM – Lowest of the three Kingdoms of Glory after death. The bad people of the world will be judged and sent there.

TERRESTRIAL KINGDOM – The middle of the three Kingdoms of Glory after death. The righteous of the world who did not become Mormons, and the non-performing Mormons will be judged and sent there.

TWELVE (THE) – The Quorum of the Twelve Apostles (part of "The Brethren"). The second tier of the Mormon Church power pyramid.

WARD – The basic ecclesiastical unit of organization in the Mormon Church. It is defined by a geographical boundary; the Christian equivalent of a congregation or local church.

WOODRUFF, WILFORD – The 4th "Prophet" of the Mormon Church. He served as President from April 7, 1889 until his death on September 2, 1898. He was the Mormon Prophet that issued the "Manifesto" which ended the practice of polygamy in the Church.

YOUNG, BRIGHAM – The 2nd "Prophet" of the Mormon Church. He served as President from December 27, 1847 until his death on August 29, 1877. He also served as President of the Quorum of the Twelve, which placed him as the head of the Church upon Joseph Smith's death. He functionally served as the head of the Mormon Church for nearly 33 years – the longest of any Mormon Prophet.

Defending Christianity From Mormon Doctrine – Jude 3

Rocky & Helen Hulse
Nauvoo Christian Visitors Center
1340 Mulholland Street
P.O. Box 93
Nauvoo, Illinois 62354
217-453-2372
www.nauvoochristian.org
http://mormonhomeevening.blogspot.com/

Are you receiving our newsletter: The Midwest Expositor? It's free. Call, write or go online: http://www. nauvoochristian.org/newsletters.php

"Truth Outreach"

Watch our weekly TV show, **"Truth Outreach,"** comparing Mormonism to Christianity. It can be viewed online via our website www.nauvoochristian.org, or www. ctni.org on Sundays at 9:30 a.m. or 10:30 p.m. Eastern Standard Time. Regular TV broadcasts are available in the following TV markets (check your local listings for air times):

WTJR TV 16 – Quincy, Illinois
KFXB TV 40 – Dubuque, Iowa City, Cedar Rapids, Waterloo, Iowa
KCLP TV 18 – Boise, Idaho
K59GS TV – Salt Lake City, Utah
K49GD TV – Spanish Fork, Utah
K55IT TV – Provo, Utah

Printed in the United States
200295BV00007B/73-420/A